The Unfinished Revolution compares the post-Second World War histories of the American and British gay and lesbian movements with an eye toward understanding how distinct political institutional environments affect the development, strategies, goals, and outcomes of a social movement. Stephen M. Engel utilizes an eclectic mix of source materials ranging from the theories of Mancur Olson and Michel Foucault to Supreme Court rulings and film and television dialogue. The two case study chapters function as brief historical sketches to elucidate further the conclusions on theory and whilst being politically oriented, they also examine gay influence and expansion into mainstream popular culture. The book also includes an appendix that surveys and assesses the analytical potential of five critical understandings of social movements: the classical approach, rational choice, resource mobilization, new social movement theories, and political opportunity structures. It will be of value to academics and students of sociology, political science, and history.

STEPHEN M. ENGEL graduated from Wesleyan University's College of Social Studies in 1998 and is currently working on his interdisciplinary MA in Humanities and Social Thought at New York University. While this is his first book, he has also published in the *Journal of Graduate Liberal Studies* (Autumn 2000).

The Unfinished Revolution

Series editors: JEFFREY C. ALEXANDER, Department of Sociology, University of California, Los Angeles, and STEVEN SEIDMAN, Department of Sociology, University at Albany, State University of New York.

The Unfinished Revolution

*Social Movement Theory and the Gay and
Lesbian Movement*

Stephen M. Engel

CAMBRIDGE
UNIVERSITY PRESS

PUBLISHED BY THE PRESS SYNDICATE OF THE UNIVERSITY OF CAMBRIDGE
The Pitt Building, Trumpington Street, Cambridge, United Kingdom

CAMBRIDGE UNIVERSITY PRESS
The Edinburgh Building, Cambridge CB2 2RU, UK
40 West 20th Street, New York NY 10011–4211, USA
10 Stamford Road, Oakleigh, VIC 3166, Australia
Ruiz de Alarcón 13, 28014 Madrid, Spain
Dock House, The Waterfront, Cape Town 8001, South Africa

http://www.cambridge.org

First published 2001

Printed in the United Kingdom at the University Press, Cambridge

Typeface Plantin 10/12 pt   *System* 3b2   [CE]

A catalogue record for this book is available from the British Library

Library of Congress Cataloguing in Publication data

Engel, Stephen M.
The unfinished revolution: social movement theory and the gay and
lesbian movement / by Stephen M. Engel.
      p.   cm. – (Cambridge cultural social studies)
Includes bibliographical references and index.
ISBN 0 521 80287 3 (hardback) – ISBN 0 521 00377 6 (paperback)
1. Gay liberation movement – History.
2. Lesbian feminism – History.
3. Social movements – Philosophy.
I. Title.   II. Series.
HQ76.5.E5 2001
305.9'0664'09–dc21   00-067496

ISBN 0 521 80287 3 hardback
ISBN 0 521 00377 6 paperback

An Author, whether good or bad, or between both, is an Animal whom every body is privileged to attack; For though All are not able to write books, all conceive themselves able to judge them. A bad composition carries with it its own punishment, contempt and ridicule. A good one excites envy, and entails upon its Author a thousand mortifications. He finds himself assailed by partial and ill-humored Criticism: One Man finds fault with his plan, Another with the style, a Third with the precept, which it strives to inculcate; and they who cannot succeed in finding fault with the Book employ themselves in stigmatizing its Author. They maliciously rake out from obscurity every little circumstance, which may throw ridicule upon his private character or conduct, and aim at wounding the Man, since They cannot hurt the Writer. In short to enter the lists of literature is willfully to expose yourself to the arrows of neglect, ridicule, envy, and disappointment. Whether you write well or ill, be assured that you will not escape from blame . . . But I am conscious, that all these sage observations are thrown away upon you. Authorship is a mania to conquer which no reasons are sufficiently strong; and you might as easily persuade me not to love, as I persuade you not to write.

Matthew Lewis, *The Monk* (1796)

Contents

Notes on language

What do I call you? Is it just gay? Or lesbians and gays? Or gay men
and gay women? Or is it lesbians and gay men?
Senator Ted Kennedy to gay delegate Bill Kraus at the 1980 Democratic
Convention Gay and Lesbian Caucus cocktail party (Randy Shilts,
And the Band Played On)

Who makes up the gay and lesbian movement?

To use the phrase "gay and lesbian movement" to describe the current
state of a social movement which includes gays and lesbians is a
misnomer. Not only is this specific movement not a unified phenomenon, but instead a collection of smaller movements differing in
ideology and political versus cultural aims, it is also not merely composed of gays and lesbians. Instead, the gay and lesbian movement has
come to represent (or perhaps not represent depending on the critique)
gay men, lesbians, bisexuals, transgenders, and queer-identified
individuals.

No single term currently exists which is adequately inclusive of this
diverse population. The label, "gay," while it often refers to men and
women, tends to connote a male identification. "Lesbian" has a restric-
tive female meaning. "Bisexual" refers to individuals who do not identify
with a bipolar definition of sexual orientation as either heterosexual or
homosexual, but fall somewhere in the middle of these extremes.
"Transgender" is the newest term; it often refers to transvestites and
transsexuals. It also reflects scholarship which suggests that gender is
socially constructed. Transgenders recognize the social construction of
their genders and thus do not fit neatly within societally prescribed
gender roles determined by biological sex.

I have refrained from using the word "queer" to be generally a
synonomous or umbrella term for the gay, lesbian, bisexual, and/or
transgender community(ies) as has sometimes been linguistic fashion. I
feel that the term connotes a specific type of confrontational politics and
identity theory that came into favor at a particular moment in gay and

lesbian politico-cultural history. When I have used the term, it has been limited to referring to this brand of political action and theory. By opting not to use "queer" as a general label for the movement, I am not judging the validity of queer ideology; rather, I am acknoledging both the term's historical context and its ultimate failure to include the entire sexual minorities community.

Finally, this work, while mentioning the expansion of the movement to include bisexuals and the transgendered, concentrates on the history of gay men and lesbians and the movement that they inspired in the immediate post-war period. To include the terms, "bisexual" and "transgender" would only mislead the reader as to the focal point of this text. At times I have used the phrases "gay men and women," "lesbians and gays," or "sexual minorities" to refer to members of this community. I have done so consciously in order to avoid potentially monotonous labeling and to provide some linguistic variety.

Preface

In the aftermath of a march

The San Francisco Gay Freedom Day Marching Band blared the opening notes of "California Here I Come," and the Parade started its two-mile trek down Market Street toward City Hall. More than 30,000 people, grouped in 240 contingents, marched in the parade past 200,000 spectators. The parade was the best show in town, revealing the amazing diversity of gay life . . . Radical gay liberationists frowned at the carnival rides that had been introduced to the rally site. Parade organizers had decided that the event had grown "too political" in recent years, so the chest-pounding rhetoric that marked most rallies was given a backseat to the festive feeling of a state fair.

Randy Shilts, And the Band Played On

We want to give GLF demos a different role to straight demos. We want to have fun as well. We want our revolution to be enjoyable.

Unnamed London Gay Liberation Front activist

This morning I was able to catch a glimpse of *The Washington Post* before I boarded the train at Washington, DC's Union Station heading back home to New York City. Sunburned and exhausted I stared at the front page trying to force my eyes to focus on the text. The article summarized the weekend's events, rehashed the controversy surrounding the latest march on Washington, and estimated the number of participants: well into the hundreds of thousands. Yet, somehow the text and corresponding photo of marchers holding banners and placards advocating an end to hate crimes and equal rights now did not ring true with my own experience.

The Millennium March on Washington (MMOW) for Lesbian, Gay, Bisexual, and Transgender Equality took place over the weekend of 29 April and 30 April 2000. It was the first such national civil rights event for the Lesbian, Gay, Bisexual, and Transgender (LGBT) community and its allies of the new millennium, and the fourth such march – others occurred in 1979, 1987, and 1993 – that invoked the template of Martin

xv

Luther King Jr.'s march on Washington in 1963. As the train pulled from the station and the newly bright May sun finally revealed some strength after an exceedingly gray April, I watched as other passengers clad in official MMOW t-shirts hoisted their suitcases into the overhead racks. I slipped my headphones on, closed my eyes, and attempted to gather my impressions of the last two days in Washington, DC.

The march had been shrouded in controversy. Opponents claimed that too few resources existed and that the march focused energy at the national level when the emphasis should be on local, municipal, and state-level reform. The Millennium March was accused of being a top-down operation, a spectacle manufactured and imposed upon this particular movement community by certain Washington-based organizations out of touch with the needs, strategies, and goals of more grassroots democratic action.

Having never before experienced a march of this magnitude – even if this one supposedly failed to draw the crowds of its 1993 predecessor – I cannot wholly agree with the assessments of the march's opponents. Many of the participants with whom I had an opportunity to talk were deeply impacted by the experience, especially those who were younger, who belonged to that new cohort of activism to whom the torch was being passed. Various speakers at the rally on Sunday afternoon stressed the possibilities of youth, of a new generation who would continue the struggle for real and total equality. Yet, there were other marchers and spectators. Some had been to the 1993 or 1987 march. Some claimed that there was something missing in this latest incarnation of marches on our nation's capital. It bordered too much on the carnivalesque perhaps; it was too reminiscent of a street fair. It somehow, in some way which is difficult at this moment to identify, lacked some degree of political import. It fell or, at least, felt flat.

Relying on caffeine and adrenaline to keep me energized after a raucous Saturday, I observed the march on Sunday morning as it proceeded down Constitution Avenue toward the Mall. Part of the weekend celebration included a Millennium Festival complete with vendors ranging from *Out Magazine* to the *Advocate* to *Instinct* to *Hero Magazine* to *Girlfriend* to *Curve* to *POZ* to Gay.com to PlanetOut to the Showtime Network to the Human Rights Campaign to the National Organization for Women to a gay rodeo and country dancing tent. Each vendor distributed piles of free merchandise, and volunteers were strategically placed to adhere Gore 2000 or HRC or Lesbian Rights stickers to anyone willing to serve as a walking advertisement. A rock concert to benefit the Human Rights Campaign Foundation, "Equality Rocks", was held that Saturday evening before the march. I was able to attend and, indeed, I marveled at the sheer vastness of the audience: 40,000 people. Forty thousand people had packed the seats of RFK Stadium to hear k.d. lang, Melissa Etheridge, Garth Brooks, George Michael, Nathan Lane, Ellen DeGeneres, Elizabeth Birch, Dennis and Judy Shepard, Kristen Johnson, Kathy Najimy, Tipper Gore, and others rally in support of full and real equality for the LGBT community. The potential future first lady of the United States even rocked out on the drums during the concert's finale to the great surprise and deafening applause of the entire stadium.

The rally on the following afternoon continued this trend of mixing celebrities and politicians, entertainment and politics. Did the march simply devolve into a capitalist commodification of identity politics or had the history of this community's political events always involved elements of fun, commercialism, and spectacle? Margaret Cho performed some standup. Corey Johnson recounted his experiences as a quarterback coming out to his teammates during his senior year of high school. President Clinton and Vice President Gore delivered taped messages both expressing support for the LGBT community and a commitment to the realization of equality in the United States. Ellen DeGeneres delivered some standup as her partner, Ann Heche, and her mom and spokesperson for the National Coming Out Project, Betty DeGeneres, offered their support and activism. Elizabeth Birch, Executive Director of the Human Rights Campaign, urged the hundreds of thousands of marchers to the polls in November, and DC mayor, Anthony Williams, welcomed the crowds to his city. Perhaps it was a cultural event sprinkled with politics or a political event broadened by culture. Much of the rhetoric focused on energizing a new generation of activists, recognizing the diversity within the LGBT community and the strength that emanates from that diversity, and a constant reminder to storm the polls in November.

Yet, as I heard these speeches, I could not help but notice that the crowd was predominantly white, and that the entire event just seemed to boil down to hanging out on the Mall on a beautiful spring day. Where was the energy? Where was the anger? Perhaps a sense of crisis was lacking. Things had changed. The LGBT community's status had no doubt improved since the 1993 march. Would there have been 40,000 people crowded in a stadium to celebrate LGBT equality with the support of the Vice President's wife twenty or even ten years ago? Would the President and the Vice President have extended at least a video-recorded message of support to this community even ten years ago? The political stage was set: the governor of Vermont had made civil unions an unprecedented reality just two days before the march, and arguments regarding the rights of gays to participate in the Boy Scouts of America had been heard before the Supreme Court earlier in the week. Yet, there was an emptiness. Was something missing? Was there no sense of urgency? Maybe, for the first time, outrage did not have to be the predominant emotion. Maybe, for the first time, we could enjoy the spring day, just as we were. Hadn't that been what the fight was all about anyway . . . just to be able to live and love like everyone else?

The 2000 march was the first of its kind in this sense: it did not respond to anything in particular. The 1979 march reacted to the assassination of Harvey Milk and the rise and success of Anita Bryant's "Save Our Children" campaign; the 1987 March was a reaction against both the *Bowers v. Hardwick* decision, in which the Supreme Court (overruled the privacy of citizens and) upheld states' rights to enact and maintain sodomy laws, as well as the Reagan administration's inadequate response to the AIDS crisis; the 1993 march came on the heels of the installment of the "Don't Ask, Don't Tell" policy, Clinton's failure to issue an executive order banning discrimination against gays in the military, and it too focused on increasing funds for AIDS research, care, and prevention.

However, to what was the Millennium March responding? It came during the last year of the most gay and lesbian-accessible presidential administration in the history of the United States. It occurred only days after civil unions – the closest step toward gay marriage taken so far – became a reality in Vermont. It happened only four months after the end of 1999, a year that the National Gay and Lesbian Task Force notes was the first in which the number of bills brought forward in the state legislatures throughout the United States that were friendly to LGBT concerns outnumbered those that were not: 214 to 81.[1] Perhaps the Millennium March marks a strategic shift in gay and lesbian movement politics: a shift from reaction to pro-action, from fighting against a conservative reactionary tide to focusing more on progressive movement goals, to getting people motivated before an election rather than picking up the pieces after one. Yet, sometimes reaction is an easier sentiment to mobilize. It is clearer to grasp, more coherent to envision. Proactive measures are sometimes harder to ascertain, especially when those affected are already experiencing unprecedented levels of freedom. This assessment is in no way meant to suggest that equality has been achieved or that somehow we can roll down our sleeves, pat ourselves on the back, and go home secure in our equality – inequality abounds. Yet, when you are a white middle-class gay man or lesbian with a secure job and home, those inequalities somehow do not seem as readily apparent as maybe they once were.

As I watched the greenery of Maryland become interrupted by the urban landscapes of Baltimore and Philadelphia on that train making its all-too-frequent stops between Union and Pennsylvania Stations, I was struck that the LGBT community may be in danger of falling victim to a misguided notion of its own success. The community faces the peculiar situation at this historical juncture of a disconnect between cultural and political achievements. Gays and lesbians are popping up endlessly on television. Every prime time show, it seems, whether it be an adolescent drama or a sitcom, whether it airs at 8 p.m. or 10 p.m., has its seemingly requisite gay or lesbian character. Indeed, most of these characters are white. Most are middle-class. Most are male. Most, in short, are not terribly threatening to the heterosexual majority, and most do not represent the varied and diverse scope of the LGBT community. Yet, the rally's speakers reminded the marchers that in thirty-nine states a person can be legally fired for being gay, lesbian, bisexual, or transgender. The rally's speakers reminded us that no national hate crimes legislation has been passed, and that gays are still banned from military service. Most states do not allow gays and lesbians to adopt children. Some ban the possibility of same-sex marriage. The possibility of being attacked, beaten, and killed for simply loving someone still lurks. Political reality lags far behind the televisual fantasy.

Did the march achieve its goals? Certainly there was coverage in *The Washington Post* and *The New York Times*. Certainly it was documented by C-Span and CNN. Certainly some of the participants left feeling energized and motivated to make greater strides towards activism and empowerment. Certainly it brought to the fore the vast achievements of the movement and the immense challenges that remain ahead. Certainly it enabled reflection on the visibility of the movement and the invisibilities within the movement. Yet, in the final analysis, the impact of the march remains, to a great extent, purely personal. And so I am left to ask myself, how did the march affect you?

I began this book with these rather brief and inconclusive remarks regarding the Millennium March on Washington for Equality because the circumstances and controversies swirling around that march encapsulate the myriad concerns and strategies that have marked the gay and lesbian movement throughout the post-war period. Does the movement attempt reform or revolutionary change? Who has the privilege of being a visible participant, and who remains invisible? How have the advances made in the cultural realms of television, film, theater, and literature kept apace, influenced, and/or been influenced by the advances and setbacks experienced within the political institutional environment?

What is the impact of a national-level march? Would the resources have been better spent at the state or local level? Why are these institutional venues perceived to be in competition? In short, should there have been a national march? Is change achieved through a top-down manner? Should change derive from grassroots democratic action at the local level? This book attempts to analyze these inquiries in order to draw out their underlying complexities. It attempts to understand how the gay and lesbian movement community developed in a unique institutional environment that governed how, where, and when to target its resources to best effect change.

This book first took shape as a jumbled and only loosely comprehensible idea locked in the recesses of my brain in May of 1997. I am indebted to numerous individuals for helping me find both the voice and the language in which to bring those thoughts out into my word processing software. My editor Sarah Caro, perhaps finding a kernel of something worthwhile in these pages, took a chance on an unknown never-before-published twenty-three year old graduate student. She imparted to me an incredible opportunity, and it is now in the hands of my readers to deem whether that opportunity was fully realized, squandered, or fell somewhere in between. Steven Seidman, the editor of the series of which this text is part, offered me invaluable critique and support as the manuscript navigated its way through the maze of editors and readers and finally to the Syndicate of Cambridge University Press. His encouragement has been much appreciated throughout the process.

Thanks must also go to the sundry professors at Wesleyan University and New York University who guided my education and imparted the knowledge and skills which come to bear on this work. Foremost among them is Giulio Gallarotti. He has been a wonderful mentor and friend believing in me despite my best efforts to dissuade him. He forced me to struggle with concepts I sometimes would rather avoid and pushed me towards a degree of thought I never believed I could attain. He gave me the freedom to tackle this project on my own terms, but also the confidence to claim it as my own. Marc Eisner introduced me to concepts like political institutions, political culture, and social movements. He pointed me in directions I never considered, offering various texts and methodologies. If I pursue a formal career in the academy, I hope that my teaching embodies the ideals I have gained from these two scholars.

Thanks must go to other key players in both my overall intellectual development and the specific drafting of this text: Donald Moon, Cecilia Miller, David Titus, David Morgan, Nancy Schwartz, Gil Skilman, Richard Adelstein, Henry Abelove, Gary Comstock, Lisa

Wedeen, Robin Nagle, and Britta Wheeler. Thanks are also extended to Sue Donnelly, the archivist at the Archive of Gay Organizations and Activists at the London School of Economics, who located hundreds of primary source documents regarding the history of the British gay and lesbian movement.

Innumerable friends scoured drafts and offered much needed support and well-timed distractions when the computer screen threatened blindness. My heartfelt appreciation to Becca Gerner, Blair Hanzlik, Jenna Minicucci, Brodie Welch, Maya Seiden, Kara Croughlio, Sarah Luchansky, Rob Finn, Matt Hunter, Audrey Goldenberg, Prana Topper, Dara Katz, Fawn Phelps, Aongus Burke, Aimee Dawson, Aaron Shield, Maureen Heacock, and Mike Whaley. Thanks to Candace Gingrich and the HRC Field Department of the summer of 1998 for introducing me to the possibilities of activism. Thanks also to Wesleyan University's College of Social Studies Class of 1998 for being fellow travelers and the CSS Class of 1999 for opening my mind to the possibilities of teaching and learning.

Finally, I have been blessed with a family whose love has exceeded all bounds and whose faith in each other has never wavered (or at least never for more than mere milliseconds). My parents, Mark and Barbara Engel, have provided me with innumerable opportunities, and, though it may seem like it, their love and care never went underappreciated. My older brother, Jarrett, has always looked out for me and inspired me more than he'll know. My sister-in-law, Jennifer, gave up much time to read and comment on numerous drafts of this work and has been a true friend throughout the many stages of bringing this text to press. My younger brother, David, has reminded me that life never really needs to be taken too seriously and that there is always time to play with Lego or show up his older brother on rollerblades. It is to these five individuals that I respectfully dedicate this book; without them, I would never have had the courage to be who I am or to make it as far as I have.

New York City
1 May 2000

Introduction

The essential link between author and reader, no matter how great the time difference, is a common humanity, a common psychological makeup or generic consciousness, that grounds the intuitive ability to empathize with other persons.   David Couzens Hoy, *The Critical Circle*

I cannot afford to believe that freedom from intolerance is the right of only one particular group . . . so long as we are divided because of our particular identities we cannot join together in effective political action.
Audre Lorde

Why this book?

It is a simple question, and often, simple questions have deceptively complex answers. My mentor on this project suggested that I should be able to summarize the objective and findings of this text in three sentences or less. Finally, somewhere nearing the end of this endeavor, I was able to convey what I had written. The following pages disclose a comparative study of the American and British gay and lesbian movements since the end of the Second World War. The aim is to discover in what ways these two social movements interact with governing structures, whether they be separation-of-powers or parliamentary-based, and how those systems influence the goals, strategies, and achievements of these movements. In so doing, I hoped to provide some useful insight into the evolution of social movement theory, its historical trends, and its future directions.

In essence the question boils down to two words: who wins? Are British queers in a better situation than American queers or *vice versa*? Through this work I attempted a strict social scientific undertaking, or so I had thought over three years ago when I began to research the project. Along the way, I discovered secondary goals. Through this text, I could help elucidate the often confusing nature of multiple social movement theories ranging from the classical and Marxist approaches to resource mobilization theory, political opportunity structures, and the political process model. I could investigate and discuss the role culture plays in a once-conceived purely political game. Through this text, I could demonstrate both the theoretical and practical similarities and distinctions between parliamentary and separation-of-powers systems. Through this text, I could introduce readers to a history to which they may never have been previously exposed.

Indeed, through the course of researching this book, I was struck by the proliferation of historical analyses that took the gay and lesbian community as its subject. However, I also could not help but notice the relative absence of work which has tied this history to a sociological frame by which to understand the gay and lesbian movements themselves. Exceptions to this observation are apparent,[1] but the vast majority of these studies have been published during the latter half of the 1990s despite the visibility of this modern movement since the 1970s. Thus, my goal became, in part, to add to the growing analysis of a movement whose goals and visibility have dramatically affected electoral and cultural politics in the United States and the United Kingdom in the closing decades of the twentieth century.

Besides accounting for my focus on the gay and lesbian movement, as opposed to the numerous other "new" social movements or other identity-based movements that have flourished in the post-war period, I feel that I must justify my choice of the United States and the United Kingdom for comparison. Selecting these two particular countries stems from my original question: How do differing political environments, including distinct political institutions such as the party structure and electoral system, on the one hand, and political culture, on the other, affect the development, maintenance, and strategies of a movement? The choice of the British and American governing structures then appears somewhat odd. Except that one is a parliamentary and the other a separation-of-powers system, the two-party structure would lead to similar tactics on the part of the movement. Indeed, the analysis, some might say, might have greater insight if I had compared the American movement to one in a country with a multi-party proportional representation system such as Germany or a non-Anglican nation such as Japan. However, the comparison of the United States and the United Kingdom raises interesting questions which belie the superficial similarities of their political party structure.[2] How does a centralized (British) versus decentralized (American) system affect a social movement? How does an independent (American) judiciary influence a movement, or does its absence (in the United Kingdom) hinder or help to concentrate a movement organization's agenda and strategies? In terms of political culture, how does a heterogeneous population, a lack of historic class cleavages, and a history of civil rights movements (all in the United States) play against a political cultural environment (in the United Kingdom) that is relatively homogenous, has a strong history of economic class-based cleavages, and a relatively minor history of identity-based and civil rights precursor movements? My analysis revealed some surprisingly counterintuitive conclusions.

I intended to accomplish all of these objectives and provide, if not direct answers, at least insights into these questions. It is in the reader's hands to estimate whether I have done so justly and with relative academic vigor. However, never at any time was this text to be clouded by emotional controversies, for staking my opinion on one side or the other of debates which afflict this movement was not within the scope of this undertaking. The value-laden debate of so-called queer nationalism versus less in-your-face tactics was not pursued. While the circumstances and facets of this debate are made clear in chapter 2, I tried to make no judgment on the validity of either side. Never was the role and seeming invisibility of the person of color in the gay and lesbian movement undertaken in a moral sense. Certainly, the issue was presented, but no judgment was made. Never was the conflict which has plagued this movement since its inception, that between liberation and legislation, between revolution and reform – often personified in the United States in the personalities of the National Gay and Lesbian Task Force on one side and the Human Rights Campaign on the other – embedded in a value judgment. The conflict was presented as one of the many schisms that has splintered the movement throughout its modern history, but no further judgments were disclosed. The same is true for commonly controversial issues within this movement: pornography, sadomasochism, barebacking, etc.

In short, my social scientific analysis was as it should be: devoid of emotion. Yet on 14 October 1998 I stood shivering on the steps of the Capitol Building in Washington, DC at a candlelight vigil for the slain Matthew Shepard. Shepard, a twenty-one year old student at the University of Wyoming, died on 12 October 1998 after being tortured, beaten, and tied to a fence by two peers for being gay. Our similarities in age and circumstance did not escape me, and I huddled with the warm light of the candle experiencing the gamut of emotions from fear to confusion to denial to sadness to anger, and I realized that an emotionally empty account of this movement fails to do justice to the individuals who work every day so that gays, lesbians, bisexuals, and transgender people can live safer and happier lives.[3]

The last two years before the close of the twentieth century witnessed a remarkable degree of activity on both sides of the "gay issue."

Throughout the summer of 1998, conservative right-wing organizations such as the Family Research Council, Focus on the Family, and the Christian Coalition poured millions of dollars into a national newspaper ad campaign claiming that gays and lesbians were diseased, an abomination in the eyes of God, and in need of a cure. These groups have manipulated the Bible's word to discriminate against gays and lesbians just as their predecessors used the same Bible to justify slavery and segregation. Their incessant and unrelenting scapegoating of gays and lesbians in an effort to score political points with a relatively apathetic electorate in an election year led unavoidably to the murder of Matthew Shepard: the exploited and twisted so-called words of a just God succeeded only in killing an innocent man.

What these right-wing groups have failed to grasp and have failed to grasp since the birth of the New Right, whether now in their battle against a sexual minority or in years past against a racial or religious minority, is that the true lesson of the Bible is not hate nor division, but love and unity. And yet, every day gays and lesbians are denied this right to express their love by the remaining criminal bans on consensual homosexual sex, the state's failure to recognize and sanction gay partnerships/marriage, the continued misguided relegation of gay and lesbian concerns and identity to the private sphere, and the continued controversy over gay parenting and adoption.

The summer of 1998 witnessed another heated debate centered on the rights of gays and lesbians. The Hefley Amendment sought to overturn Executive Order 13087, which stated that discrimination on the basis of sexual orientation would not be tolerated in the hiring and general employment practices of the federal work-force. After arguments were heard in the House of Representatives, the amendment was defeated, and the Executive Order remained in place. Yet, in nearly forty states in these United States of America, an individual can still be denied the ability to earn a living simply because he or she may be gay, lesbian, bisexual, or transgender.

Why am I writing all this? Is this merely an ill-placed emotional catharsis on the part of the writer? The purpose of this brief section, and, in a sense, of all the pages that follow it, is to reveal that in the shadow of the next millennium, we have a long journey to travel.

The title of this work is *The Unfinished Revolution*. Hidden in the word "revolution" is "evolution." Such evolution refers to a primary theme of this work: the continuous development and expansion of social movement theory over the past sixty years. The unfinished *revolution*, an idea and phrase borrowed from an observation by British scholar Jeffrey Weeks – quoted in chapter 3 – refers to the unfinished revolution in values of the heterosexual majority not merely to tolerate sexual minorities, but to do away entirely with the cultural power dynamic of the acceptor and the accepted as well as the unfinished nature of the gay and lesbian movement itself. Even my subtitle, in reference to the "gay and lesbian movement" as opposed to the gay, lesbian, bisexual, and transgender movement reminds the reader of the continued internal conflict within the sexual minorities movement. Does the bisexual or transgender person have a role in this movement? Are issues surrounding transgenderism in line with the gay and lesbian equal rights agenda? Are gays and lesbians committing the same sexual squeamishness or worse, prejudice, towards transgenders as heterosexuals commit against gays and lesbians? The movement has accomplished so much in the past fifty years (as this book endeavors to illustrate). Yet, its achievements have been fraught with setbacks, such as Anita Bryant's "Save Our Children" campaign, the onset of AIDS, the "Don't Ask Don't Tell" policy, the passage of the Defense of Marriage Act (DOMA), or the frustrating 1996 defeat of the Employment Non-Discrimination Act (ENDA). As I now reflect on that title, as I relive the emotions of that chill October evening's vigil, I come to understand that *The Unfinished Revolution* has a far greater meaning. It embodies all revolutions in which people struggled and died in the name of personal freedom. And thus, it includes, but its scope is not limited to, the American Revolution, and how even that revolution remains unfinished. For that revolution, in its most base terms, was a fight for "life, liberty, and the pursuit of happiness." As long as people, any people, whether gay, straight, bi, male, female, black, white, Asian, Latino, or transgender, are denied the right to be who they are, are forced to live in fear of being who they want to be, are indeed violently murdered for loving another human being, then even the American Revolution will remain an unfinished revolution.

That is why I wrote this text. Certainly it was to cover all those issues and questions raised at the beginning of this passage, but more importantly, it was to reveal the struggle and strength of gay, lesbian, bisexual, and transgender people, and thereby to promote greater understanding of the movement's goals. It was with the hope that maybe a person would read this book and realize that those newspaper ads issued by right-wing conservatives were ill-spirited, misguided, and inspired only by hate. It was to help prevent another tragic hate crime. My only regret is that I know this book to be fundamentally incapable of these goals and that it will be seen (perhaps) as just another interesting commentary on the applicability of social movement theory. And the revolution will remain sadly unfinished until enough tragedies force us to realize our own *in*humanity. Only at that point will we be able to rediscover together

our common humanity – our collective empathy – and embrace our
diversity and the strength it necessarily provides.

Navigating through this text

The American and British gay and lesbian movements, despite seemingly parallel developmental histories, have experienced distinct legal
and political outcomes. In the year 2000, private consensual homosexual
sex between two individuals at least eighteen years of age is legal in the
United Kingdom, while any homosexual relations are still criminal acts
in approximately twenty states in the United States. This fact, like
numerous other current circumstances, is quite paradoxical given that,
as this book endeavors to illustrate, the post-war American movement
has historically functioned as the leader among similar movements
throughout the world: it developed first, it has the largest number of
participants and highest level of resources, and its tactics and ideologies
have been appropriated by other nations.[4] How can we account for this
paradox?

Of course, this question encompasses a series of other inquiries. What
is the gay and lesbian movement? Who makes up this movement? Or
even more fundamentally, what is a social movement? Are the movement and the gay community separate, merged, and/or mutually reinforcing? How does the American movement compare to its British
counterpart? Did these respective movements develop according to
similar patterns? What are the aims of these movements? Have the
movements achieved their goals? Has the American movement been
more or less successful than the British variant? What accounts for
distinct levels of social movement success? This book attempts to
answer these questions in the hope of elucidating not only the current
status, but also providing perspective and possible prediction regarding
the future fates of the movements in both countries.

In order to analyze the gay and lesbian movement in either country,
we must first understand the nature of a social movement and collective
behavior in general. Hence, chapter 1 provides a multifaceted model to
comprehend collective behavior commonly referred to as the political
process model (PPM). The discussion of social movement theories is
fleshed out in the appendix. The appendix provides a more thorough
survey of common theoretical explanations of collective social insurgency from both the American and Marxist schools, including the
classical model, rational choice, resource mobilization, new social movement theory, and political opportunity structure. By including the
appendix, I provide not so much a literature review as a timeline of the

evolution of thought on social movements. The appendix relays a foundational knowledge of important theories while grounding them in empirical examples. Both chapter 1 and the appendix explore the ability of theory to distort historical reality, how each of these theories utilize different levels of analysis, how they are interrelated, and, indeed, how each, save the political process model, falls short of providing satisfactory explanations of movement development and existence.

The political process model (PPM) exists in two parts. The first section isolates three critical variables necessary for movement emergence: changing opportunity structure, pre-existing organizations to exploit this opportunity, and some type of cognitive liberation which promotes positive collective identity and legitimizes mass participation. These factors interact to produce a social movement. In the second part, the interest groups spawned by the movement interact with political institutions to produce outcomes that can either support or hinder the movement's agenda. By the end of the chapter, we are prepared to apply the theoretical tools provided by the two-part paradigm of the political process model (PPM).

Chapter 2 is an historical sketch of the American post-war gay and lesbian movement. I refer to it as a "sketch" because the chapter does not go into great detail regarding much of the tempestuous nature of many internal debates within the movement community nor does it relay a copious account of influential leaders, although key players and their contributions are mentioned in due fashion. Rather, it provides a *foundational* knowledge with which to apply and test the validity of our theoretical model – the primary aim of the text. Starting with an interpretation of the Second World War as the necessary opportunity for movement development, it traces the establishment of homophile organizations such as the Mattachine Society and the Daughters of Bilitis in the 1950s and 1960s. It then turns to an evaluation of gay liberation and the politicization of "coming out" as the necessary cognitive liberation to engender mass mobilization. The critical turning point in modern American gay history, as cited by numerous historians, is the Stonewall Riots of 1969. In this text, however, the riots are not only seen as the foundation of the modern movement, but also as the concrete example which bridges the theoretical Parts I and II of the political process model. The impact of the AIDS crisis on the movement's equal rights agenda is assessed. Lastly, sundry events of the past decade, including the gays-in-the-military debate, the 1992 presidential election, and the increase in mainstream visibility of gays and lesbians, are discussed to demonstrate the extent of movement success. The analysis reveals a movement which has traditionally functioned at local and state levels and has been plagued by gender rifts and struggles between militant versus moderate approaches; the AIDS crisis has served to expand its agenda and methodology to include federally oriented interest groups and nationwide goals.

Chapter 3 tracks the developmental history of the British gay and lesbian movement in the same time period, and it too functions as a foundational sketch with which to test the applicability of the political process model. We witness that the Second World War provided a similar opportunity as it did in the United States, but also that various other events, including the 1954 Wildeblood–Montagu trial and the establishment of the Wolfenden Committee on Prostitution and Homosexuality later that same year, fostered an environment amenable to homosexual legal reform. The chapter explores the role of the parliamentary lobby, the Homosexual Law Reform Society, the liberal culture of social reform which characterized the United Kingdom in the 1960s, and the implementation of the Wolfenden recommendations to decriminalize homosexuality – with certain restrictions on the age of consent and the definition of privacy – in the 1967 Sexual Offences Act. This reform subsequently deflated further impetus for collective behavior, and we see that British gay liberation of the 1970s is only a partially successful appropriation of the American model. Lastly, the chapter examines the effect of AIDS, evaluates how mobilization against Section 28 of the 1988 Local Government Bill provided the cognitive liberation that gay liberation failed to do (to the extent it had in the United States), and assesses the prospects of the movement given the election of Labour in 1997 after eighteen years of Conservative rule. This evaluation reveals a movement that has both paradoxically attained legal reform before it was fully formed, i.e., no great degree of cognitive liberation nor collective identity formation had taken shape, and is now potentially better situated (with regard to institutional opportunity) than its American contemporary to attain its goals, despite the fact that much of its foundational ideology was appropriated from the American model.

If the book ended at this point, the reader might walk away with the misguided belief that both the American and British movements (being similar) would have attained the same level of political and legal reform with respect to gay and lesbian equal rights, or that the American movement, being more diverse, having more constituents, amassing more resources, and thereby being generally stronger, should have attained more favorable legislation. *While they follow similar developmental patterns – each displaying instances of changing opportunity, pre-existing organizations, and cognitive liberation – they have, in fact, achieved different levels of political and legal success.* Why? Chapter 4 answers this question by utilizing part two of the political process model. It compares the parliamentary and separation-of-powers systems and seeks to ascertain how these political structures influence the tactics and achievements of social movement organizations. Essentially, the American separation-of-powers system provides interest groups with more agenda access, but the centralized British parliamentary structure establishes both greater capability for policy implementation and increased interest group access *if* a supportive political party is in power. The difference in political institutions and the subsequent different opportunities and venues they provide resolve the paradox that the larger American movement has still failed to attain any national level rights-protection legislation while its smaller British contemporary has done so or that the British ban on gays serving openly in the military has been lifted while the American ban, despite or because of "Don't Ask, Don't Tell," remains intact. British political institutions engendered national gay legal reform under a Labour majority in 1967 despite the relative non-existence of a mass movement comparable to that emerging across the Atlantic. The American federalist separation-of-powers has hindered national legislation by promoting multiple veto points while simultaneously encouraging gay-related issues to be debated at the local and state levels as well as through litigation.

Although the political process model has been explored and its robust quality demonstrated, new research in social movement theory may indicate that the analysis is not thorough enough. The inherent problem may be more clearly understood if we start with sociologist Ken Plummer's concept of the gay and lesbian movement as "a broadly based overlapping cluster of arenas of collective activity lodged in social worlds in which change is accomplished: some of it is overtly political, and some of it is economic (the Pink Economy), but much of it is cultural."[5] Plummer acknowledges that a key component of the movement is what has been discussed to this point, namely formally structured organizations that work through the existing political institutional environments to promote and preserve legal change concerning equal rights. However, the movement consists of scenes such as bars or social organizations, gay and lesbian media, self-help organizations, academia, that is, the development of gay and lesbian studies and queer theory, rituals and marches, and the burgeoning community on the Internet.[6] Many of these other areas that comprise this movement are hinted at and discussed throughout the case study presentations in chapter 2 and chapter 3. Yet, as the concept of movements as not merely political but also as containing a *cultural* component has been a recent topic of debate and research by students of social movements, this text would be incomplete and the gay and lesbian movement inaccurately portrayed if some degree of cultural analysis is not performed. An increasing number of sociologists, anthropologists, historians, and political scientists are examining not only how the dominant culture affects movement development, but how the movement itself generates its own reinforcing culture through the use of interpretive ritual and collective identity formation.

Thus, in chapter 5 we come full circle to the central premise of chapter 1, namely that no theoretical model is collectively exhaustive. This chapter introduces the element of culture as it influences movement behavior. The political process model fails to account for the role of culture both used as a tool manipulated by the gay and lesbian movement and as a variable which conditions the political environment in which interest groups act. The purpose of the chapter is not to discount the validity of PPM; rather, it is to *augment* an already useful theoretical framework and to flesh out a description of the movement that, to this point, is perhaps too unidimensional and overly political. The goal is not, as has been done in the past, to propose a paradigm shift from the more structural political process model to a more culturally based understanding reminiscent of new social movement theories, but simply to provide a useful evaluative tool with another facet of analysis. Besides revealing how the movement fosters its own culture, maintaining its cohesiveness and sustainability relatively *independent* of political opportunity, the chapter also utilizes statistical and historical analysis to demonstrate that homophobia – the hatred and fear of homosexuals – is alive in both the United States and the United Kingdom, but to a lesser extent in the latter nation. This greater degree of cultural tolerance may be another reason why British national legal reform concerning gay equality has been more easily passed and promises to expand more readily in the future, given the election of a Labour majority.

1 Asked and answered: how questions can condition conclusions in social movement theory

> There are two mistakes to be avoided in trying to explain collective behavior. The crudest is to believe that there exists one privileged motivation – self-interest, for example – that explains all instances of cooperation. A more subtle error is to believe that each instance of cooperation can be explained by one motivation. In reality, cooperation occurs when and because different motivations reinforce each other.
>
> Jon Elster, *Nuts and Bolts for the Social Sciences*

Theory provides a conceptual framework by which to comprehend a series of events. It allows linkages to be drawn between the present and the past while simultaneously enabling predictions regarding the future. Often when explaining a certain event or era, multiple theories exist; some may be compatible, others may not, but usually and most importantly, *no one theory is able to elucidate all aspects of these events.* No one theory is either mutually exclusive or collectively exhaustive. Historical interpretation is highly dependent upon the framework adopted to investigate a particular phenomenon. In other words, the theory conditions the evaluation by allowing only certain variables to come under the scope, only certain questions to be asked.

Given the parameters of theory, it is often helpful to evaluate how distinct social movement theories account for the same historical event. Divergent understandings derive from the different questions that are asked. This chapter offers a brief overview of various social movement theories including the classical approach, rational choice, resource mobilization, new social movement, and political opportunity structure. A more detailed survey of these theories can be found in the appendix. An explanation of the political process model (PPM), the theory that grounds this analysis, is the chapter's primary focus.[1]

The post Second World War era has witnessed the proliferation of social movements in the United States and throughout most, if not all, Western democracies. This rise of collective behavior – what John McCarthy and Mayer Zald refer to as a social movement industry[2] –

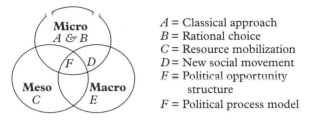

A = Classical approach
B = Rational choice
C = Resource mobilization
D = New social movement
E = Political opportunity
    structure
F = Political process model

Figure 1.1 *Social movement theories*

focuses on the evolution of supposedly "new" social movements which tend to be identity and not class-based and which include the civil rights movement, the feminist movement, and the gay and lesbian movement among others. These movements simultaneously constitute a social psychological, political, sociological, and historical phenomenon revealing the existence of multiple levels of theoretical analysis.

A social movement, although it may have secondary aims to promote the development of a subculture,[3] is inherently and fundamentally a political phenomenon since its target is the state.[4] This contention is more clearly demonstrated if we start with Max Weber's definition of the state as "a human community that (successfully) claims *the monopoly of the legitimate use of physical force* within a given territory."[5] Since the state holds this legal use of coercive power, it reserves a position as the primary distributor of rights and resources. A social movement, in its attempt to acquire these resources to promote structural change, must view the state as both an objective and an antagonist.[6] Thus, a movement requires the resources of the state it abhors in order to alter that state. An antagonistic relationship exists between the state and the social movement, or between those individuals who hold political power and those who are effectively disenfranchised. Hence, *social movements embody sustained collective challenges against political elites and authorities led by people with a common purpose and who lack regular access to existing political institutions.*[7]

Various theories have been constructed to understand the existence, methods, and achievements of collective action. Each theory operates within three particular analytical spheres or at the juncture of these spheres as depicted in Figure 1.1.

Classical and rational choice theories are micro-level analyses, which means that they focus on individual motivation to participate in a social movement. Why does an individual choose to participate? As such, these theories concentrate on the existence of individual grievances. Given their base assumption that democratic society is essentially pluralistic or that all voices are heard, classical and rational choice theories perceive collective behavior as fundamentally irrational and indicative of some kind of psychological imbalance; collective action thereby falls outside the realm of legitimate politics.[8]

Encountering the increase of collective behavior in the 1960s, the evidence that participants in such action did not suffer from some psychological dysfunction, and increasing belief that American politics was elitist rather than pluralistic, students of social movements developed a new theory, resource mobilization, to understand the formation of such activity. A caveat of an elite-managerialist theory of democracy is that grievances perpetually exist: "there is always enough discontent in any society to supply grass-roots support for a movement if a movement is organized and has at its disposal the power and resources of some established elite group."[9] Accordingly, grievances alone are insufficient to instigate the formation of social movements;[10] the centrality of organizational needs and resources, e.g., money, labor, office space, is established as a primary factor in movement development. The research question is altered from *why* individuals participate to *how* such participation is possible. In short, resource mobilization is a meso-level analysis focusing on *organizational* requirements of social movements.

Classical theory, rational choice, and resource mobilization cluster about the stereotypical American school, which emphasizes individual or collective *agency*, as opposed to the more Marxist perspective, which places stress on *structure*. In none of the three theories discussed above is any reference made to traditionally Marxist notions of solidarity, collective identity, or collective (class) consciousness. The aim of new social movement theory is to explain the existence of post-1960 movements which do not turn on class consciousness, but on identity – a phenomenon of advanced industrial and/or late-capitalist society – while simultaneously reviving a traditional Marxist interpretation through the incorporation of the participants' collective identity.[11] New social movement theory is a collection of neo-Marxist theories operating at the intersection of micro- and macro-analytic spheres; it seeks to understand *why* individuals participate in collective behavior via reference to grievance articulation while also claiming the structuralist view that identity is *shaped* by the overarching circumstances and dynamics of advanced industrial society.

In response to new social movement theory, the American school was forced to focus more fully on macro-level analysis, that is, the interaction between the state and the social movement without relying on a Marxist interpretation. Political opportunity structure (POS) filled this theoretical gap. Political opportunity structures refer not to necessarily permanent nor formal configurations of political institutions and historical precedents for social mobilization which protesters can exploit to promote collective action.[12] In essence, at a macro-level then, social movement formation boils down to a question of timing; as sociologist Sidney Tarrow notes, "People join in social movements in response to political opportunities and then, through collective action, create new ones. As a result, the 'when' of social movement mobilization – when political opportunities are opening up – goes a long way towards explaining its 'why.'"[13] Therefore, political opportunity structure is a macro-analysis that evaluates how different governing structures affect mobilization by providing possible institutional opportunities such as electoral realignments; hence, POS is useful when comparing and contrasting similar movements in different countries.

Since the purpose of this book is to explore the development of the gay and lesbian movement in two nations with distinct political institutional arrangements, the political process model (PPM), a variant of POS, will be used as a foundation. The use of this particular theory implies a pragmatic fit between an existing theory and a methodological approach to interpreting and comparing empirical data regarding the American and British gay and lesbian movements. The political process model will be used to make sense of the political relevance of the historical case studies discussed in later chapters. PPM avoids the macro-structural bias of POS because it is a multifaceted theory which navigates the linkages among the micro, meso, and macroanalytic levels. Critical understanding of social movements occurs most fully at the overlap of these spheres. By operating at this analytical juncture, PPM utilizes both the essential components of the theories introduced above and realizes the potential complementary nature of traditionally American and Marxist perspectives.

The political process model: a multi-faceted analysis

All theories are relatively incapable of accurately depicting and evaluating historical circumstance; however, some are better able to minimize the distorting lens. The aim, when understanding social movements, is not to develop a totalizing theory that accounts for every potential variable, but to derive a model which can answer the foundational questions of any given analysis. In this case: *why* people participate (micro-level), *how* they (afford to) participate (meso-level), and *when* they participate (macro-level). Each of these questions underlies a specific focus whether it be oriented toward individual motivation, organizational resources, or the external/institutional environment. *A theory which can address the interrelated nature of each of these questions without necessarily privileging one above the others will provide the most comprehensive understanding of social movements and the communities that they foster.* The political process model (PPM) accomplishes this by successfully navigating the junctures of the micro-, meso-, and macro-analytical levels to isolate three crucial factors in the development of collective insurgency: changing opportunity, pre-existing organizational strength, and cognitive liberation coupled with collective identity formation. PPM is essentially made up of two distinct but related dynamics: movement formation and movement maintenance. The first part is represented by the tri-factor interaction of a changing opportunity structure, organizations to seize control of this opportunity, and the psychological alteration of a minority group from an isolated victimized perspective to a sense of collective empowerment. The second part of the model refers to the actions of the organizations that make up the movement. These networks are sometimes called pressure groups, special interests, or interest groups. Unlike a movement, interest groups are characterized by defined membership, permanent staff, and fiscal responsibilities. More importantly, whereas a movement is sometimes characterized as acting outside of the political system, interest groups navigate from within it.[14] They interact with the political institutions – the legislative-executive system, the judiciary structure, and the political party dynamics of a state – in an attempt to reform the ruling ideology. Hence, this two-step design of PPM neatly parallels the notion of social movements and interest groups as existing on a continuum of non-elite political action:

At one end are those social actions based on contagious spontaneity and lack of structure (a crowd or a riot). At the other end are the established, structured interest groups; and in the middle are the social movements having an element of spontaneity and some structure, but not characterized by well-defined formal organization. A social movement may have one or several core organizations among the mass of people who support the movement. The core organizations can often mobilize these followers, but they cannot always control them as a disciplined force.[15]

Thus, as the movement moves beyond the initial insurgency generation stage to an emphasis on sustainability, the pre-existing organizations are replaced by new, more enduring groups which, emerging from the movement itself, attempt to impose some centralized direction on the movement. This shift demarcates the schism inherent in the two parts of the political process model.

The diagram illustrates that a change in the opportunity structure creates the possibility of insurrection by a group which usually has little

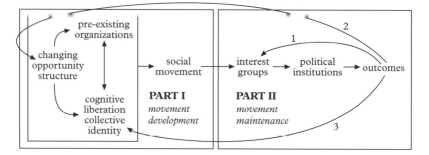

Figure 1.2 *The political process model*

or no access to political power. Yet, an opportunity for insurrection is quite different from and does not guarantee the actual existence of a movement. Some type of pre-existing organizational network which can enable further member recruitment, select leaders, and facilitate communication must exist to harness this opportunity and convert it into an organized and sustainable protest.[16] Finally, the disenfranchised minority must experience a cognitive shift characterized by a relinquishment of fatalism and victimized self-perception, an endorsement of a rights-based agenda, and a new sense of efficacy and agential power.[17] This psychological liberation is enabled by the potential implications inherent in the shift in political opportunities and the possibility of newly grasped political power.[18] Thus, all three factors are integrally tied in the evolution of a movement. Yet, while PPM asserts that all of these three initial factors are interdependent and necessary for successful collective action, the model presupposes the existence of some type of vulnerability in the socioeconomic and political environment.[19] In other words, it assumes that some type of initial opportunity, what Tarrow refers to as a changing opportunity, must exist.

For a movement to maintain itself after its initial generation, the initial opportunity becomes irrelevant, collective identity must be sustained, and the pre-existing organizations must give way to new networks – created by the movement itself and therefore inherently better able to mobilize the movement – that respond to social control. Such control may take the form of government-facilitated repression or the development of a countermovement.[20] As each outcome occurs, whether it be a legislative or legal reform achieved by the social movement or a backlash by a countermovement, the social movement organizations or interest groups are forced to reorient and reshape themselves. As the arrow labeled "1" depicts, any outcome inevitably instigates some opportunity shift causing the organization(s) to respond and possibly the movement's collective identity to reformulate itself. Arrows "2" and "3" also demonstrate how outcomes can affect movements. Arrow "2" illustrates how an outcome can create new changing opportunity structures. As chapter 2 and chapter 3 will detail, the unwillingness of both the American and British conservative regimes to provide adequate funding for AIDS research and care throughout the 1980s promoted a reinvigorated wave of grass-roots organizing within the gay and lesbian community. Arrow "3" shows that outcomes, or even the marked lack of outcomes, can foster and reinforce collective identity and cognitive liberation. As further illustrated in the following two chapters, the lack of reform in the United States was partly responsible for the cognitive liberation illustrated by 1970s gay liberation; the prospect of Clause 28 in the United Kingdom also fostered the emergence of this psychological shift from victimization to pride and political empowerment. No arrow exists connecting outcomes to pre-existing organizations because an outcome presupposes a social movement; outcomes affect the social movement organizations or interest groups which have replaced the pre-existing organizations.

The political process model has five obvious advantages over other theories. First, it achieves the theoretical flexibility and comprehensiveness so clearly desired in the beginning of this chapter; as a theory, it exists in that central overlapping of the three analytical spheres depicted in Figure 1.1. Second, it successfully combines aspects of the American and Marxist tradition into a coherent theory. The PPM adopts an elite-managerialist perspective in its depiction of political power as unequally spread throughout different groups in society. Yet, it also takes a potentially Marxist stance by positing the existence of latent political leverage embodied by the non-elite. Third, it explains individual participation through the concept of collective identity formation. It goes beyond NSM by linking this collective identity to organizational strength, a concept usually discussed by resource mobilization theory.[21] Fourth, by focusing on the interaction between movements and the state through the exploitation and creation of political opportunities, PPM abandons the psychological bias of the classical model (where activists are perceived as dysfunctional) and reasserts the primarily *political* nature of social movements. Fifth, by emphasizing the role of political institutions in structuring the methodology and goals of social movements, the model enables a comparative study of similar movements in different nations to be undertaken. Such a study, which is the ultimate purpose of this book, should tell us much about distinct forms of government and how each responds to its citizens.

Conclusion

After briefly exploring the various theoretical explanations of collective action, the political process model appears most useful in our attempt to comprehend a comparative history of the American and British gay and lesbian movements and how the governing structures affect movement development and movement sustainability. Its isolation of three inter-dependent factors – changing opportunity, pre-existing organizations, and cognitive liberation – provides a useful framework to track the emergence of these two movements. Theoretically, the differences in political institutions as defined by the British parliamentary or the American separation-of-powers system should not necessarily influence the evolution of the movement if a changing opportunity, a network of pre-existing organizations, and some form of psychological liberation occur in both nations. Since both systems are democratic, each will experience short-term political opportunities such as electoral shifts; long-term opportunities including war or industrialization historically occur without necessary regard for political systems (at least if both are democratic). The differences in ruling systems should appear to have their primary effect on the second stage of social movements, that is, movement maintenance, when interest groups interact with the political elite. To apply this theory, we must turn our attention to the emergence and growth of the gay and lesbian movements in the United States and the United Kingdom.

2 Tracing the rainbow: an historical sketch of the American gay and lesbian movement

> To be overtly homosexual, in a culture that denigrates and hates homosexuals, is to be political.
>
> Michael Bronski

An historical analysis of the American gay and lesbian movement utilizing the political process model seeks to answer a variety of questions. What changing opportunity enabled the movement even to be contemplated? What types of organizations existed to capitalize on this opportunity? When did members of this disenfranchised minority realize their inherent agential power thereby experiencing cognitive liberation? What organizations did the movement spur? What type of response did the movement elicit from both the government and other citizens? How has the movement changed over the course of its existence? What factors have influenced this change? This chapter attempts to address these questions by sketching the evolution of the American gay and lesbian movement throughout the post-war period. Starting with an analysis of the effect of the Second World War on homosexual identity and community, this chapter traces the development of the homophile movement of the 1950s and 1960s, explores the effect of the Stonewall riots of 1969, examines the ideology of gay liberation in the 1970s, analyzes the complex impact of AIDS on the movement, and assesses current notions of gay and lesbian visibility and the present status of the movement. Although homosexuals have obviously existed before this time, and a homosexual subculture had been emerging since the late nineteenth century, the onset of the Second World War ushered in a new era of visibility that would profoundly shape not just the lives of American gay men and lesbians, but question the understanding of sexuality itself.

No longer alone: World War II and changing opportunity

Despite and sometimes because of the mounting political war against them, the generation of the Second World War gay veterans did find ways to break through their isolation. They responded to a hostile environment by expanding their "closet," making it a roomier place to live. Previous generations had invented the closet – a system of lies, denials, disguises, and double entendres – that had enabled them to express some of their homosexuality by pretending it didn't exist and hiding it from view. A later generation would "come out of the closet," learning to live as proud and open gay men and women and demanding public recognition. But the World War II generation slowly stretched their closet to the limits, not proclaiming or parading their homosexuality in public but not willing to live lonely, isolated lives. (Allan Berube, *Coming Out Under Fire*)

The emergence of the gay and lesbian movement in the United States is sometimes pinpointed to an exact date and time: 1:20 a.m. on Saturday, 28 June 1969. On this day, police officers from Manhattan's Sixth Precinct raided a well-known gay bar, the Stonewall Inn, on Christopher Street in Greenwich Village.[1] The police raid was not so uncommon; innumerable gay bars experienced such hostile actions from law enforcement. Yet, the reaction of the patrons was extraordinary: they fought back sparking two days and nights of riotous confrontation between approximately four hundred New York police officers and two thousand gay men and women, especially people of color.[2] This event is so crucial because it signifies the emergence of group action among a previously docile, powerless, and seemingly invisible minority. Soon after the riots, various organizations, such as the Gay Liberation Front (GLF), were created to help mobilize gay men and lesbians into a viable political force. Yet, as historian John D'Emilio demonstrates, a curious contradiction developed between the GLF rhetoric and the reality of the homosexual community. Activists of the early 1970s excoriated the invisibility and silence which many felt characterized the homosexual lifestyle. However, leaders of liberation movement organizations demonstrated a remarkably uncanny ability to mobilize these supposedly silent and isolated men and women: by the middle of the 1970s over one thousand gay and lesbian organizations existed in the United States.[3] This apparent inconsistency can be resolved if we take D'Emilio's advice: "clearly what the movement achieved and how lesbians and gay men responded to it belied the rhetoric of isolation and invisibility. Isolated men and women do not create, almost overnight, a mass movement premised upon a shared group identity."[4] In other words, the gay and lesbian movement did not suddenly start at a given hour on a certain day following a specific event; rather, it embodies an historical process marked by diverse opportunities, multiple organizational networks, and instances, such as the Stonewall riots, which ushered in some shift in the personal perspectives of gay men and lesbians themselves.

If we acknowledge that the gay and lesbian movement is a movement grounded in a shared and community identity, then we must also recognize that such identity formation takes time. Numerous theorists, including Michel Foucault, contend that the homosexual *per se* does not inherently exist but is a social construction dating from the late nineteenth century:

As defined by the ancient civil or canonical codes, sodomy was a category of forbidden acts; their perpetrator was nothing more than the juridical subject of them. The nineteenth-century homosexual became a personage, a past, a case history, and a childhood, in addition to being a type of life form, and a morphology, with an indiscreet anatomy and possibly a mysterious physiology. Nothing that went into his total composition was unaffected by his sexuality. It was everywhere present in him: at the root of all his actions because it was their insidious and indefinitely active principle; written immodestly on his face and body because it was a secret that always gave itself away. It was consubstantial with him, less as a habitual sin than as a singular nature . . . Homosexuality appeared as one of the forms of sexuality when it was transposed for the practice of sodomy onto a kind of interior androgyny, a hermaphrodism of the soul. The sodomite had been a temporary aberration; the homosexual was now a species.[5]

Foucault contends that the transformation from homosexual behavior to homosexual identity was induced by a shift in societal norms, particularly from a medical angle. Foucault isolates the transference of a type of *behavior* to a type of *person*, indeed the confluence of the behavior with the person and thereby the construction of a new identity. The characterization of the Victorian era as prudish and sexually repressed is entirely incorrect according to Foucault; rather, this age saw a proliferation of studies and discourses which attempted to categorize various forms of sexual deviancy including prostitution and homosexuality.[6] In doing so, sexual acts were no longer mere practices, but, instead, became reflections of the individual essence; the acts became symptoms and expressions of a deeply ingrained identity.

Even if homosexuality is considered an identity and not an act, it does not necessarily follow that homosexual individuals would come together to form a community and a unified social movement. If homosexuality was no longer an act to be avoided, but a description of a person, that person could still remain isolated from similar individuals. However, the altered social conditions of the Second World War, i.e., a sex-segregated society marked both by men under the strain of warfare and a predominantly female domestic labor force, provided a critical opportunity for gay men and lesbians to come into contact with one another.

John D'Emilio refers to the Second World War as fostering "a nationwide coming out experience."[7] The sex-segregated atmosphere created by militarization immensely disrupted the heterosexual patterns of peace-time life; this phenomenon is no more apparent than in the armed forces. The war functioned as an opportunity to promote homosexual visibility in a variety of ways. First, by asking recruits if they had ever felt any erotic attraction for members of the same sex, the military ruptured the silence that shrouded a tabooed behavior, introducing some men to the concept for the first time.[8] Furthermore, the act of considering a homosexual unfit for service illustrates both a sharp shift in the language of military policy as well as a change in the common perception of the homosexual. Previously the sexual act was the problem; individuals discovered in sexual relations with a member of the same sex were punished accordingly through the military's criminal justice system. Yet, the drafting procedure initiated by the Second World War viewed the person as mentally ill. In an interesting parallel to Foucault's argument, the homosexual act was *not* banned, rather the homosexual himself was banned.[9] Second, the war functioned to bring previously isolated homosexuals together. Given that the recruits could merely lie about their sexual inclinations and that the draft preferred young and single men, it was likely that the armed forces would contain a disproportionately high percentage of gay men.[10] Third, soldiers often resorted to antics which exaggerated common homosexual stereotypes to alleviate sexual tension. Soldier slang utilized derogatory homosexual terms to heterosexualize military life. Soldiers called each other "cocksucker" or "sweetheart." When reproached by a commanding officer, the private was said to have "his ass reamed," and a close friend of the soldier was called his "asshole buddy."[11] The practice of pairing off with another intimate friend, or "asshole buddy," was quite common. Howard Brotz and Everett Wilson, two sociologists who studied military life, commented that "covering up for, defense of, and devotion to one's buddy [were] expected"[12] and that these buddies often expressed "sentiments that would be considered maudlin under other circumstances."[13] In his work, *The Great War and Modern Memory*, historian Paul Fussel explores the homoerotic feelings that soldier buddies expressed for each other during the First World War; one soldier, Anthony French, wrote to his "buddy," Albert William Bradley, who had been killed in combat:

'This, my dear Bert, is your day, and I'm more than ever reminded of you . . .' As I wrote a deep sadness afflicted me . . . I drafted some verses of a lyric of unadulterated sentimentality that told of a friendship and what it had meant to me. It ended with

> . . . one happy hour to be
> With you alone, friend of my own,
> That would be heaven to me.[14]

Not all soldiers who experienced homoerotic feelings toward other soldiers or who even engaged in sex with other men were gay. Often heterosexual men engaged in "situational homosexuality," having sex with other men only to attain a level of physical intimacy deprived by the war experience.[15] It was not uncommon for men to dance together at canteens, to share beds at hotels when on leave, or to share train berths while in transit.[16] The critical point is not that the Second World War led to an increase in the number of homosexuals; such a statement can neither be confirmed nor denied. Rather, *the war created a sexual situation where individuals with homosexual feelings or tendencies could more readily explore them without the absolute fear of exposure.*

As men were sent abroad, women were increasingly needed to fill the gap left in the labor force. Often women moved to urban centers and lived in boarding houses and apartments occupied mostly by other women. The lack of men forced women to reorient their social lives around female companions. Just as the military environment did not necessarily foster the expression of homosexuality among soldiers, this predominantly female environment did not necessarily cause heterosexual women to become lesbians. However, the social space in which women could interact with one another greatly expanded, and, as a result, lesbians had an increased chance of meeting one another within the cover of the primarily female environment.[17]

Approximately 150,000 women participated in the Women's Army Corps (WACS). Like the draft, WACS recruitment isolated a population likely to include a disproportionately high percentage of lesbians. The vast majority of WACS were single, childless, and under thirty. Coupling this population with the popular conception that military service was a masculine pursuit, WACS acquired a reputation for being overridden with lesbians.[18] Furthermore, the official military response to lesbianism was relaxed. Training manuals praised the formation of intense friendships among women, and officers were instructed not to speculate about the prevalence of lesbians in the corps, to ignore damaging hearsay, and to attempt to provide guidance rather than punish a known lesbian.[19] In other words, the military provided women with a relatively safe outlet to explore their sexuality.

The Second World War altered the prevailing heterosexual gender dynamic by creating the necessary single-sex segregation of the military leaving women home to take on traditionally male roles. As D'Emilio notes, "the war temporarily weakened the patterns of daily life that channeled men and women toward heterosexuality and inhibited homosexual expression."[20] Men and women who were aware of a same-sex attraction, but had not acted upon it, could explore it in a relatively safe environment. Individuals already aware of their homosexuality could meet others, embark on relationships, and build further ties to help foster the development of a gay community. The point is not that the war experience fostered homoerotic feelings and a rise in homosexuality. Rather, the disruption in the social environment caused by the war provided the *opportunity* for homosexuals to meet, to realize others like themselves existed, and to abandon the isolation that characterized the homosexual lifestyle of the pre-war period.

The return of peace brought with it the re-establishment of pre-war heterosexual gender norms; men replaced women in the work force, and women resumed their role in the home. Yet, the war had enabled gay men and women to discover one another and to start building networks than could not easily be torn down; thus, the immediate post-war years witnessed early forms of homosexual-oriented organizations. The Veterans Benevolent Association was established by several honorably discharged gay men in New York City in 1945 to function as a social club for gay ex-servicemen hosting parties and dances. In Los Angeles, interracial couples organized the Knights of the Clock to discuss mutual problems of their relationships.[21]

The late 1940s and the early 1950s also saw a proliferation of novels which featured predominant gay characters and themes. Claire Morgan's *The Price of Salt* (1951) and Jo Sinclair's *The Wasteland* (1946) relayed the stories of strong lesbians and their acceptance of their sexuality while Charlie Jackson's *The Fall of Valor* (1946) discussed the homoerotic social environment experienced by men during the war. While these texts tended to bow to contemporary beliefs on homosexuality portraying the characters as usually unhappy and fundamentally tragic, their publication signaled a small opening of social mores and a shift in the traditional attitude toward homosexuality.[22]

The most significant indication of this transformation was the publication of Donald Webster Cory's, a.k.a. Edward Sagarin,[23] *The Homosexual in America: A Subjective Approach* in 1951. In this text, Cory touches on some fundamental issues that still confront the movement today: the need to come out, the controversy of same-sex marriage, and the use of popular culture as a tool of visibility.[24] He was also remarkably ahead of his time in both his contention that the United States was not a heterosexual society, but rather an anti-sexual society in which all sex is viewed as dirty – heterosexual acts are only privileged due to their procreative function – as well as in his notion that homosexuals were inherently progressive.[25] Such ideas were not common until the formation of the Gay Liberation Front in the early 1970s; they resurfaced with Queer Nation in the early 1990s, and now are common themes of academic queer theory.[26] Cory cites the dilemma in which the homosexual found himself or herself locked in the 1950s:

If he [the homosexual] does not rise up and demand his rights, he will never get them, but unless he gets those rights, he cannot be expected to expose himself to the martyrdom that would come if he should rise up and demand them. It is a vicious cycle, and what the homosexual is seeking, first and foremost, is an answer to this dilemma.[27]

Cory suggests that the answer lies in the liberalization of the media and the discussion and inclusion of homosexuality in the newspapers, radio, and theater.[28] If the heterosexual majority becomes more comfortable with the concept of homosexuality through film, literature, and press coverage, then the danger of identifying as homosexual significantly declines. The tone of this idea is obviously mild as it seeks heterosexual tolerance rather than affirmation on one's own terms. However, this type of inclusion in popular culture (as well as more affirmative representations) is precisely how the movement could be characterized today. Adamantly fought for since the 1960s and expanded in later decades, this visibility in television and film has opened new questions regarding what kind of gay men and lesbians are seen and who remains invisible. Such selective visibility has led some activists to question whether it is undermining the movement itself.[29]

Gay subcultural institutions proliferated in the immediate post-war period. Gay bars, while more common in large cities such as New York City or Los Angeles before the war, now opened in smaller cities including Worcester, Massachusetts, Kansas City, Missouri, and Richmond, Virginia.[30] The gay bar provided a relatively safe place for gay men to meet each other without having to maintain a facade of heterosexuality.[31] The bars also shaped a gay identity that went beyond a so-called individual "affliction" toward a sense of community.[32] The bar therefore functioned as a vehicle by which to promote a primitive notion of collective identity before the era of gay liberation. As Urvashi Vaid, former Executive Director of the National Gay and Lesbian Task Force notes, the bars helped to establish a "nascent post-war community of gay men and women [which] was, like its nongay counterparts, ripe for political organizing. As the climate grew more overtly hostile toward gay men and lesbians, a new social movement came into being."[33] Given the importance of the gay bar as a community-building institution, it should come as no surprise that the first major backlash by the gay community toward heterosexual oppression emerged at a gay bar, the Stonewall Inn.

Despite these advances in gay subcultural and community development, gay men, lesbians, and any other individuals who failed to fit into the heteronormative pattern of post-war life encountered oppression from the religious, legal, and medical fields. Judeo-Christian tradition denounces homosexuality as a sin.[34] At this time, engaging in consensual homosexual sex was a criminal act throughout the United States. The medical sphere tended to view homosexuals as diseased or mentally ill.[35] Yet, within this last field, homosexuals tended to make the most advances even if they were merely indirect and unplanned. Since homosexuals were believed to suffer from a psychological disease, they could elicit compassion and a sympathetic attempt to find a "cure." Indeed, Foucault suggests, as homosexuality became a subject of scientific inquiry, further theories could be suggested which differed from the disease model. Medicine, unlike religion, could suggest dissenting ideas without blasphemously confronting the Bible's teachings.[36]

The foremost example of medical studies of sexuality put forth at this time was Alfred Kinsey's *Sexual Behavior of the Human Male* and *Sexual Behavior of the Human Female*, both published in 1948 and 1953. Although widely discredited now, Kinsey's survey provided the most comprehensive study of the sexual behavior of Caucasian Americans. After interviewing more than ten thousand subjects of both sexes, Kinsey recorded the following observations. Approximately fifty percent of men had at some time experienced a homoerotic feeling, thirty seven percent had reached orgasm in a post-adolescent homosexual act, four percent considered themselves exclusively homosexual, and slightly more than twelve percent engaged in same-sex encounters for at least three years. Twenty-eight percent of females recorded having homoerotic feelings at some point in their life, thirteen percent had reached orgasm with another woman, and about two percent considered themselves to be exclusively homosexual.[37] Kinsey drafted a seven-point scale to detail the fluidity of sexual orientation in which at least eighteen percent of Americans did not consider themselves universally or mostly heterosexual.[38] Such results led Kinsey to conclude that "persons with homosexual histories are to be found in every age group, in every social level, in every conceivable occupation, in cities and on farms, and in the most remote areas of the country."[39] These findings helped to tear away the ideological barriers that hindered equality for gays and lesbians by opening up for discussion the formerly taboo topic of sexuality. *In short, the reports enlarged the already existing opportunity structure provided by the war; the political environment was ripening for the formation of a homosexual movement.* Yet, the Kinsey reports were also utilized throughout the repressive decade of the 1950s as ammunition against the increased visibility of homosexuality in the United States.

The onset of Cold War anti-Communist repression spearheaded by

Senator McCarthy marked the 1950s as a decade rife with political repression. Yet, communists were not the only target; individuals who did not conform to the mainstream heteronormative image reminiscent of the pre-war period were perceived as enemies of the state.[40] According to historian Barry Adam,

in McCarthyism as in other reactionary ideologies, psychosymbolic connections between gender and power assigned a place to homosexuality. For the authoritarian mind, male homosexuality signified the surrender of masculinity and the 'slide' into 'feminine' traits of weakness, duplicity, and seductiveness . . . the McCarthyites drew together personal feelings of self-esteem expressed in terms of 'manhood' with national self-esteem and belligerence. Working within a gender discourse that associated maleness with toughness and effectiveness, in opposition to supposedly female weakness and failure, male homosexuality symbolized the betrayal of manhood – the feminine enemy within men.[41]

In March of 1950, John Peurifoy of the State Department classified homosexuals as "security risks." A month later, Guy Gabrielson, national chairman of the Republican Party sent a letter to seven thousand party employees declaring that "perhaps as dangerous as the actual Communists are the sexual perverts who have infiltrated our Government in recent years."[42] A month later, the Republican Governor of New York, Thomas Dewey, "accused the Democratic national administration of tolerating spies, traitors, and sex offenders in the Government Service."[43] Amidst these growing fears that homosexuals were infiltrating the highest levels of government and threatening national security, the Senate Investigations Subcommittee of the Committee on Expenditures in the Executive Department began an inquiry in June of 1950 and released its report, "Employment of Homosexuals and Other Sex Perverts in the US Government," in December of 1950.

The report's attack on homosexuals was twofold: it degraded the personal character of gay men and lesbians, and it contended that homosexuals embodied a threat to national security.[44] The report used Kinsey's data regarding the greater prevalence of homosexuality than previously thought to promote a sense of paranoia: these diseased individuals were everywhere and, worse yet, they could not be detected by any physical features. The committee concluded that gay men, lesbians, and bisexuals exhibited emotional instability, and their tendency to engage in so-called "perverse" sexual acts was indicative of weak moral integrity.[45] The committee contended that

the presence of a sex pervert in a Government agency tends to have a corrosive influence upon his fellow employees. These perverts will frequently attempt to entice normal individuals to engage in perverted practices . . . Government officials have the responsibility of keeping this type of corrosive influence out of the agencies under their control . . . One homosexual can pollute a Government office.[10]

According to the Senate report, employing homosexuals would not only put fellow workers at risk, but would endanger the security of the entire nation. The notion that homosexuals were inherently a security risk was defended by using a story of Russian spies blackmailing an Austrian counterintelligence officer in the First World War by threatening the exposure of his homosexuality.[47] The report asserted that

It is the experience of intelligence experts that perverts are vulnerable to interrogation by a skilled questioner and they seldom refuse to talk about themselves . . . The pervert is easy prey to the blackmailer. It follows that if blackmailers can extort money from a homosexual under the threat of disclosure, espionage agents can use the same type of pressure to extort confidential information or other material they might be seeking.[48]

The ultimate conclusion of the report was that gay men and women were fundamentally unsuited for employment in the federal government. The report profoundly affected the ability of gay men and lesbians to maintain their government positions. Between 1947 and 1950, the dismissal rate of homosexuals from an executive branch office averaged five per month.[49] By mid-1950, between forty and sixty dismissals per month were based on homosexuality. This rate continued through 1955, and homosexuals were officially banned from the government with the passage of Executive Order 10450 under President Eisenhower in April of 1953.[50] In total, between 1947 and 1950, 1,700 applicants for government positions were turned away because of professed homosexuality, 4,380 individuals were discharged from military service, and 420 gay men and lesbians were dismissed or forced to resign from government posts.[51]

While the national government endorsed an anti-homosexual stance, gay men and lesbians encountered the more immediate danger of police harassment. Bar raids became quite prevalent. In the 1950s, approximately one hundred gay men were arrested each month in Philadelphia on misdemeanor charges, and approximately one thousand gay men were arrested each year in Washington, DC. During the 1953 New York City Mayoral election, raids on gay bars increased dramatically.[52] The wearing of drag was outlawed in Miami in 1953, and a year later, after the murder of a gay man in Miami, newspapers "demand[ed] that the homosexuals be punished for tempting 'normals' to commit such deeds."[53] In such a seemingly backward environment where the victim is blamed for murder, the American Civil Liberties Union refused to support gay and bisexual individuals in their attempts to attain equality.[54]

The Second World War coupled with the Kinsey studies of the late 1940s created the *opportunity* for men and women unsure of their sexual orientation or already aware of their homosexuality or bisexuality to meet others like themselves and realize their commonality. The proliferation of gay bars enabled the community development and identity formation initiated during the war to continue. However, anti-Communist repression, military and government witch hunts, and bar raids continued to demonstrate the enormous challenges that gay men and women encountered daily. The increasing attacks on homosexuals may have actually promoted community development by making homosexuality a topic for national-level discourse; indeed, in their analysis of sexual minority movements around the world, sociologists Barry Adam, Jan Willem Duyvendak, and Andre Krouwel, found that "politicization of a social group seems to be facilitated, rather than hampered, when political repression is evident but not too strong."[55] D'Emilio makes a similar point by contending that these attacks "hastened the articulation of homosexual identity and spread the knowledge that they [gay men and women] existed in large numbers. In other words, the repression was enough to make people want to fight it, but not strong enough to quell any reactionary spirit. Ironically, the effort to root out the homosexuals in American society made it easier for them to find one another."[56] Yet, even if they could find one another, the widespread condemnation of homosexuality led many gay men and lesbians to consider homosexuality to be an individual problem not indicative of injustice but disease.[57] Nevertheless, the juxtaposition of the opportunity provided by the Second World War for gay men and lesbians to explore their identity and the subsequent repressive environment of the 1950s fostered a dissonant atmosphere from which the first politically active gay and lesbian organizations emerged.

Making a minority: the homophile movement and expanding opportunity

Above all, audacity. (Henry (Harry) Hay)

The important difference between the male and the female homosexual is that the Lesbian is discriminated against not only because she is a Lesbian, but because she is a woman. Although the Lesbian occupies a "privileged" place among homosexuals, she occupies an under-privileged place in the world. (Shirley Willer, "What Concrete Steps Can be Taken to Further the Homophile Movement?")

I say that it is time to open the closet door and let in the fresh air and the sunshine; it is time . . . to discard the secrecy, the disguise, and the camouflage;

it is time to hold up your heads and to look the world squarely in the eye as the homosexuals that you are, confident of your equality, confident in the knowledge that as objects of prejudice and victims of discrimination you are right and they are wrong, and confident of the rightness of what you are and the goodness of what you do; it is time to live your homosexuality fully, joyously, openly, and proudly, assured that morally, socially, physically, psychologically, emotionally, and in every other way: *Gay is good*. It is. (Frank Kameny, "Gay is Good")

A historical sketch of the American gay and lesbian movement reveals that the movement's guiding ideology exhibits a bipolar pattern exacerbated by gender-based rifts. Movement philosophy tends to swing between periods of moderation or assimilationism on one side and militancy and liberationism on the other. These seemingly oppositional ideologies have divided the movement throughout the post-war era. The homophile movement, initiated in 1951 with the formation of the first modern gay rights organization, the Mattachine Society, illustrates the effect of these conflicting ideologies on mobilization. The history of the Mattachine Society specifically, and of the homophile movement in general, follows a pattern of brief militancy followed by a long period of assimilation and moderate leaders leading to a crescendo of renewed radicalism climaxed by the Stonewall riots.

Founded by Harry Hay in April of 1951 in Los Angeles, and modeled after the communist party, the Mattachine Society became the first organization of what would become the homophile movement.[58] The secret hierarchical and cell-like organization adapted from the communist party was necessitated, according to the founders, by the oppressive environment fostered by McCarthyism. Yet, Mattachine drew on the communism for more than just a structural guide; Marxist ideology functioned as a means to mobilize a mass homosexual constituency for political action. Utilizing a Marxist understanding of class politics, that is, a class as merely a socioeconomically determined entity until it gains consciousness enabling recognition of its inherent political power, Hay and the other founding members theorized that homosexuals constituted a similarly oppressed minority group. Homosexuals, like members of the proletariat, were trapped in a state of false consciousness purported and defended by the heterosexual majority which maintained homosexuality to be a morally reprehensible individual aberration.[59] Hence, the early Mattachine attempted to promote a measure of cognitive liberation and homosexual collective identity. During a time when both religion and law condemned homosexuality, and medicine viewed it as an individual psychological abnormality, the Mattachine Society was advocating the development of a group consciousness similar to that of other ethnic minority groups in the United States.[60] The parallel to Jews, Catholics, and African-Americans as conscious minority groups is readily apparent in the Mattachine statement of purpose:

1 TO UNIFY: While there are undoubtedly individual homosexuals who number many of their own people among their friends, thousands of homosexuals live out their lives bewildered, unhappy, alone – isolated from their own kind and unable to adjust to the dominant culture. Even those who may have many homosexual friends are still cut off from the deep satisfactions man's gregarious nature can achieve only when he is consciously part of a larger unified whole. A major purpose of the Mattachine Society is to provide a consensus (sic) of principle around which all of our people can rally and from which they can derive a feeling of "belonging."

2 TO EDUCATE: The Mattachine Society holds it possible and desirable that a highly ethical homosexual culture emerge, as a consequence of its work, paralleling the emerging cultures of our fellow minorities . . . the Negro, Mexican, and Jewish Peoples . . . The Society . . . is in the process of developing a homosexual ethic . . . disciplined, moral, and socially responsible.

3 TO LEAD: It is necessary that the more far-reaching and socially conscious homosexuals provide leadership to the whole mass of social deviants if the first two missions (the unification and the education of the homosexual minority), are to be accomplished . . . Only a Society, providing an enlightened leadership, can rouse the homosexuals . . . one of the largest minorities in America today . . . to take the actions necessary to elevate themselves from the social ostracism an unsympathetic culture has perpetrated upon them.[61]

Phrases such as "own people," "derive a feeling of 'belonging,'" "homosexual culture," and "homosexual ethic" illustrate a fundamental shift in the way the leaders of Mattachine perceived themselves and how they wished to be viewed by others. The influence of Marxist notions of an oppressed group are clearly visible in the description of the "unsympathetic" and "dominant" heterosexual culture. The bourgeoisie is now the heterosexual, and the proletariat has become the homosexual. By asserting that homosexuals constituted a minority comparable to other ethnic groups, Mattachine defined itself rather than being defined by the dominant culture: homosexuality was distinct from and morally equivalent to heterosexuality. Self-definition is a recurring theme in the attempts to create a validating and positive collective identity, and the sexual minorities community continued the trend with the adoption of "gay" in the 1970s and the less widespread adoption of "queer" in the 1990s.[62] Furthermore, the comparison to ethnic minorities provided a model for action; homosexuals should follow the lead of other groups and politically organize for equal civil rights.[63]

In order to help develop the homosexual consciousness, the

Mattachine Society coordinated public discussion groups. By late 1951, approximately twelve discussion groups existed throughout southern California; Mattachine billed these events as positive alternatives to the anonymous sexual encounters fostered by the bar and bathhouse sub-culture.[64]

Mattachine increased in popularity and visibility during 1952 when Dale Jennings, a founding member, was arrested for lewd behavior and claimed to be a victim of police entrapment.[65] The organization received many letters of support and financial contributions. After thirty-six hours of debate, the jury returned deadlocked; the charges were dismissed, and the Mattachine Society declared a victory.[66]

After this initial small show of political force, Mattachine guilds proliferated throughout southern California. By 1953, the Society had an estimated two thousand members and one hundred discussion groups stretching from San Diego to Santa Monica.[67] In that same year, the organization launched *One*, a magazine expressly devoted to discussion of homosexual concerns.[68] As the organization expanded, members became increasingly uncomfortable with its secretive structure and leftist orientation. Given the rise of McCarthyism, some members wanted to distance themselves from communism as much as possible. Already putting themselves at political risk by joining a homosexual organization, these individuals did not want to endanger their lives any further.

In order to mitigate some of the growing dissension, the original five members called for a convention in April of 1953 to convert the Mattachine Society into an above-ground organization. However, rather than ameliorating tension, the conference merely exacerbated the rift between the moderate and militant perspective. Chuck Rowland and Harry Hay were confronted by the demands of Kenneth Burns, Marilyn Reiger, and Hal Call. The former individuals stressed the need to build an ethical homosexual culture and to end the prejudice that privileges heterosexuality as morally superior.[69] Burns, Reiger, and Call took the opposite stance. They emphasized assimilation and suggested that homosexual behavior was a minor characteristic that should not foster a rift with the heterosexual majority. Reiger contended that

we know we are the same . . . no different than anyone else. Our only difference is an unimportant one to the heterosexual society, unless we make it important . . . [equality will result from] integrating . . . not as homosexuals, but as people, as men and women whose homosexuality is irrelevant to our ideals, our principles, our hopes and aspirations.[70]

By declaring homosexuality to be an unimportant difference that the heterosexual majority cares little about, Reiger failed to take into account the staunch anti-homosexual campaigns associated with McCarthyism. Yet, by reaffirming that homosexuals were human beings, she managed to strike a chord in an audience that still, despite the Mattachine discussion groups, internalized the negative views of homosexuality espoused by dominant culture. Reiger's speech coupled with growing fears about the current leaders' communist backgrounds led to a dramatic shift in leadership. Burns, Reiger, and Hall took control of the organization and steered it towards what historian John D'Emilio calls a "retreat to respectability."[71]

Abandoning its communist-based ideology, the post-convention Mattachine Society no longer sought to promote a homosexual culture or mass movement. Instead, it established an assimilationist tendency emphasizing homosexuality as primarily an individual problem, and it turned to psychology to provide theories on homosexuality. The new leadership proposed, and members endorsed, an elimination of any mention of "homosexual culture" from the statement of purpose. Indeed, the statement no longer even identified the Mattachine Society as a homosexual organization; the word "homosexual" was eliminated from the passage altogether.[72] Shortly after the conference, attendance at discussion groups fell off sharply. Despite the decline in Mattachine, *One* magazine remained vibrant, attracting the more radical elements of the Society and maintaining its reputation as a forum for topics relating to homosexuality.[73]

By the end of 1955, membership in the Mattachine Society increased and chapters developed in San Francisco, New York, and Chicago. On 21 September 1955, another homophile organization, the Daughters of Bilitis (DOB), was established by four lesbian couples in San Francisco though Del Martin and Phyllis Lyon are mostly credited with maintaining it in early years.[74] This organization, similar to the assimilationist Mattachine, emphasized education and self-help activities. The DOB's "Statement of Purpose" cites as its main goals "education of the variant, with particular emphasis on the psychological, physiological and sociological aspects, to enable her [the lesbian] to understand herself and make her adjustment to society in all its social, civic, and economic implications."[75] Despite its commitment to legal reform, stated as its final aim in its statement of purpose, the DOB functioned ultimately as a safe meeting space for lesbians and bisexual women who did not feel comfortable in the lesbian bar scene. As one flyer notes, the DOB was "a home for the Lesbian. She can come here to find friendship, acceptance and support. She can help others understand themselves, and can go out into the world to help the public understand her better."[76] In contrast to the early Mattachine, the DOB had no interest in collectively organizing lesbians for political action; it had no agenda to promote group identity. Rather, its main function, like that of Mattachine as directed by Ken Burns, was to help integrate the homosexual into heterosexual society by de-emphasizing the importance of sexual difference and seeking the acceptance of the majority culture.

Yet the ascension of the assimilationist and moderate perspective did not drown out the voices of more radical homosexuals who desired to end oppression through direct action. One such individual was Frank Kameny who started a Washington, DC, branch of the Mattachine Society (MSW) in 1961. Kameny unabashedly asserted his beliefs in a speech at a convention of the Mattachine Society of New York (MSNY) in 1964. Tired of the homophile obsession with discovering the cause of homosexuality and the organization's deferment to the psychology establishment's labeling of homosexuality as a mental sickness, Kameny criticized his colleagues. There was no reason to find a cure for homosexuality because homosexuality was not an illness; rather it was a characteristic marking a particular group of people. In his discussion he utilized the cultural frame established by the African–American civil rights movement. He contended

I do not see the NAACP or CORE worrying about which chromosome and gene produces [a] black skin or about the possibility of bleaching the Negro. I do not see any great interest on the part of the B'nai B'rith Anti-Defamation League in the possibility of solving the problems of anti-semitism by converting Jews to Christians . . . we are interested in obtaining rights for our respective minorities as Negroes, as Jews, and as homosexuals. Why we are Negroes, Jews, or homosexuals is totally irrelevant, and whether we can be changed to whites, Christians, or heterosexuals is equally irrelevant.[77]

Beyond a mere scolding of the current homophile leaders for guiding the movement down a useless path that failed to promote full homosexual equality, the above passage reveals a resurgence of the ethnic minority model utilized by Hay and the original founders of the Mattachine. Yet, by the middle and late 1960s, activists no longer had to rely on Marxist teachings to learn about the development of group consciousness and social insurgence. Kameny merely drew on the burgeoning civil rights movements and feminist movements in the United States. Both of these movements, especially the later stages in which black power and radical feminism took hold, exemplified the development of New Left politics. The New Left engendered renewed militancy in the homophile movement and led to a situation ripe for the full emergence of a gay rights movement by the end of the 1960s and the beginning of the 1970s.

Kameny utilized the civil rights movement and the role played by the NAACP, Students for a Democratic Society (SDS), and the Student

Non-violent Coordinating Committee (SNCC) as a model of coalition building. In 1963, he organized a regional confederation, the East Coast Homophile Organizations (ECHO), composed of MSW, MSNY, DOB – New York, and the Janus Society of Philadelphia. Kameny aimed to promote a more militant ideology that endorsed direct action. Yet, ECHO soon splintered when the DOBNY withdrew in June of 1965 claiming that Kameny's use of picketing was too extreme.[78] The presidents of DOBNY defended their withdrawal on the basis that "demonstrations which define homosexuality as a unique minority defeat the very cause for which the homosexual strives – *to be an integral part of society.*"[79] The tendency to cling to its more moderate stance was not the only reason the DOB pulled out of ECHO. Lesbians and bisexual women were in the unique position relative to gay and bisexual men of having to navigate a dual identity that suffered a dual oppression. Lesbians were oppressed because they were lesbians, but also because they were women; consequently, an internal debate erupted in many women about whether to remain active in the homophile movement through DOB or whether to defect to the women's movement through networks such as the National Organization of Women. The struggle was embodied in the personality of activist Shirley Willer. In an address to the National Planning Committee of Homophile Organizations in the summer of 1966, Willer contended that problems such as police harassment and sodomy law, which seemed to make up the majority of the homophile agenda, did not affect women.[80] Willer further claimed that:

there has been little evidence however, that the male homosexual has any intention of making common cause with us [lesbians] We suspect that should the male homosexual achieve his particular objective in regard to his homosexuality he might possibly become more of an adamant foe of women's rights than the heterosexual male has been. (I would guess that a preponderance of male homosexuals would believe their ultimate goal achieved if the laws relating to sodomy were removed and a male homosexual were appointed chief of police.)[81]

Such harsh comments were mitigated by Willer's simultaneous desire to maintain the DOB's participation in the homophile movement so as to at least expand the perspective of the male-dominated movement. In May of 1967, the DOBNY sponsored the first meeting of the Eastern Regional Conference of Homophile Organizations (ERCHO) to replace ECHO after its collapse in 1965.[82]

Besides experiencing gender-based conflict, the homophile movement was increasingly embroiled in the moderate versus militant debate throughout the late 1960s. The former perspective was embodied in the commentary of Dick Lietsch of MSNY whereas the latter was symbolized by Frank Kameny of MSW. The debate was most clearly depicted in an ongoing dialogue between the two individuals. Lietsch asserted that Kameny's emphasis on building a homosexual communal identity was inappropriate. Only approximately 4 percent of the population was exclusively homosexual according to Lietsch. He saw the purpose of Mattachine to reach people who engaged in homosexual acts only on occasion, and "help them come to grips with themselves. We're not interested in 'bringing them out' and encouraging them to give up their heterosexual activities . . . We . . . encourage them to swing both ways and enjoy themselves, and try to help them avoid trouble."[83] Kameny recognized that Lietsch's emphasis on helping the individual cope with his homosexuality reflected not only a moderate approach, but more importantly and more dangerously, an unquestioning acquiescence to the dominant image of homosexuality as something that even necessitated coping with and avoiding trouble.

Kameny's response chides his colleague's assimilationist tendencies:

we must instill in the homosexual community a sense of the worth of the individual . . . We must counteract the inferiority which ALL society inculcates into him in regard to his homosexuality . . .

Our people need to have their self-esteem bolstered – singly, and as a community.

The very idea of changing to heterosexuality . . . is a tacit acknowledgment of inferiority . . .

People who are TRULY equal, and TRULY not inferior, do NOT consider acquiescing to the majority and changing themselves . . .

To submit to the pressure of immoral societal prejudice is immoral. Self-respecting people do not so submit. Self-respect is what *I* am trying to inculcate in my people, even if you are not.

When you acquiesce to "therapy" and "change" in the manner which you do, you simply confirm . . . all of the feelings of inferiority, wrongness, and self-contempt with which society has inculcated the individual homosexual. You harm the homosexual, and you harm the movement.[84]

Kameny's stress on the movement reveals an understanding for the desperate need to forge a collective identity-based movement if gay men and women were ever to achieve political, legal, and social change. As opposed to Lietsch, Kameny attempted to provide a more lasting equality by fundamentally confronting the prejudice of the heterosexual majority rather than attaining immediate objectives in a piecemeal fashion. Furthermore, Kameny's emphasis on repudiating acquiescence to the heterosexual norm suggests a prideful homosexual identity. As such, the ideology that Kameny espoused not only signaled a degree of cognitive liberation from victim to empowered agent, but it was also a subtle foreshadowing of the liberationist theories purported after the

Stonewall riots. This psychological shift took its cue from similar more militarist tendencies taking shape in the civil rights and feminist movements.

While various organizations of the homophile movement were mired in this unending debate, mainstream attitudes toward homosexuality continued to shift. The Mattachine Society defended its right to publish *The Mattachine Review* to the US Supreme Court in 1958. Throughout the 1960s, gay and lesbian-oriented novels such as Jean Genet's *Our Lady of Flowers*, Hubert Selby's *Last Exit to Brooklyn*, and John Rechy's *City of Night* were published. Best-sellers of the decade including Allen Drury's *Advice and Consent* and James Baldwin's *Another Country* all contained gay characters and gay-themed subplots. In October of 1961, the Production Code Administration of Hollywood allowed homosexuality to be portrayed in film. In 1962 and 1963, films such as *The Children's Hour*, *Walk on the Wild Side*, and *The Best Man* all had gay characters. These films still usually portrayed the gay and lesbian characters as having some kind of tragic end. In December of 1963, *The New York Times* published a front-page feature detailing the emergence of a gay subculture, and related articles appeared in *Newsweek*, *Time*, *Harpers*, and *Life*.[85]

Relative to the previous decade, the 1960s embodied a great deal of reform and liberalization of attitudes toward homosexuality. In the legal field, this change was not necessarily represented through an actual alteration or repeal of existing laws, but rather a broadening of support among the heterosexual community for an expansion of civil rights and the attainment of full gay and lesbian equality. For example, only Illinois and Connecticut repealed their anti-sodomy legislation; in 1961, Illinois became the first state to adopt the Model Legal Code of the American Law Institute that decriminalized private consensual homosexual sex.[86] Yet, Americans for Democratic Action, the New York Liberal Party, Wisconsin's Young Democrats, and the American Civil Liberties Union (ACLU) all accepted the principle of a basic right to private consensual sex. Many legal writers of the middle and late 1960s favored complete decriminalization of homosexuality altogether. The supreme courts of California, New Jersey, New York, and Pennsylvania all recognized the basic right of gay men and women to congregate thereby providing legal protection to the bar scene and recognition of the growing gay subculture. More gay-related legal cases were reaching federal appellate courts. Between 1960 and 1964 only twelve cases were heard, but this number increased 250 percent between 1965 and 1969. Finally, in 1967, the ACLU accepted the premise that individuals have a fundamental right to privacy, reversed its policy towards homosexuals, and guaranteed them legal support.[87]

The religious and medical spheres, also traditional harbingers of anti-homosexual rhetoric, demonstrated some tendency towards reform. The Committee on Religion and the Homosexual (CRH) was established in 1964 in San Francisco. This organization sought to re-evaluate the traditional Judeo-Christian stance on homosexuality as sinful. While religious bodies continued to consider homosexuality to be immoral, numerous Protestant and Roman Catholic churches, following the lead of those in the United Kingdom, advocated the decriminalization of homosexuality.[88]

In the medical field, the model of homosexuality as indicative of psychological disturbance came under increasing attack. Columbia University students picketed a forum on homosexuality sponsored by the medical school. Dick Lietsch of MSNY was invited by NBC to discuss and debate homosexuality with numerous physicians on national television. In 1967, Evelyn Hooker was appointed by the National Institute of Mental Health to study homosexuality; the investigative committee's report, released in 1969, gave credence to the liberal notion that human sexuality covered a wide spectrum of behavior and that homosexuals exhibited no inherent signs of mental illness.[89] *In short, the political and cultural environment had undergone a liberalizing shift which had created the opportunity for the emergence of a mass homosexual movement.*

Despite this increasingly liberal environment and consequent ripening of opportunity initially provided by the Second World War, and despite a multitude of gay and lesbian organizations throughout the country, a mass gay rights movement failed to materialize at this time for three reasons. First, few examples of positive effects of gay mobilization existed. Coming out was considered too risky if social change had not yet been proven to be feasible, and the DOB and Mattachine had yet to demonstrate its ability to make any significant political changes. Second, while the political environment was entertaining more debate around homosexuality both in popular culture and medical circles, the vast majority of this debate was led by heterosexuals. While research proliferated, it was conducted by individuals lacking the experience of oppression.[90] Third, the homophile movement, after the 1953 convention and before the resurgence of militancy, engaged in the paradoxical process of disassembling itself. By advocating that homosexuals should assimilate, and that the only difference between homosexuality and heterosexuality was fundamentally unimportant, it destroyed any possibility of mass mobilization because it devastated the potential for collective identity formation.[91] Not until many more gay men and women were willing to participate, overcome their self-perception as diseased persons, and recognize themselves as an oppressed minority with potential for collective action, would a full movement become possible.

Becoming gay: Stonewall and liberation

You know, the guys there were so beautiful. They've lost that wounded look fags all had ten years ago. (Allen Ginsberg a few days after the Stonewall riot)

Exclusive heterosexuality is fucked up. It reflects a few people of the same sex, it's anti-homosexual, and it is fraught with frustration. Heterosexual sex is fucked up too; ask women's liberation about what straight guys are like in bed. Sex is aggression for the male chauvinist; sex is obligation for the traditional woman. And among the young, the modern, the hip, it's only a subtle version of the same. For us to become heterosexual in the sense that our straight brothers and sisters are is not a cure, it is a disease. (Carl Wittman, *A Gay Manifesto*)

What we now perceive as the lesbian, gay, bisexual, and transgender (LGBT) movement at the beginning of the twenty-first century planted its roots in the 1970s; yet, the movement that took shape in that decade bears little resemblance to its modern form of various and highly organized state and national-level organizations. To conceive of a gay and lesbian rights movement in the 1970s is to confront a decentralized history of numerous short-lived organizations, clashing personalities, grassroots, local, and state-level activism, the rise of a religiously based conservative backlash, and the curious denouement of a movement before it seemingly reached political climax. The struggle for gay and lesbian rights in the 1970s unfolded in New York City, San Francisco, Los Angeles, Washington, DC, Miami, Boston, Minneapolis-St. Paul, Eugene, Oregon, and Wichita, Kansas. The cast of activists is wide and varied: Craig Rodwell, Jim Owles, Jim Fouratt, Marty Robinson, Frank Kameny, Elaine Noble, Harvey Milk, Virginia Apuzzo, Barbara Gittings, Rita Mae Brown, Bruce Voeller, Steve Endean, Kerry Woodward, Jean O'Leary, Midge Costanza, Reverend Troy Perry, Barney Frank, Allan Spear, David Goodstein, Sheldon Anderson, David Mixner, and countless others. For the first time, the gay and lesbian rights movement attracted nationally known or soon-to-be-known politicians: Senator Edward Kennedy, President Jimmy Carter, President Ronald Reagan, Governor Jerry Brown, Senator Diane Feinstein, and Washington, DC Mayor, Marion Barry, among others.

The movement fostered a powerful countermovement. Spearheaded by Anita Bryant's "Save Our Children" Campaign to repeal Dade County, Florida's gay rights ordinance, the message of "traditional family values," carried forth by Jerry Falwell and Pat Robertson, led to a rash of anti-gay initiatives and/or the repeal of recently won expanded civil rights protections inclusive of sexual orientation throughout the late 1970s. Yet, as the movement took shape in the 1970s, it suffered also from repeated internal fractures as lesbians fought to distinguish and ultimately separate from a gay male culture seemingly preoccupied with sodomy reform and other laws related to sexual activity. The movement struggled through each internal rupture managing to establish numerous lobby organizations and political action committees including the Gay Liberation Front, the Gay Activist Alliance, the National Gay Task Force, the Municipal Elections Committee of Los Angeles, and the Gay Rights National Lobby. The decade ended with the unprecedented March on Washington for Lesbian and Gay Rights on 14 October 1979 that attracted anywhere from the Parks Service estimate of 25,000 to marchers' estimate of 250,000 participants.[92]

By the end of the decade the political side of the movement almost seemed to fizzle faster than any of its predecessors. Spun out of similar concerns that grounded the civil rights and feminist movements, the gay and lesbian rights movement emerged as much of the leftist energy began to wane and as the national culture turned conservative. Having established a vibrant culture and exuberant lifestyle in safe enclaves of San Francisco's Castro district or New York City's Greenwich Village, the movement appeared to de-politicize just as it acquired the numbers, public visibility, and cultural confidence to become political. Characterizing the culture of the gay male community as it entered the 1980s, Dudley Clendinen and Adam Nagourney note: "These men had no inkling of gay liberation . . . and, by all appearances, very little notion of oppression, at least now that they had escaped their hometowns for the gay life of San Francisco. Gay liberation had somehow evolved into the right to have a good time – the right to enjoy bars, discos, drugs and frequent impersonal sex."[93] Afraid to come out of the closet at the end of the 1960s, only ten years later gay men enjoyed an unprecedented hedonism and visibility that pushed political activism into an increasingly secondary position relative to embracing the new liberating gay lifestyle.

Gay liberation evolved from one transcendental moment that symbolized the shift from victim to empowered agent. It came in the late evening of Friday, 27 June 1969 at a seedy gay bar, the Stonewall Inn, in Greenwich Village. Despite the bar's lack of running water and rumors that its filthy glasses caused a hepatitis outbreak, the Stonewall was popular because it was one of the few gay bars in New York City that allowed dancing.[94] Patrons of this particular bar usually ranged in age from late teens to early thirties and included what historian Toby Marotta has called "particularly unconventional homosexuals,"[95] e.g., street hustlers, drag queens, and "chicken hawks."[96] When officers raided the bar at 1:20 a.m., numerous customers did not flee the scene. As the police arrested some of the drag queens, the crowd became restless, and, as some escapes were attempted, rioting broke out. The *Village Voice* reported that

the scene became explosive. Limp wrists were forgotten. Beer cans and bottles were heaved at the windows and a rain of coins descended on the cops . . . Almost by signal the crowd erupted into cobblestone and bottle heaving . . . From nowhere came an uprooted parking meter – used as a battering ram on the Stonewall door. I heard several cries of "let's get some gas," but the blaze of flame which soon appeared in the window of the Stonewall was still a shock.[97]

Perhaps their unconventionality freed these particular gay individuals from the more reserved tactics advocated by MSNY. Arrest or public embarrassment carries no substantial threat for a street hustler. Most likely, none of the patrons were particularly worried about losing a government or corporate job. Those individuals who rioted could do so because their personal circumstances enabled them to proclaim actively their homosexuality without the threat of gravely negative circumstances. Before the end of the evening approximately two thousand individuals battled nearly four hundred police officers.[98]

On Saturday morning a message was haphazardly scrawled on one of the bar's boarded-up windows: "THEY INVADED OUR RIGHTS, THERE IS ALL COLLEGE BOYS AND GIRLS AROUND HERE, LEGALIZE GAY BARS, SUPPORT GAY POWER."[99] Rioting continued on Saturday evening; by most official accounts, it was less violent than the previous evening. On Sunday morning a new sign was posted on the outside of the bar: "WE HOMOSEXUALS PLEAD WITH OUR PEOPLE TO PLEASE HELP MAINTAIN PEACEFUL AND QUIET CONDUCT ON THE STREETS OF THE VILLAGE – MATTACHINE."[100] These two messages encapsulate the growing rift of ideology in the existing homophile movement. The former advocated a militant, adversarial, and radical position while the latter maintained more staid and conformist tactics. Phrases such as "gay power" belie how dependent the gay liberation movement was on the precedent-setting frames used by both the black power and radical feminist movements.

The movements that embodied the New Left – the student movement, the anti-war movement, the black power movement, and the feminist movement – began to utilize a new vocabulary to describe their present circumstances. Instead of viewing them in terms of discrimination, minority groups spoke of structural oppression inherent in the capitalist system. *Instead of aiming for equality and integration, the goal shifted to liberation and self-determination.*[101] These movements represented a new blend of politics and culture that moved beyond standard Marxist leftist thinking to incorporate other areas of oppression which were perhaps more relevant at this time than economic class. Black power perceived oppression as fundamentally racial; feminism introduced the notion of gender as systematically enforced; and gay liberationists contended that underlying sexism was heterosexism.[102] Gay men and lesbians often participated in both the civil rights and feminist movement although often without disclosing their sexual orientation. Carl Whitman, who wrote "A Gay Manifesto" in 1970, was a national president for Students for a Democratic Society (SDS). Robin Morgan, Charlotte Bunch, and Leslie Kagan were lesbians who were all heavily affiliated with the women's movement.[103] Yet, despite the New Left's commitment to equality, the movements that composed it were rampant with sexism and homophobia. Stokely Carmichael, one of the leaders of the SNCC, remarked that "the only position for a woman in the SNCC is prone"[104] and that "homosexuality is a sickness, just as are baby-rape or wanting to be head of General Motors."[105]

The gay liberation theory which emerged in the post-Stonewall era was essentially New Leftist in that it was not concerned with the goals of gays and lesbians alone, but with overturning the white male hegemony which characterized modern capitalism. The theory entailed a shift away from the class-based Marxist principles to a struggle over cultural representation. Gay liberation theory assumed that all individuals are innately sexually androgynous. By asserting this supposition, it attempted to destroy the limitations of the patriarchal sex and gender dynamic that insists on a masculine/feminine and homo/hetero division.[106] Yet, gay liberationists contended that since they questioned the very notion of heterosexuality itself, they were also necessarily combating notions of sexism. In this sense, they saw themselves as not only integrally tied to the New Left but as the vanguard of New Left political action.[107]

Liberation theory was organizationally embodied in the Gay Liberation Front (GLF) established in July of 1969. Gay men and women, but especially the former, disgusted with the moderate tactics and assimilationist aims of MSNY, established this new group as a militant arm of the New Left. The distinctions between Mattachine and Liberation philosophies are summarized by the GLF's statement of purpose:

we are a revolutionary homosexual group of men and women formed with the realization that complete sexual liberation for all people cannot come about unless existing social institutions are abolished. We reject society's attempt to impose sexual roles and definitions on our nature . . . Babylon has forced ourselves to commit to one thing . . . revolution![108]

This statement makes no reference to fighting the ban on gay men or lesbians in the civil service or the military. It does not address discriminatory employment practices, the end of police harassment, or the repeal of anti-sodomy laws. In other words, the GLF made no explicit statement on the attempt to achieve civil rights legislation or work through the existing political system at all. Rather, as its name suggests, GLF sought liberation from constraint inherent in capitalism itself. It intended to work in concert with all oppressed minorities: women, blacks, workers, and the third world.[109]

In order to end structural oppression, the GLF, following the lead of radical feminists, sponsored consciousness-raising sessions. Consciousness-raising served to bring gay men and women together, to share their experiences, and to discover commonality. Discussion topics ranged from sexual attraction to relationship problems. Similarity of experience fostered a collective identity. It also encouraged the notion that such similarity could not exist if oppression were not inherent in the system itself.[110] The liberationist ideology that infused consciousness-raising sessions inspired cognitive liberation; it provided gay men and women with a basis to reject legal, medical, and religious definitions of homosexuality and, for the first time, to define themselves. Such definition is apparent in the name "Gay Liberation Front." The term homosexual was imposed upon gay men and women by the medical establishment as a term of illness. The term "homophile" symbolized the assimilationist and tactics of the Mattachine and DOB.[111] Radicals chose the word "gay" because it was how homosexuals referred to each other; the word symbolized self-definition and, as such, was a recognition of internal power.

Gay liberation also fundamentally restructured the definition of "coming out" in order to build and strengthen a mass movement. Whereas the phrase had previously referred to an individual acknowledgment of homosexuality to oneself, gay liberationists transformed it into an extremely public and political act. Coming out symbolized a total rejection of the negative definitions which society inflicted on the homosexual and substituted both acceptance and pride in one's gayness. Coming out was the ultimate means to conflate the personal and political. Coming out was no longer perceived as a simple one-time act, but as the adoption of an affirmative identity.[112] Furthermore, by acknowledging one's gayness, a person exposed himself or herself to social injustice ranging from verbal discrimination to physical violence. Hence, individuals who did come out had a personal tie to the success of a gay liberation movement.[113] Through the process of coming out, the victim status was discarded; homosexuality was transformed from a stigma to be hidden to a source of pride to be celebrated. *Indeed, by coming out, the homosexual became gay.* Coming out was the necessary psychological break to do what the homophile movement could never accomplish – attract a large following.

The ideology of the GLF was that critical element that had been missing from the earlier attempts to mobilize gay men, lesbians, and bisexuals. Even if individuals did not actively participate in the political movement, notions of prideful identity trickled into the subculture. Yet, despite their importance in promoting mobilization and insurgency, the GLF, like Mattachine before it, was soon wracked with internal division. The disagreement centered on the extent to which the GLF should foster the aims of other New Left organizations as opposed to focusing on gay oppression as a single issue. Numerous activists such as Jim Owles and Marty Robinson contended that the GLF was spreading its energy too thin, and its avoidance of hierarchical structure (assumed to be part of the evil innate in American capitalism) led to a fundamentally disorganized group.[114] Recognizing the benefits of the liberationist philosophy, i.e., the emphasis on consciousness-raising and coming out, and also understanding that MSNY was regressive in its approach, these activists established an organization in December of 1969 that lay between these two extremes: the Gay Activist Alliance (GAA). The GAA stressed working *within* the system to promote improvement in the everyday concerns of gay men and women by sponsoring candidates, holding rallies, converting its firehouse headquarters into a fund-raising massive gay disco on the weekends, and utilizing chaotic mixes of street theater and politics called zaps to attain media attention. Indeed, its first act, the promotion of a gay rights bill prohibiting employment discrimination against gays and lesbians, could not have more starkly marked the different guiding principles of the GLF and GAA.[115]

As the 1970s progressed and the ideological rift between a single-issue and multi-issue perspective widened, the movement experienced further gender-based schisms. The dual oppression of lesbians as both homosexuals and women strained their allegiance to both the women's movement and the gay liberation movement. In the late 1960s, Betty Friedan denounced lesbianism as a "lavender menace" that threatened the integrity and credibility of feminism. Yet, in 1971, following the Second Congress to Unite Women in New York, NOW reversed its stance declaring that the oppression of lesbians was a legitimate feminist issue. With the women's movement's relative acceptance of lesbians, women began to abandon the gay movement in increasing numbers between 1971 and 1973.[116] The GLF and GAA, which were overwhelmingly male from their beginnings, tended to ignore the structural oppression which lesbians faced as women. As activist Marie Robertson claimed, "Gay liberation, when we get right down to it, is the struggle for gay men to achieve approval for the only thing that separates them from the 'Man' – their sexual preference."[117] Gay organizations responded to the female exodus too late and often viewed these lesbians with confusion and/or resentment as they established an autonomous feminist–lesbian subculture throughout the decade.

The 1970s ushered in an entirely new stage of gay and lesbian rights. Whereas the GLF collapsed by 1973 and the GAA did the same in 1974, the cognitive liberation produced by a redefinition of "coming out" and homosexuality itself profoundly affected gays throughout the nation. While the revolution for which liberationist theorists hoped never occurred, the movement witnessed incredible growth. In 1969, before the Stonewall riot, fifty homophile organizations existed in the United States; by 1973, there were over eight hundred gay and lesbian groups, and by the end of the decade they numbered into the thousands. One such organization, the National Gay Task Force established in 1973 and renamed the National Gay and Lesbian Task Force in 1986, would become one of the leading LGBT rights organizations in the United States. Gay bars continued to proliferate, but now gay-friendly and gay-owned health clinics, book stores, cafes, law offices, travel agencies, and churches and synagogues (most notably Troy Perry's Metropolitan Community Church) also sprung up. In 1974, the American Psychiatric Association de-listed homosexuality from its register of mental illnesses. In 1975, the ban on gays in the Civil Service was lifted.[118] The gay press expanded producing magazines and newspapers such as the *Advocate, Washington Blade, Gay Community News, Philadelphia Gay News*, and the *Windy City Times*.[119] Before the end of the decade, Detroit, Boston, Los Angeles, San Francisco, Houston, and Washington, DC, incorporated sexual preference into their civil rights codes. Openly gay and lesbian officials were elected to office including Elaine Noble to the Massachusetts State Assembly, Karen Clark and Allen Spear to the Minnesota State Assembly, and Harvey Milk to the San Francisco Board of Supervisors. In 1980, the Democratic Party adopted a gay and lesbian rights plank at the national convention and an African–American gay man, Mel Boozer, was nominated to be the Democratic Vice Presidential candidate.[120] Before the end of the decade, a national gay and lesbian civil rights bill had been introduced in both the House and Senate.[121] As historian Dennis Altman notes, the 1970s produced a gay male who was "non-apologetic about his sexuality, self-assertive, highly consumerist and not at all revolutionary, though prepared to demonstrate for gay rights."[122] Perhaps the most stunning example of the effect that cognitive liberation had on the growth of the movement is that the 4 July 1969 gay rights march at Independence Hall in Philadelphia attracted seventy-five participants whereas the first National March for Lesbian and Gay Rights on 14 October 1979 – a mere decade later – attracted between 100,000 and 200,000 participants.[123]

Despite these strides, by the end of the decade a new political conservatism swept across the United States, and the gay and lesbian movement encountered an active New Right countermovement. Anita Bryant spearheaded "Save Our Children" and rallied for the repeal of a gay rights ordinance in Dade County, Florida in 1977. Following Bryant's precedent, recently passed gay rights ordinances were repealed in Wichita, Kansas, Eugene, Oregon, and St. Paul, Minnesota.[124] These defeats fostered a massive initiative by gays and lesbians to prevent passage of the Proposition 6 (the Briggs Initiative) in California. This bill, which advocated the removal of homosexual teachers from public schools, was defeated fifty-eight to forty-two percent after then-governor Ronald Reagan came out against it.[125]

In another blow to the gay and lesbian community, San Francisco Supervisor Harvey Milk was assassinated on 11 November 1978 by Dan White, an ex-Supervisor; White was convicted of manslaughter and received an eight-year and seven-month sentence. Shock at the lenient sentencing on 21 May 1979 led to massive riots at San Francisco's city hall. By the end of the 1970s, opportunity for movement expansion dissipated. Gay liberation as a tenable ideology had died, the movement was weakened by diverse aims among gay men and lesbians, and political conservatism bolstered by a growing radical Christian right began to tear away at the inroads that movement organizations had made earlier in the decade. In short, the 1970s ushered into existence and concretized a highly visible gay male and, to a lesser extent, lesbian culture. By the end of the decade, gay politics appeared to be subsumed by an ever-expanding gay cultural lifestyle; however, the increased media attention given to that subculture by both mainstream media and a backlashing countermovement testify to the political impact of that cultural visibility. By the early 1980s, gay and lesbian rights was being actively debated at all levels of government despite or because gay cultural institutions were coming out of the closet. Yet, the nature and content of these debates on civil rights and privacy would dramatically shift after the discovery of a microscopic retrovirus that would come to be known as the Human Immuno-deficiency Virus.

A new crisis: the double-edged impact of AIDS

The only way we'll have real pride is when we demand recognition of a culture that isn't just sexual. It's all there – all through history we've been there; but we have to claim it, and identify who was in it, and articulate what's in our minds and hearts and all our creative contributions to this earth. And until we do that, and until we organize ourselves block by neighborhood by city by state into a united visible community that fights back, we're doomed. That's how I want to be defined: as one of the men who fought the war. Being defined by our cocks is literally killing us. Must we all be reduced to becoming our own murderers? ("Ned" in Larry Kramer's play, *The Normal Heart*)

AIDS IS A GAY DISEASE! . . . AIDS is a gay disease because a lot of gay men get AIDS . . . More important, most of what has been noble about America's response to AIDS has been the direct result of the lesbian and gay community. (Michael Callen, *PWA Coalition Newsline*)

In 1981, *The New York Times* reported that five gay men had acquired a curious cancer; in the seventeen years between 1981 and 1998, over 300,000 Americans have died from that disease now identified as Acquired Immune Deficiency Syndrome (AIDS), approximately 210,000 of whom were gay men.[126] If only measured in terms of its massively destructive impact, AIDS has fundamentally altered the gay and lesbian movement. Yet, to measure the disease's influence only by citing the death rate within a specific community dramatically and dangerously oversimplifies how AIDS has affected the movement. In numerous ways, the AIDS crisis produced a variety of positive externalities; on the other hand, not only did AIDS provide further anti-gay fodder for the New Right, it also spawned a related but distinct movement increasingly at odds with the equal rights agenda of the gay and lesbian movement. The AIDS movement had distinct aims from the gay and lesbian movement, but, perhaps more importantly, it achieved those aims through strategies never conceived as possible by gay rights activists in the 1970s. AIDS, therefore, dramatically shifted the tactics of sexual minority movement organizations throughout the 1980s and 1990s.

The most immediate impact of AIDS is the incredible rapidity with which it spread throughout the 1980s. By the end of 1981, 225 cases were reported nationwide. In the spring of 1983, this increased to 1,400; only two years later, AIDS cases rose by over 900 percent to 15,000. In 1987, this figure increased to 40,000 cases reported.[127] The disease's seemingly unstoppable nature coupled with the government and mainstream media's silence and lack of concern regarding both the virus itself and its most prominent class of victims in the United States, i e , gay men, forced the gay community to mobilize itself. Hundreds of community-based organizations including Shanti, Coming Home Hospice, Project Open Hand of San Francisco, and, most notably, Gay Men's Health Crisis (GMHC), developed to provide services to individuals coping with the virus.[128] With a staff of over two hundred individuals and an annual budget of twenty million dollars, GMHC has become the largest AIDS service organization in the world. The sexual minorities community also shaped the early response by supporting more open and frank discussions of sexuality in the media and by spearheading campaigns for "safer sex."[129]

The onset of the AIDS crisis also fostered a dramatic increase in the amount of people who were willing to come out. The lack of an adequate response – or any response at all – from the Reagan or Bush administrations forced gay men and women to realize that they were being abandoned by their government. Men who would not publicly express their homosexuality in the pre-AIDS era were becoming involved. Early executive director of GMHC, Robert McFarlane, asserted that "for a white man with a graduate degree and a good job who can pass, [discrimination was] not an issue. Never was. Until [AIDS] really got down to it and you realized they want you to die. If you want to be the way you are and not play their way, you're dead meat. You are literally left to die."[130] GMHC itself was started by men who were relatively uninvolved in gay and lesbian politics during the 1970s including Larry Kramer, Nathan Fair, Paul Popham, Paul Rapoport, Dr. Larry Mass, and Edmund White. Many of these individuals brought money, contacts, and business experience that pre-AIDS organizations never could have mustered.[131]

AIDS also forced a variety of celebrities including film stars, fashion designers, and government officials out of the closet, the most notable of whom was Rock Hudson in 1986.[132] Furthermore, with the realization that the virus was not contained within the gay male population but that anyone – gay, straight, male, or female – was susceptible, media visibility of the gay and lesbian community dramatically increased. Books such as *And the Band Played On* by Randy Shilts, published in 1987, and films including *Philadelphia*, released in 1993, demonstrated the greater willingness of heterosexuals to come to terms with both the AIDS epidemic and a politically active gay and lesbian minority.[133] Urvashi Vaid notes that "perversely put, we won visibility for gay and lesbian lives because we died in record numbers."[134] Gay visibility also increased as a result of many pre-AIDS organizations becoming nationally oriented in order to lobby the government more effectively for support. While gay liberation was predominantly a grassroots and local political movement, the

AIDS movement functioned at a national level. The National Gay and Lesbian Task Force (NGLTF) moved its headquarters from New York City to Washington, DC, and the ACLU hired a lobbyist specifically to cover AIDS issues for its Washington office.[135] Hence, AIDS enabled gay and lesbian politics to be heard in national public policy debates and electoral politics. Whereas most movement interest groups had acted with local and state political institutions, they now began to promote agenda implementation through Congress and the President.

AIDS reestablished and strengthened ties with both the lesbian and straight communities. Whereas lesbians often wavered in their commitment to the gay movement throughout the 1970s, opting to join the feminist movement instead and fostering an independent subculture of women-only festivals, bookstores, and cafes, AIDS, or rather the Right's exploitation of and the government's ignorance of AIDS, showed many lesbians and bisexual women that homophobia was still deeply ingrained in American culture.[136] Furthermore, the families of people with AIDS (PWAs) became involved in movement politics taking part in marches such as the 1987 March on Washington for National Gay and Lesbian Rights. AIDS and straight allies featured prominently in this demonstration which attracted approximately 650,000 participants. The Names Project AIDS Quilt was displayed on the Washington, DC Mall on 11 October 1987, and the parents of PWAs were invited to lead a candlelight march that evening.[137] Whereas the gay liberation movement of the 1970s attracted predominantly young countercultural white participants, the AIDS movement of the 1980s attracted Caucasians, African-Americans, Asian-Americans, Latinos, women, men, gays, straights, and bisexuals.

Lastly, the intransigence of the Reagan and Bush administrations as well as the relative lack of visibility in the more mainstream press revitalized direct action protest tactics reminiscent of the liberationist zaps of the 1970s. The AIDS Coalition to Unleash Power (ACT UP) was created in March 1987 to promote media attention to the AIDS crisis in hopes of raising universal awareness and acquiring political leverage. ACT UP was bolstered by the above-mentioned silence of the Republican-dominated executive branch, experiences at the 1987 march on Washington, increased media coverage, and the inability of more conservative AIDS groups to compete for participants. On 11 October 1987, the day following the march, five thousand individuals staged a National Civil Disobedience protest on the steps of the Supreme Court. The demonstration ignited enthusiasm for such direct activism. ACT UP's rallies, speak-outs, spray-painting, placard-painting, and leaflet-distribution both represented a wide range of opportunities for participation and were all oriented to attract media coverage. Early ACT UP leaders included media experts such as Ann Northrop, Michaelangelo Signorile, and Bob Rafsky. Protests incorporated political artwork and graphic design by popular artists such as Keith Haring. Placards such as the lime green portrait of Ronald Reagan with the word "AIDSGATE" emblazoned in pink or the "Bush AIDS Flag" which replaced the fifty stars with fifty skulls were designed to relay a highly charged political message as well as catch the eye. Finally, ACT UP's popularity derived from its ability to acquire media exposure even if only in the short term. ACT UP leaders claimed, and supporters agreed that, the organizations espoused a democratic and participatory culture reminiscent of the GLF; it often belittled more reform-orientated and "political insider" organizations such as the Human Rights Campaign or GMHC for working too slowly and utilizing behind-the-scene tactics that were so-called undemocratic and failed to represent anyone except the middle-class white gay male.[138]

Yet, just as AIDS enabled many of these positive externalities – media visibility, further political organization at the local and national levels, expanded support from both the gay and straight communities, a resurgence of direct action – many of these same benefits carried with them negative impacts on the movement. To mention nothing of the death toll or the vehement attack orchestrated by the New Right, AIDS engendered negative visibility for the gay, lesbian, and bisexual community, fundamentally derailed the movement's original agenda from equal rights to medical and social service provision, and produced an offshoot movement that increasingly distanced itself from the gay and lesbian movement utilizing different methods and having distinct goals.

The New Right exploited AIDS as a weapon with which to maintain inequality, to overturn the achievements of the 1970s, and to return the nation to an era of more traditional heterosexual values. After fighting for and winning the de-listing of homosexuality as a mental illness, gays and lesbians now confronted conservatives' exploitation of AIDS to re-link homosexuality with sickness. In 1985, Representative Newt Gingrich stated that "AIDS will do more to direct America back to the cost of violating traditional values and to make Americans aware of the danger of certain behavior than anything we've seen. For us, it is a great rallying cry."[139] Two-time Republican candidate for President, Pat Buchanan, was less subtle in furthering the myth that AIDS was a gay disease: "The poor homosexuals – they have declared war upon nature, and now nature is exacting an awful retribution."[140] Conservatives discussed quarantining early identified high risk groups, i.e., gay men,

IV drug users, and black and Hispanic men. The United States military imposed mandatory testing. Congress required all immigrants to be tested and forbade entry to anyone who was HIV-positive. Bathhouses and bars, staples of the gay subculture, shut down in record numbers.[141] The ultimate legislative achievement of the New Right was the passage of the Helms Amendment in 1987 which prohibited the use of federal funds to "provide Aids education, information, or prevention materials and activities that promote or encourage, directly or indirectly, homosexual sexual activities."[142]

Far more damaging than any attack from conservatives was the derailing effect AIDS had on the celebratory concepts of coming out and gayness introduced by gay liberation philosophy. The visibility that AIDS has conferred on gay men and women has been characterized by prominent queer theorist Leo Bersani as "the visibility of imminent death, of promised invisibility. Straight America can rest its gaze on us, let us do our thing over and over in the media, because what our attentive fellow citizens see is the pathos and impotence of a doomed species."[143] According to this analysis, the heterosexual majority is currently permitting a greater degree of gay and lesbian visibility because AIDS will eventually wipe out the movement anyway. Homophobic reactions in the media are declining because AIDS has essentially usurped the role of the homophobe.

In an effort to attain media coverage and government support in combating the virus, many gay and lesbian organizations attempted to "de-gay" AIDS and de-sexualize homosexuality. Existing institutionalized homophobia meant that AIDS could not be successfully combated if it was continually thought of as a "gay disease." In promoting the truthful notion that heterosexuals were also susceptible, the gay and lesbian movement abandoned the overarching and long-term aims of equality and fighting institutionalized homophobia for the immediate need of survival. "De-gaying" the disease also inhibited people from coming out since people could donate to AIDS organizations without the stigma of being associated with a gay organization.[144] "De-gaying" has also paradoxically led to a measure of invisibility of a minority which accounts for 70 percent of all AIDS cases. For example, at the 1987 march on Washington, no mention was given to the gay or lesbian community in the program regarding the Names Project AIDS Quilt nor during the five speeches delivered during the candlelight vigil.[145]

While AIDS did attract wider participation from the gay and straight communities, especially among upper middle-class gay men, such participation further steered the movement away from its traditionally leftist orientation. The influx of this group, while bringing immense resources, also brought political conservatism: "in place of liberation, the AIDS movement substituted nondiscrimination; instead of building a movement, it built agencies and bureaucracies; instead of placing its political faith in training and organizing gay and lesbian people, and our allies, into an electoral coalition, it placed faith in friends in high places."[146] AIDS brought into question the underlying point of gay liberation: was gay liberation about the right to have sex? Was gay liberation only about sex? In some sense, AIDS helped to bring back to the surface the same questions that impelled a lesbian-separatist movement to form in the 1970s. This time however, the question was dividing gay men on their response to the health crisis.[147] This more conservative tendency also led to a de-sexualization of homosexuality itself disregarding the connection between sexual freedom and gay liberation; since AIDS exposed gay sexuality, gay men and women often responded by de-emphasizing that sexuality and promoting a new image espousing monogamy and safer sex.

While the virus may have caused higher rates of involvement in various AIDS-related organizations, such groups rarely maintained the civil rights oriented agendas of earlier social movement groups. Most AIDS organizations did not directly promote sodomy reform or employment non-discrimination based on sexual orientation, and were instead primarily social service groups that focused on goals enabling survival rather than the long-term objective of overcoming homophobia.[148] The immense public health crisis that AIDS had created pushed gay and lesbian rights organizations to focus on national-level politics and concentrate less on grass-roots activism aiming for legislation at the local and state level. In this sense, the gay and lesbian and the AIDS movements are distinct entities. The latter grew out of the former, but the latter also dramatically impacted and altered the strategies of the former: "The spread of the AIDS epidemic also drew more and more gays and lesbians to the view that federal intervention on gay-related issues was essential."[149] Furthermore, the AIDS movement responded to a fundamentally different opportunity – the onset of a medical crisis – and, as such, it more readily attracted non-gay allies, increasingly distanced itself from the gay and lesbian movement, and became a competitor[150] with that movement for legislative and popular support. As Clendinen and Nagourney note, the creation of an AIDS movement was one instance of the "gay movement turning on its parents."[151] Just as the Gay Liberation Front encouraged the downfall of its predecessor, the Mattachine Society, now AIDS-related concerns overtook those of gay civil rights. The AIDS movement had an "urgent agenda [that] stood in contrast to the unhurried civil rights agenda that had dominated the gay rights movement for so long . . . The ground was shifting again. Faced with the AIDS epidemic, many homosexuals had originally turned in anger on doctors, the health system, and the government . . . many of them were now turning on the homosexual rights movement itself."[152] AIDS activists advocated the shut down of bath houses and sex clubs, venues often perceived as integral to the core freedoms connoted by gay liberation. In short, the AIDS movement attracted a different constituency (with some obvious overlap), pursued distinct goals, and adopted different strategies than the gay and lesbian rights movement.

The double-edged nature of AIDS is symbolically embodied in the Helms Amendment. This amendment, which prevented the use of federal funds to "promote" homosexual behavior, appears to have only a wholly negative impact on both the AIDS and the gay and lesbian movements. Yet legal theorist, Carl Stychin, suggests that "the paradox, though, is that in seeking to silence an identity and to deny a right of sexual citizenship, the prohibition on expression creates discursive space for the identity to be excluded. A prohibition must acknowledge the existence of the prohibited and this brings the prohibited practices into the public domain of discourse."[153] In an argument similar to Foucault's addressed earlier in this chapter, Stychin contends that while the Amendment harmed the movement, it represents a shift in political attitudes toward homosexuality. Whereas in previous decades the topic would rarely be discussed, now it is the subject of heated public debate. Sexuality has acquired a political connotation; the attempt to prohibit its expression only makes it more visible.

Just as the Helms Amendment represents such dual implications, so do most circumstances engendered by the AIDS crisis. Visibility was gained, but much of it was negative. It acquired national prominence, but AIDS overshadowed gay and lesbian rights at the national level. The movement expanded, but became increasingly mainstreamed into the Washington political power structure at the expense of grassroots participation. Direct action was rejuvenated, but at the expense of both movement solidarity and heterosexual support. These dramatic changes brought about by the AIDS crisis established the gay and lesbian movement as a major minority constituency in mainstream American politics; yet, as the various circumstances of the 1990s illustrate, this achievement, so vigorously fought for since the early 1950s, is now paradoxically threatening to weaken the movement itself.

Does *Will and Grace* help?: the movement today

Well, yes, "gay" is great . . . But when a lot of lesbians and gay men wake up in the morning we feel angry and disgusted, not gay. So we've chosen to call ourselves queer. Using "queer" is a way of reminding us how we are perceived by the rest of the world. It's a way of telling ourselves we don't have to be witty or charming people who keep our lives discreet and marginalized in the straight world . . . Yeah, QUEER can be a rough word but it is also a sly and ironic weapon we can steal from the homophobe's hands and use against him. (Anonymous, "Queers Read This; I Hate Straights")

Is everybody gay?! (Emily Montgomery (Joan Cusack), *In & Out*)

The American gay and lesbian movement, or rather gayness in general, has become increasingly visible in politics and popular culture throughout the 1990s. Enormous volumes of both pro- and anti-gay legislation have been debated, passed, and rejected mostly at the state level, but also at the national level, and the movement has continued to fight against an increasingly powerful Christian right. Yet, such visibility, while further enabling the promotion of the civil rights-based agenda of the movement, has revealed the multiple factions that currently exist in the movement – most importantly, the exclusion of people of color – as well as threatened the viability of earlier liberationist aims to end institutionalized heterosexism. While gays and lesbians may have received new prominence in national electoral politics – revealed by the 1992 presidential election – the movement also demonstrated its political weakness and lack of cultural acceptance at the national level by its inability to achieve a full lifting of the ban on homosexuals in the military, its failure to secure passage of the Employment Non-Discrimination Act (ENDA) in 1996, and its failure to prevent passage of the anti-gay Defense of Marriage Act (DOMA).

Throughout the 1970s and much of the 1980s, the gay and lesbian movement has been viewed as a primarily white male movement. The concerns of women and people of color were never foremost on the gay agenda. The essential "whiteness" of the movement becomes startlingly visible as gay African–Americans, Asians, and Latinos established separate sexual minority rights and AIDS organizations to help members of those particular minorities cope with the illness. The establishment of the Latino/a Lesbian and Gay Organization (LLEGO), the Native American AIDS Task Force, the National Gay Asian and Pacific Islander Network, and the National Black Gay and Lesbian Leadership Forum revealed that mainstream gay and AIDS organizations failed to recognize internalized elements of racism and sexism.[154]

Queer Nation attempted to overcome internal division within the movement and set forth a new seemingly post-identity-based agenda in which all elements of the gay, lesbian, bisexual, and transgender community could come together under a single unifying banner. Queer Nation developed in the summer of 1990 and drew upon the direct action tactics of ACT UP. Unlike ACT UP, which sought to attain media visibility and subsequent political response for the AIDS crisis, Queer Nation aimed to bring to the forefront the fundamental issues that AIDS had subsumed and sidetracked, namely combating institutionalized homophobia and achieving full gay equality.[155] In doing so, Queer Nation sought to move away from the racial and gender divisions that plagued the movement by asserting a new unitary identity of "queer":

Being queer means leading a different sort of life. It's not about the mainstream, profit margins, patriotism, patriarchy or being assimilated. It's not about executive director, privilege and elitism. It's about being on the margins, defining ourselves; it's about gender-fuck and secrets, what's beneath the belt and deep inside the heart; it's about the night. Being queer is "grass roots" because we know that everyone of us, every body, every cunt, every heart and ass and dick is a world of pleasure waiting to be explored. Everyone of us is a world of infinite possibility.[156]

Queer Nation attempted to create a unified group of all individuals considered sexually marginalized: gays, lesbians, bisexuals, transgenders, transvestites, etc. Furthermore, by uniting under the label, "queer," these activists take a once derogatory term and transform it into a statement of pride, power, and militancy. Assuming the label of "queer" is, in this sense, a second form of cognitive liberation that many activists experienced. The Stonewall generation, through coming out and proclaiming their gayness overcame the self and societally inflicted victimization of being homosexual. These "queer nationals," by asserting their queerness, counter the psychological damage incurred by the AIDS crisis and the resurgence of the far Right. The queer manifesto, "Queers Read This" states that "fear is the most powerful motivator. No one will give us what we deserve. Rights are not given, they are taken, by force if necessary."[157] This militancy reveals an ultimate expression of agential power that flows from the mental and emotional liberation of the post-AIDS movement.

Defining oneself as queer, as the Stonewall generation defined themselves as gay, is as much an expression of individuality as it is one of collective identity. In some sense, being queer is not so much identifying as something as it is identifying as what someone is not. Such negative and reflexive identification enables such a disparate group of individuals to come under one banner; yet, it paradoxically prevents that group from taking unitary action. By attempting to stand as a representative for all disempowered individuals, Queer Nation affirms a unity built out of difference. By blaming heterosexual society for constructing this difference, it denies the existence of any essential distinctive identity ultimately suppressing the internal differences which it seeks to represent.[158] Hence, instead of working through the gender and racial rifts that have damaged the movement, queer nationalism subsumed and belittled them in order to preserve cohesion. Film maker, Marlon T. Riggs found the centrality of white middle-class concerns of Queer Nation profoundly alienating: "the New [Queer] Nationalists, on the rare occasion they acknowledged my existence at all, spoke of me with utter contempt, spat and twisted my name like the vilest obscenity."[159] Queer Nation did not, as its advocates contended, become the ultimate unifier, but rather an expression of the internal factions – assimilationism versus militancy, age, gender, race, and class – that the movement has confronted since its emergence in the immediate post-war period.

Similar to ACT UP, the prevalence of Queer Nation chapters and other queer groups such as Lesbian Avengers and Women's Action Coalition and the occurrence of direct action tactics have declined steadily throughout the 1990s. Some activists became tired of the protests that were extremely energy-intensive. Some members of the gay and lesbian community could not relate to the "in-your-face" brand of activism and were disinclined to contribute. Queer Nation was heavily identified as a youth movement to which many in the sexual minorities community could not subscribe. In its attempts to avoid labels and promote an ideology of fluid sexuality, Queer Nation struggled to find an organizational premise, and thus succumbed to a similar problem which afflicted the Gay Liberation Front. Many of the original supporters succumbed to AIDS. Urvashi Vaid has astutely and eloquently summarized the paradoxical and shaky foundation of Queer Nation:

Queer Nation should more aptly have been called Queer Anti-Nation. The group consisted of people united more by what they stood against than what they stood for. Defined by style, individualism, and an opposition to the idea of normality, the group resisted any definition by substantive politics, political practice, or old notions of community. Queer activists may have been ideologically diverse, but they quickly established a new and fairly orthodox tribal language. QN had a dress code (leather, shaved heads, Doc Martens, and T-shirts with big lettering), an anti-establishment stand (the target mattered little: it simply needed to be more "fixed," and therefore regarded as more "mainstream" than the Queer Nationalist), and an attitude that spoke to the nineties (postmodern, in their faces, militant). The flourishing underground 'zines published by defiant queers ranted against the assimilation stance of those who used the words *gay* and *lesbian* to identify themselves. Queer became the vanguard; everything else was retro.[160]

Queer Nation may have been a short-lived organizational network, but its long-term legacy lies in cultural transformations ranging from the advent of queer theory to the positive connotation of "queer" to the fashion craze of body piercing which queer identity popularized. Yet Queer Nation not only succumbed to internal disorganization and disunity, but failed because the in-your-face politics which it espoused no longer appeared as relevant or appropriate given the political climate taking shape by 1992. Both the political and popular environment became increasingly willing to promote gay visibility to the extent that Andrew Kopkind wrote in *The Nation* in 1993, "Gay invisibility, the social enforcement of the sexual closet, is hardly the problem anymore. Overexposure is becoming the problem."[161] By then, especially in the presidential election of 1992, it seemed that gay issues had become mainstreamed and up for discussion, and suddenly the gay and lesbian community was no longer to be shunned, but to be courted. That is, at least, by the Democratic Party.

The 1992 election found the incumbent Republican President Bush battling an economic recession, a gay minority and its straight supporters increasingly disillusioned with the Republican response to AIDS, and an increasingly powerful Christian right which aimed to reinstate "traditional" family values. AIDS and the Right's negative response towards the disease brought gay issues to the forefront of the election forcing each Democratic contender to take a stance on gay rights. The position they took contrasted starkly to their Republican opponents. Every major Democratic candidate promised to increase AIDS funding and to lift the ban on gays in the military. Jerry Brown was supportive of gay rights and endorsed gay marriage. Paul Tsongas demonstrated early support when he introduced a federal non-discrimination bill to protect gays and lesbians during his first term as senator in 1979. However, the gay community was not courted merely on principle; gay rights had been a topic on which the Democratic Party had wavered since as early as the 1972 election,[162] and which party leadership had chosen to downplay after the disastrous loss of Walter Mondale to Ronald Reagan in 1984. However, the appeal of the gay constituency was money and votes. Indeed Bill Clinton's emergence as the candidate to receive the overall endorsement of the gay community had less to do with his stance on gay rights – a law criminalizing same-sex sodomy was passed while he was attorney general of Arkansas – and more to do with the fact that he actively sought the gay vote in direct contrast to anti-gay Republican sentiment couched in traditional family values rhetoric.[163] Nor did the help of an openly gay political consultant, David Mixner, harm Clinton's campaign. Mixner advised Clinton to tailor his speeches to stress the inclusion of gays and lesbians in his cabinet as well as a sincere desire to use federal resources to stem the AIDS crisis. An estimated 75 percent of the gay vote helped Clinton secure the presidency.[164]

The unprecedented visibility of gays and lesbians at the 1992 Democratic Convention and the prevalence of the "gay issue" in the election, especially in relation to the military ban, brought the movement into the realm of mainstream politics. Gay visibility increased in popular cultural arenas as well; however, such visibility had both positive and negative consequences. This visibility promotes and reflects greater tolerance of homosexuality; homosexuality is considered a legitimate topic of exploration, as demonstrated by the proliferation of gay and lesbian studies at the university level as well as the increased portrayal of gays on the small and large screen. Popular musicians such as Melissa Etheridge, Ani DiFranco, and k.d. lang, and actors including Ellen DeGeneres, Anne Heche, Rupert Everett, and Nathan Lane are all open about their homosexuality or bisexuality. The musical *Rent*, which discusses AIDS and gay sexuality, won the 1996 Tony Award for best musical. Tony Kushner's gay-themed play *Angels in America* won a Pulitzer Prize. Films such as *Philadelphia* (1993) – for which Tom Hanks won an Academy Award for best actor and which was also nominated as best picture of the year – confronted the impact of AIDS on gay men. Popular films that have reached a mainstream audience and that have explored gay themes or had gay characters include *My Own Private Idaho* (1991), *Threesome* (1994), *Reality Bites* (1994), *Clueless* (1995), *The Birdcage* (1996), *Chasing Amy* (1997), *My Best Friend's Wedding* (1997), *In and Out* (1997), *As Good as it Gets* (1997), *High Art* (1997), *L.A. Confidential* (1997), *The Object of My Affection* (1998), *Wild Things* (1998), *Gods and Monsters* (1998), *Go* (1999), *Cruel Intentions* (1999), *Big Daddy* (1999), *Trick* (1999), the Academy Award-winning *American Beauty* (2000), *The Next Best Thing* (2000), and *Groove* (2000). Gay and lesbian characters abound on television. MTV's *The Real World* is always careful to select a gay, lesbian, or bisexual individual as one of its seven housemates on the popular docu-drama (now in its ninth season). Other mainstream prime-time shows that have had recurring gay characters or have had episodes exploring gay themes include: *L.A. Law*, *Thirtysomething*, *The Golden Girls*, *Friends*, *Mad About You*, *Frasier*, *Roseanne*, *Melrose Place*, *Beverly Hills 90210*, *Party of Five*, *My So-Called Life*, *Veronica's Closet*, *South Park*, *E.R.*, *Chicago Hope*, *Spin City*, *NYPD Blue*, *Oz*, *Sex and the City*, *Ally McBeal*, *That Seventies Show*, *Felicity*, *Buffy the Vampire Slayer*, *Popular*, *The West Wing*, *Popular*, *Grosse Point*, *Boston*

Public, Normal, Ohio, and Showtime's Americanized version of *Queer as Folk.* A huge amount of media attention was focused on openly lesbian comedian Ellen Degeneres when her character, Ellen Morgan, came out of the closet on the sitcom *Ellen,* aired on 30 April 1997. The show earned the highest ratings the American Broadcasting Company (ABC) had all season, and DeGeneres became the first and only gay leading role in a television show.[165] In 1998, the National Broadcasting Company (NBC) premiered its now-popular sitcom, *Will and Grace,* which features two gay men – Will Truman and Jack McFarland – as lead characters. This television show has become so popular it is slated to begin the Fall 2000 season as part of the coveted Thursday evening "Must-See-TV" line-up. In 1999, the Warner Brothers (WB) Network introduced Jack McFee, a gay high school student, as a lead character to its immensely popular teen drama, *Dawson's Creek,* which explores the lives and personal trials of six immensely articulate and emotionally savvy adolescents. While such visibility suggests a high degree of mainstream cultural acceptance for gays, lesbians, and bisexuals, the inherent danger in this visibility is that it legitimates only particular elements of the movement. The gay image that mainstream culture has appropriated tends to be that of the middle-class white gay male.

The cultural appropriation of gay images is reminiscent of a form of mainstream backlash against the feminist movement detailed by Susan Faludi in her book, *Backlash: The Undeclared War Against American Women.* According to her model, heterosexist society utilizes popular culture as one means to undermine the gains of the feminist movement by contending that it is "equality" which makes women unhappy. By appropriating feminist terminology, institutional sexism can be masked to appear pro-feminist while simultaneously impeding the aims of feminism.[166] This theory can be applied to the gay and lesbian movement. Gay imagery has, to some extent, become chic, especially in the fashion industry. Aspects of gay life are addressed in such mainstream male magazines as *Details, Esquire,* and *GQ; Esquire Gentlemen* has asserted that "just about everyone dresses a little gay."[167] The inherent danger in this statement is that if the dominant heterosexist institutions appropriate and legitimate particular elements of the movement, for example, the middle-class white male element, it undermines the potency of that movement; it diffuses the queer threat to heteronormativity.

Indeed, the graver danger is that movement organizations, viewing that certain representations of the gay subject are acceptable to the heterosexual majority, will privilege that identity at the expense of silencing non-conforming members of its own community. This has been the experience of gay and lesbians of color who throughout the

1980s and 1990s led a backlash against "mainstream" gay culture. Theorist Barbara Smith claims that the creation of a separatist lesbian–feminist subculture "seems much like a narrow kind of politics and . . . it seems to be only viably practiced by women who have certain kinds of privilege: white-skinned privilege, class privilege."[168] Joseph Beam isolated the inherent racism in the gay and lesbian movement:

> It is possible to read thoroughly two or three consecutive issues of the *Advocate* [a national gay and lesbian news magazine] . . . and never encounter, in the words or images, Black gay men . . . It is possible to leaf through any of the major men's porno magazines . . . and never lay eyes on a Black Adonis . . . We ain't family. Very clearly, gay male means: white, middle-class, youthful, Nautilized, and probably butch, there is no room for Black gay men within the confines of this gay pentagon.[169]

The gay and lesbian movement demonstrates the major obstacle of invisibility of certain individuals despite similar identities. This invisibility is reinforced in commodity culture, one of the vehicles by which queer visibility is spread, which has appropriated this image of the bourgeois gay white male and has given it universal status. Many of the mainstream films and television shows mentioned above have gay characters that conform to this white middle-class stereotype; this kind of visibility both promotes and reflects greater tolerance of homosexuality thereby signaling the potential erosion of patriarchal norms and institutions. Yet, in doing so, it exploits a narrow, but presently widely accepted and innocuous image of the homosexual.[170]

Even more problematic is that many of the organizations which have gained national prominence in the late 1980s and early 1990s such as the National Gay and Lesbian Task Force, Human Rights Campaign, or the Gay and Lesbian Victory Fund, do not necessarily have staffs or constituents which represent the diversity inherent in the sexual minorities communities. Demographically speaking, individuals involved in political lobbying efforts have tended to be highly educated, middle- and upper-class, and white. Tickets to HRC's major fund raising tool, black tie dinners, held in over twenty cities around the country cost between $150 to $175, and participation is therefore cost-prohibitive. Furthermore, given that the Victory Fund's existence is reliant on donations to sponsor gay-identified candidates, their constituents, that is, those people able to give monetary support and therefore on the higher end of the class structure, will necessarily not be wholly representative of the gay and lesbian community. Thus, the national voice(s) of the gay and lesbian community, or at least those that mainstream media venues will hear, tend to reinforce this atypical image of the community along class, gender, and racial lines. However, these organizations have taken strides to diversify their staffs and expand their reach to new constituencies.[171]

The constrained image of the gay subject as white and middle-class also enables the heterosexual community to ignore those individuals who do not fit this stereotype. Visibility is gained at the exclusion of potential members of the movement. Representations of gay individuals who do not conform to the class, gender, and race stereotypes of the gay male are relatively rare. Political theorist, Rosemary Hennessy, notes the potentially devastating consequences that this limited visibility can produce:

Redressing gay invisibility by promoting images of a seamlessly middle class gay consumer or by inviting us to see queer identities only in terms of style, textuality, or performative play helps produce imaginary gay/queer subjects that keep invisible the divisions of wealth and labor that these images and knowledges depend on. The commodified perspectives blot from view lesbians, gays, queers who are manual workers, sex workers, unemployed, and imprisoned.[172]

The queer visibility that currently predominates in media and consumer culture is exclusive. This limited visibility inherently undermines the movement's ability to achieve radical change. The image of the middle-class white gay male is that precise level of visibility which the heteronormative patriarchy can accept without becoming threatened. It represents those aspects of queer lifestyles that are "hip" and that the straight culture can adopt without fear of any great degree of destabilization. By appropriating these images, heteronormativity is slowly making the gay and lesbian movement invisible. The accepted images of queerness are appropriated while marginalized images are ignored.

The consequences of this limited visibility which the movement currently enjoys are most clearly expressed in the outcome of the military ban debate resulting in the "don't ask, don't tell" compromise. The policy suggests heterosexual culture's unwillingness to cope with the possibility of homosexual soldiers. Furthermore, no longer is the homosexual act or homosexual identity grounds for discharge, but rather the mere verbal expression of that act or identity. Coercing soldiers to keep their sexual orientation secret illustrates an awareness of the potential threat of queer politics to the maintenance of patriarchal institutions. The enforced silence further bolsters or at least avoids the destabilization of heteronormativity.[173]

The gay and lesbian movement's inability to pressure for a successful lifting of the ban also indicates how politically weak the American movement was at the national level during the early 1990s. The military ban was not at the forefront of the gay and lesbian agenda when the movement started to organize at a national level; AIDS was.

Furthermore, the leftist ideological bias of the post-Stonewall generation included a heavy anti-militarist bent.[174] Thus, despite the creation of the Military Freedom Project (MFP) in 1988 which aimed to repeal the ban, the ban itself did not receive much media attention until Pete Williams, the Department of Defense's chief spokesperson – who gained national prominence during the Gulf War – was outed as gay in the *Advocate*, a national gay and lesbian news magazine. This event forced Dick Cheney, the Secretary of Defense, to assert that the military ban was outdated and that its repeal should be considered. Yet, despite increasing media attention on gays in the military and high-level support for change, the vast majority of activists were concerned that the military ban replaced AIDS as the prominent gay-themed issue of the election.[175]

Once Clinton was elected, national movement organizations such as the National Gay and Lesbian Task Force (NGLTF) and the Human Rights Campaign (HRC) were unaware of how to interact with the first gay-friendly administration. Instead of coordinating with each other, different organizations lobbied on their respective issues. They organized independent demonstrations and failed to put together a coherent agenda that could be presented to the Clinton administration.[176] Furthermore, movement organizations and the Clinton administration underestimated the conservative culture of Washington as well as the increasing power of the religious right. While NGLTF and HRC pushed for an executive order to lift the military ban, i.e., a fundamentally top-down approach, the Christian Coalition was conducting a more successful grassroots campaign to ensure that the ban remained intact. Organizations such as MFP (which now included HRC, NGLTF, ACLU, and NOW), the Ad Hoc Military Group, the Joint Chiefs, the Gay and Lesbian and Bisexual Veterans, and the respective staffs of Representative Gerry Studds, Representative Barney Frank, Senator Bob Dole, and Senator Sam Nunn failed to coordinate their efforts and often engaged in outright conflict despite working on the same issue.[177] Furthermore, despite amassing vast resources relative to both their past history and to any other movement around the world, the American gay and lesbian movement organizations could in no way compete with the resources of an ever growing Christian right countermovement that fought for fiercely for the maintenance of the ban.[178] In short, the movement ignored signals that the administration was deeply divided on the issue, failed to muster a grassroots campaign to counter that of the right, and President Clinton, lacking military credibility for being an alleged "draft-dodger," latched onto Representative Barney Frank's "don't ask, don't tell" compromise as political cover.[179]

The failure to lift the ban and the implementation of a far more homophobic standard – the institutionalization of the closet in the armed forces – demonstrates that the American gay and lesbian movement is at a dramatic crossroads at the turn of the new millennium. First, movement organizations are much more successful at attaining legislation at the state than at the national level.[180] Second, and more importantly, gays, lesbians, bisexuals, and all others who do not conform to the heterosexual norm, have achieved a potentially dangerous kind of pseudo-equality, what Urvashi Vaid terms "virtual equality."[181] The movement has secured a large degree of civil rights legislation at the state level. It has achieved positive Supreme Court litigation outcomes such as *Romers v. Evans* (1996), which deemed unconstitutional laws that forbade barring discrimination based on sexual orientation. The 1990 Hate Crimes Bill included sexual orientation. The ban on gay immigrants was lifted in 1991. AIDS funding has increased significantly under the Clinton administration. Despite its failure in 1996, the Employment Non-Discrimination Act missed passage by only one vote – a remarkable achievement given that most politicians considered the bill untenable only three years prior.[182] These successes do not include the gay and lesbian community's unprecedented degree of mainstream cultural visibility attained over the last decade. Yet such achievements threaten to destroy the movement since they inadvertently misrepresent the movement's level of success, providing a false sense of security for the sexual minorities community. The movement is still far from achieving its most fundamental aim: the destruction of institutionalized homophobia. The maintenance and indeed strengthening of the military ban as well as the power and popular resonance of Christian right anti-gay rhetoric vividly reflects this failure. In order to counter successfully the mobilization of the far right, the movement must create a dual agenda focusing on civil rights legislation at all government levels on the one hand and liberation and cultural reform on the other. It must combine a grassroots with a top-down approach to ensure that its constituents are both mobilized and their voices heard.

Conclusion

In a certain sense, the modern American gay and lesbian movement *did* commence at 1:20 a.m. on Saturday, 28 June 1969. At that exact moment, the cognitive liberation necessary to spark a movement took shape. The organizations and the opportunity were there, but until a shift from victim to empowered agent occurred, there was no modern

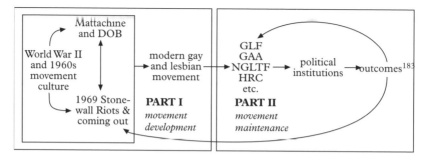

Figure 2.1 *Political process model applied to the American gay and lesbian movement*

movement. The changing opportunity structure provided by the Second World War and the development of a social movement culture throughout the 1960s coupled with homophile organizations such as the Mattachine Society and the Daughters of Bilitis which exploited these opportunities testify that proto-movement developments existed before the Stonewall riots. Yet, the riots themselves were the symbolic critical moment for gays, lesbians, and bisexuals all over the country (indeed, across the world) that provided that crucial cognitive liberation without which no cohesive social movement could occur. The riots, fostered in part by the lack of response by local, state, or national governments, inspired gay men and women to shed the victim status that heteronormative society imposed upon them and that they had internalized. Coming out was transformed into a profoundly political act that helped accomplish what the homophile organizations could not: attract a large number of participants.

Figure 2.1 graphically applies the political process model illustrated in Figure 1.2 to the American case study. Changing opportunity was fostered by the Second World War, the publication of the Kinsey reports in the late 1940s and early 1950s, and the expansion and legitimization of a movement culture throughout the 1960s. Black power and radical feminism especially provided the model which would inspire gay liberation of the 1970s. Pre-existing organizations such as the Mattachine Society and Daughters of Bilitis exploited these opportunities to some degree and did conduct protests for law reform; however, they were unable to establish a mass movement because their assimilationist tendencies failed to provide the basis for an affirmative and prideful collective identity. Such an identity emerged after the Stonewall riots in the shape of gay liberation.

Once the movement started to accomplish its aims within the realm of

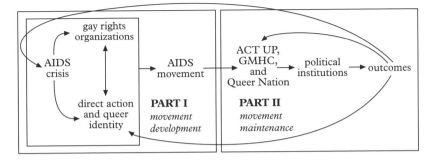

Figure 2.2 *Political process model applied to the American AIDS movement*

civil rights legislation at the local, state, and national level, it was confronted with a countermovement orchestrated by a backlashing religious right and, far more devastatingly, by AIDS. AIDS, perceived as a crisis, is also an inherent opportunity; it fostered the development of more movement organizations, helped to mobilize non-gay allies, provided another policy angle by which to achieve gay visibility and legislation, reoriented the strategies of gays and lesbians toward national-level politics, further broke down the closet door, and vastly increased the number of movement participants. AIDS created an offshoot movement with its own organizations, such as GMHC and ACT UP. As Figure 2.2 demonstrates, the AIDS crisis acted as the changing opportunity that interacted with the pre-existing gay rights organizations and affirmative collective gay identity to produce the AIDS movement with its own interest groups already named above. Queer identity or queer nationalism, while not directly linked to the AIDS movement, was inspired by ACT UP and provided another element of cognitive liberation to overcome the victimized status that gays and lesbians confronted as a result of the dramatic destructive capability of the disease. The "outcome," defined as the inadequate response to the AIDS crisis by the conservative Reagan government (and to a less extent by the Bush government), also provided an opportunity which helped to foster this new form of cognitive liberation expressed as queer identity. Hence, Figure 2.2 depicts a feedback arrow connecting outcomes with direct action and queer identity.

Presenting the gay and lesbian movement and the AIDS movement as separate, while illustrating that the latter came out of a fundamentally different opportunity and demonstrating the dramatic ways in which the crisis derailed the original civil rights goals of the gay and lesbian movement, is somewhat contrived. The separation does illustrate the different aims and strategies, but perhaps a more realistic conception would suggest that the AIDS movement should be seen as a component part of the gay and lesbian movement pushing the latter towards national and mainstream politics while reintroducing direct action and developing the notion of queer identity.

The gay and lesbian movement aims to achieve the long-term end of dismantling institutionalized homophobia whether through legislative reform or cultural transformation (more often the first method, though the second is perhaps an extraordinarily positive consequence which reinforces and enables the reformist strategy). To accomplish this goal, the movement and its organizations, which developed in accordance with Part I of the applied political process model detailed above, act through the political institutions – the executive-legislative structure, the judicial branch, the federal system, and the party structure. How the movement organizations' tactics are determined by the composition of the American political system will be further discussed in chapter 4. In other words, this future chapter seeks further to explore the dynamics of the second part of the political process model. Yet, as a comparative analysis will facilitate an illustration of the political structure's influence on movement tactics, we must first understand how the British counterpart of the American gay and lesbian movement emerged in the post-war period.

3   Tracing the rainbow: an historical sketch of the British gay and lesbian movement

> The love that dare not speak its name in this century is such a great affection of an elder for a younger man as there was between David and Jonathan, such as Plato made the very basis of his philosophy, and such as you find in the sonnets of Michelangelo and Shakespeare . . . on account of it I am placed where I am now. It is beautiful, it is fine, it is the noblest form of affection. There is nothing unnatural about it.
> Oscar Wilde, 1895

The emergence and growth of the gay and lesbian movement in the United States during the post-war period is not an isolated phenomenon. Similar movements developed throughout the world, most notably in the democracies of western Europe and Canada. This chapter seeks to ascertain to what degree the British and American gay and lesbian movements resembled each other. As mentioned in the introduction, the British movement was selected for comparison because of the political institutional environment in which it evolved. That environment is discussed further in chapter 4. This chapter focuses on the movement history itself. What type of changing opportunity existed in the United Kingdom during the immediate post-war period? Did a British homophile movement exist? Did gay liberation take hold in Britain? What effect did AIDS have on the movement? Starting with the political opportunity provided by the Second World War, this chapter will trace the development of the British homophile movement, evaluate the law reform of 1967, assess the impact and effect of gay liberation, consider the influence of AIDS, and arrive at sundry conclusions regarding the movement's present status. Furthermore, the aim is not merely to lay out the similarities and differences, but to arrive at some conclusion as to why these movements both paralleled and diverged from each other. The ultimate aim is to discover if the variations in American and British movement development derive from the distinct political institutional structures of each nation, the dissimilar cultural environments, or some combination of these factors.

Opportunity and vice: the paradoxical 1950s

If you could have written a survival guide for gay men at that time it would have said: never, never give anybody your surname or address. Never tell anybody where you work. Never take anybody to your home and never write letters, whether affectionate or otherwise, to anybody you're sexually involved in or anybody you know to be gay. And I think that would have been sound advice. (Allan Horsfall, law reform campaigner)

One is as likely to cure a homosexual of his perversion by sending him to an all-male prison as one is likely to cure a drunkard by incarcerating him in a brewery. (Anthony Greenwood, Labour MP, 26 November 1958)

The Second World War had a similar effect on British gays and lesbians as it did on their American counterparts. By promoting single-sex segregation, the war enabled gay men and women to come into contact with each other and gave individuals questioning their sexual orientation the opportunity to explore their feelings. Historical legend even links the impact of the Blitz on sexual experimentation and promiscuity. The blackout caused by the Blitz provided an opportunity for everyone, gay and straight alike, to engage in far more risky sexual behavior than during peacetime.[1] Since London was enveloped in darkness, a park became as private as a bedroom.[2]

The onset of the Cold War established a bipolar world in which the United Kingdom, nestled within the United States sphere of influence, followed American example to seek out potential communist infiltration. The anti-homosexual undercurrent of the American red scare also took root in the United Kingdom. Homosexual purges increased after the appointment of Sir Theobold Mathew as Director of Public Prosecutions in 1944. Whereas in 1939, only 299 cases of male "indecency" were registered, 1,686 were registered in 1952. Furthermore, the Kinsey Reports, whose findings were known in the United Kingdom, suggested that as many as 650,000 men in England and Wales were exclusively homosexual and almost two million additional men entertained homosexual tendencies.[3] Such findings only aggravated the popular misconception – holding strong since the Victorian era as further elucidated in chapter 5 – that homosexuality was contagious and indicative of moral degeneracy which threatened the British empire.[4] Furthermore, the connection between homosexuality and the communist threat to national security was concretized in the popular press in 1951 with the defection of two British spies, Guy Burgess and Donald Maclean, to the Soviet Union. Burgess was a known homosexual, and Maclean was bisexual. Shortly after this incident, the United States put further pressure on its allies to crack down on homosexuality.[5]

The anti-homosexual purges reached to the highest levels of British political and intellectual society. Alan Turing, who was responsible for helping to break the Nazi Enigma code and whose research laid the foundations for the first computer, was prosecuted for "gross indecency" as understood under the 1885 Labouchere Amendment;[6] he was forced to take estrogen hormone treatment and subsequently committed suicide. In 1953, Labour MP William Field was arrested and charged with soliciting a male prostitute in Piccadilly Circus; he was found guilty and resigned his seat in October of that year. Rupert Craft-Cooke, a well-known author, was arrested for indecency in January of 1953 and sentenced to nine months imprisonment. Sir John Gielgud, a well-known actor, pleaded guilty to soliciting sex in a public bathroom and was fined ten pounds; yet, interestingly, Gielgud received a standing ovation at his first performance following the arrest.[7] Historian Jeffrey Weeks notes that these prosecutions were often staged to set a dramatic example for the media. They usually involved socially prominent but politically expendable figures. This characterization is most apparent in the trial of Lord Montagu of Beaulieu and Peter Wildeblood.

On 16 October 1953 Lord Montagu and film director Kenneth Hume were charged with indecency in connection with two Boy Scouts; yet, their trial resulted in a hung jury. In December of 1953, Conservative MP Robert Boothby and Labour MP Desmond Donnelly, alarmed at the rise in chain prosecutions of homosexuals,[8] called for a Royal Commission to examine the feasibility of law reform given recent scientific evidence concerning homosexuality. The Home Secretary denied the request.[9]

Lord Montagu was arrested on new charges on 9 January 1954 regarding a conspiracy involving Peter Wildeblood, a diplomatic correspondent for the *Daily Mail*, and Montagu's cousin, Michael Pitt-Rivers, to seduce Corporal Edward McNally and Aircraftsman John Reynolds. While the latter two individuals received immunity for turning Queen's evidence, Montagu received a one-year prison sentence, and Wildeblood and Pitt-Rivers were sentenced to eighteen months imprisonment.[10]

Some of the popular press utilized the trial to sustain the homosexual stereotype as effeminate and decadent men who were a corrupt influence on youth – an image congealed by the Oscar Wilde trials.[11] Yet, public opinion was not as anti-homosexual as Parliament had assumed. Whereas McNally and Reynolds were harassed for receiving immunity, Wildeblood recalls that

the crowd began to press around us shouting. It was some moments before I realised that they were not shouting insults, but words of encouragement. They tried to pat us on the back and told us to "keep smiling," and when the doors were shut they went on talking through the windows and gave the thumbs-up sign and clapped their hands.[12]

By 1954 the average homosexual in Britain found him or herself trapped in a contradictory environment marked by an ever-increasing homosexual witch hunt coupled with an increasingly vocal call for law reform from the medical, church, and legal establishments as well as the general public. In 1952, the Church of England Moral Welfare Council, composed of physicians, lawyers, and clergymen, began an in-depth study of homosexuality; its report, published as *The Problem of Homosexuality*, in 1954, called for reform of the Labouchere Amendment. The Council concluded that heterosexual and homosexual behavior should be equal before the law with a common age of consent set at seventeen. More importantly, the committee suggested that male homosexuality was no worse than sins like adultery and lesbianism and, as such, should be perceived as violations of private morality but not public law. By making this assertion, the Council intellectually nullified any legislation which used religiously dictated morality as grounds for anti-gay legislation.[13]

Similar to the United States, the 1950s in Britain witnessed the development of an urban gay subculture centered around the gay bar. Bars that attracted a predominantly male clientele included the Fitzroy, the Coleherne, and the Boltons in London and the Union bar in Manchester. Lesbians formed social circles at bars such as the Raven, the Robin Hood, and the Gateways. Also, a number of gay coffee bars, centered in London's West End, attracted a wide range of people.[14] Relatively positive homosexual images pervaded popular novels such as Mary Renault's *The Charioteer* and Rodney Garland's *The Heart In Exile*. Peter Wildeblood's autobiography, *Against the Law*, was published shortly after his release from prison.[15] In this book, Wildeblood writes "I think it is more honest, and less harmful for a man with homosexual tendencies to recognize himself for what he is. He will always be lonely; he must accept that . . . but he will at least have the austere consolations of self-knowledge and integrity. More than that he cannot have, because the law, in England forbids it."[16] The passage reveals a growing consciousness of homosexuals as an unfairly oppressed minority, an idea similar to the early ideologies of the American Mattachine society. Yet, this idea is overshadowed by a continued sense of victimization. This feeling of second-class citizenship also afflicted American homosexuals throughout the 1950s and 1960s; it colored Mattachine's attempts to achieve substantive change and conditioned its assimilationist tendencies.

Astonishing in its absolute contrast to the situation in the United

States, the first signs of reform came from *within* the government itself. The Montagu–Wildeblood trial had revealed that the existing law was applied unevenly and that the defendants' rights to lawful search had been violated. Two members of Parliament, Robert Boothby and Desmond Donnelly, reiterated their desire to have a commission study the existing law regarding homosexuals. In April of 1954, the Government announced that it would establish such a committee in hopes of diffusing some of the controversy that had arisen both in popular newspapers as well as within the House of Commons.[17]

In August of 1954, Sir John Wolfenden took the position as chair of the Committee on Homosexual Offences and Prostitution, more commonly referred to as the Wolfenden Committee.[18] After sixty-two meetings and countless interviews with members of the legal, medical, and religious fields, the Committee released its report on 4 September 1957. The Committee's recommendations were grounded in utilitarian philosophy:

Unless a deliberate attempt is made by society, acting through the agency of law, to equate the sphere of crime with that of sin there must remain a realm of private morality and immorality which is, in brief and crude terms, not the law's business. To say this is not to condone or encourage private immorality. On the contrary, to emphasize the personal and private nature of moral or immoral conduct is to emphasize the personal and private responsibility of the individual for his own actions, and that is a responsibility which a mature agent can properly be expected to carry for himself without the threat of punishment from the law.[19]

The law was not a tool to legislate morality, but to maintain public order, and, as such, it could not invade the realm of private behavior. The Committee concluded that private consensual homosexual acts between men aged twenty-one or over be decriminalized.[20]

Since general elections were less than two years away upon the release of the Wolfenden Report, Home Secretary Butler avoided considering the recommendations. Yet, since the House of Lords is an unelected body, it held a debate on the Wolfenden findings on 4 December 1957. Although no official vote was taken, the Lords were evenly split as to whether or not reform should be implemented; thus, they fairly represented the popular opinion of England and Wales. Thirty-eight percent of the surveyed public supported reform as detailed in the Report, 47 percent were against reform, and 15 percent were undecided.[21]

To capitalize on the existing controversy and *opportunity* created by the Wolfenden Report, A. E. Dyson and Reverend Halladie Smith established the Homosexual Law Reform Society (HLRS). Unlike the Mattachine Society or the Daughters of Bilitis, HLRS was not a self-help or consciousness-raising organization. It was a single-issue interest group that established a separate fundraising arm, the Albany Trust, directed by Antony Grey. As its first public action, HLRS published a letter in *The Times* on 7 May 1958 citing

> general agreement with the recommendation of the Wolfenden Report that homosexual acts committed in private between consenting adults no longer be a criminal offence. The present law is clearly no longer representative of either Christian or liberal opinion in this country, and now that there are widespread doubts about both its justice and its efficacy, we believe that its continued enforcement will do more harm than good to the health of the community as a whole . . . we should like to see the Government introduce legislation to give effect to the proposed reform at an early date; and are confident that if it does so, it will deserve the widest support from humane men of all parties.[22]

This letter was signed by thirty prominent individuals in British academic and political circles including former Prime Minister Lord Attlee, A. J. Ayer, Isaiah Berlin, Julian Huxley, Sir Robert Boothby, Bertrand Russell, Barbara Wootton, and the Bishops of Birmingham and Exeter.

HLRS also lobbied members of Parliament by distributing its pamphlet, "Homosexuals and the Law," as well as Eustace Chesser's book, *Live and Let Live*, which was sympathetic to law reform.[23] Yet, the heavy lobbying approach backfired as many MPs became increasingly wary of the HLRS campaign. Memories of the anti-homosexual witch hunts held earlier in the decade were still fresh; the high pressure with which HLRS confronted Parliament evoked paranoid visions of well-placed homosexual officials who used their position to push through reform that would ultimately sanction vice and threaten national stability. Parliament rejected the Wolfenden proposals for the time being. Approximately forty-eight percent of the population supported the government's decision. More importantly, after the HLRS campaign, only twenty-five percent of the population supported reform compared to thirty-eight percent who had done so only a few months earlier.[24]

By the end of 1958, a tremendous degree of opportunity existed in the United Kingdom for gay men and women both to develop a subculture as well as to achieve some measure of equality through national legislation. While the Second World War provided the impetus for the subcultural development in the United States and the United Kingdom, legislation seemed particularly feasible only in the latter nation. The high profile Montagu–Wildeblood trial exposed the inequity of the existing anti-homosexual law and, as such, was causally linked to the formation of the Wolfenden Committee. The Committee's recommendations and the subsequent call for legislation led to a dramatic difference in the operations and tactics of the American and British homophile movements. While both chose to downplay an explicit connection to homosexuality by seeking heterosexual allies in legal, medical, and religious fields, the American movement concentrated on building a "bottom-up" grass roots campaign that pursued equality through various local and state levels. The British counterpart, perhaps adhering to Wilde's advice to educate public officials rather than public opinion, utilized a "top-down" approach. The British homophiles developed a single-issue interest group to lobby directly at the national level to achieve reform through Parliamentary legislation. These distinct mobilization patterns not only indicate the different levels of institutional access and diverse political cultural histories, but they would profoundly affect the ability of the respective movements both to mobilize participants as well as attain reform in the following decades.

"Swinging" sixties: cultural shift and law reform

The road is long and red with monstrous martyrdoms. Nothing but the repeal of the Criminal Law Amendment Act would do any good. That is essential. It is not so much public opinion, as public officials that need educating. (Oscar Wilde to George Ives, 1898)

The backlash against its high pressure lobbying forced the Homosexual Law Reform Society to take a more moderate stance not unlike the Mattachine Society and the Daughters of Bilitis across the Atlantic. HLRS, like the American organizations, began the long and tedious project of educating the public about homosexuality in hopes of more fully exposing the prejudicial nature of the existing law. HLRS directed its primary work outward into the more progressive elements of heterosexual society. Unlike Mattachine and the DOB, HLRS was not intended to be a support group for men or women struggling with their sexual orientation; rather, it was similar to any other predominantly middle-class single-issue pressure group prominent during the late 1950s and 1960s in areas such as abortion and capital punishment reform. As such, not only did the Society attempt to sway public opinion in its favor, but more importantly, it aimed more narrowly at attaining the support of MPs.[25]

The Homosexual Law Reform Society held its first *public* meeting on 12 May 1960 attracting an audience of nearly one thousand people. Taking his cue from this event, Labour MP Kenneth Robinson introduced a Private Member Bill in the House of Commons in June of 1960 calling for action on the Wolfenden Report. The motion was defeated 213 votes to 99 votes.[26] Yet, while the scale of defeat was large, the preceding debates isolated a number of Labour politicians, particularly

Leo Abse, who were receptive to the implementation of the Report,[27] In March of 1962, Abse introduced a diluted version of the Wolfenden recommendations that merely limited the ability to prosecute homosexuals while it maintained the illegality of homosexuality itself. The bill lapsed without a vote.[28]

The government's reluctance to take a firm stand on homosexual law reform was interpreted by the police and courts as free license to continue to harass and arrest gay men and lesbians. A rash of chain prosecutions occurred in the spring of 1958, and during the years before the appointment of a new Director of Public Prosecutions in 1964, there were indications that more people were arrested and sentences were more severe with each passing year.[29] Bar raids were prevalent and plain clothes police officers continued to entrap men in public lavatories as well as use cameras and mirrors to spy on men in these lavatories.[30] When Sir Peter Rawlinson was appointed Director of Public Prosecutions, the era of arrests and trials seemed to have climaxed. Rawlinson issued instructions that all cases involving "gross indecency" be referred to him before proceeding to trial. The change in attitude stemmed from Rawlinson's reformist orientation; he had defended Peter Wildeblood at the latter individual's trial in 1954, and sponsored Abse's reform bill in Parliament in 1962.[31]

Yet, more had changed than merely a new Director of Public Prosecutions. By attempting to decrease the rate of prosecutions for homosexual offenses, Rawlinson's actions paralleled a cultural shift toward a more liberal and sexually relaxed environment embodied in the growth of the "swinging" scene.[32] Gay men and lesbians epitomized what *Time* magazine called "Swinging London"; popular playwright, Joe Orton, avant-garde artist, Francis Bacon, and composer, Benjamin Britten, were all openly gay.[33] Furthermore, Lord Chamberlain's ban on homosexual content in drama was lifted in November of 1958.[34] As a result, film makers explored gay themes which were hugely popular in the 1960s. In 1960, two film versions of the Oscar Wilde trials were released. Later that decade, *The Killing of Sister George*, a film detailing the life of a fallen radio soap opera actress and her relationship with a female lover, was also a hit.[35] Even more popular and daring was the film *Victim* starring the well-known actor, Dirk Bogarde. Bogarde portrayed a married man, Melville Farr, with homosexual tendencies who becomes enmeshed in a blackmail plot. *Victim* is often touted as the first film to attempt an objective and serious investigation of gay life. Bogarde himself noted that "it was the first film in which a man said 'I love you' to another man. I wrote that scene in. I said, 'There's no point in half-measures. We either make a film about queers or we don't.'"[36]

The film was immensely sympathetic to the case for law reform. At its premiere, five hundred copies of the HLRS journal, *Man and Society*, were distributed.[37]

The small screen also became more willing to cover the controversial topic of homosexuality. In 1960, Granada Television ran a show called *On Trial* about Oscar Wilde. In June of 1963, the popular BBC police drama *Z Cars* featured an episode revolving around a blackmailed homosexual couple. Homosexuality became a prevalent topic on discussion-oriented shows such as *Table Talk*. In 1964, the show, *This Week*, aired a documentary contrasting the situation of British and Dutch homosexuals featuring men dancing together and kissing one another in Dutch discos.[38]

Numerous gay-themed books were published during the 1960s further testifying that this decade was more relaxed and sexually liberating than the previous one. Elliot George's *The Leather Boys* and a book version of *Victim* were available early in the decade. The autobiography of Lionel Fieldon, *The Natural Bent*, as well as John Morris's *Hired to Kill* were also popular. Sociological studies included Gordon Westwood's *A Minority* in 1960 and Richard Houser's *The Homosexual Society* in 1962. Finally, W. H. Allen's *Queer People* was published in 1963.[39] Magazines such as *Timm*, *Jerry*, and *Sparticus* catered to both the "swinging" and the gay scenes.[40]

This cultural shift gained political expression in the general election of 1964 when the Labour Party returned to power after thirteen years of being the opposition party. Both major parties entered the 1960s with a commitment to "modernizing" Britain. Since the worst excesses of capitalism appeared to have been overcome, a Keynesian welfare state firmly grounded, and a measure of affluence pervaded the nation, the government and the populace turned to social issues and/or issues of conscience. This tendency was paralleled in the United States and is one of the factors which contributed to the rise of the civil rights movement, Johnson's Great Society Program, and the feminist movement. These more personal, social, and lifestyle issues became the new focus of political party, especially Labour, philosophies thereby fostering the reform movement. Conscience issues also did not necessarily contradict a more old-fashioned liberalism reminiscent of the philosophies of John Stuart Mill to which many Liberals, such as Lord Arran, adhered. Most importantly, the Labour Party was known for a utilitarian view of the law; if the law did not work, then it ought to be altered in some fashion.[41] Given that this pragmatic philosophy was adhered to by the majority of Parliament after the 1964 elections, numerous MPs and the HLRS considered it merely a matter of time before the Wolfenden recommendations, or some variant of them, were implemented.

Given the appointment of Rawlinson, the Labour majority – even if it only amounted to four seats in the House of Commons – and abundant evidence that British society was becoming more liberal and potentially more amenable to homosexual law reform, the Homosexual Law Reform Society reinitiated a campaign to convince Parliament to implement the Wolfenden proposals. Yet, the point must be stressed that the United Kingdom in the 1960s was ripe for change; *HLRS did not unlock a new door, rather it merely pushed a door wide open that was already ajar.* The Society functioned mainly as a Parliamentary resource in the latter half of the 1960s as the debate on homosexual law reform was reignited. It supplied information, provided lists of MPs favorable to reform, and accomplished mostly clerical work. Furthermore, similar to Mattachine philosophy, but grossly oppositional to later liberation theory, HLRS stressed that reform had no greater implications; HLRS ignored issues of institutionalized homophobia and gender role socialization.[42] In the grand scheme, then, any reform regarding decriminalization of homosexuality had as much, if not more, to do with the liberal culture of the times than with the actions of a single-issue lobby.

When the Labour government took power, it advised HLRS not to press for reform since the party majority was so minimal. Despite this warning, Lord Arran initiated a debate regarding the Wolfenden recommendations in the House of Lords on 12 May 1965. The Government chose to remain neutral citing that the issue was one of personal conscience. Two weeks later, Arran introduced a single-clause bill seeking to overturn the illegality of private consensual homosexual acts between individuals over age twenty-one. After a second debate, the bill passed by a vote of 94 to 49.[43]

Since the Bill was not sponsored by the Government, it had to be introduced through a Private Member Bill in the House of Commons.[44] Labour MP Leo Abse introduced the Bill under the Ten-Minute Rule on 26 May 1965. The Bill was defeated in the first vote which registered 178 against reform and 159 for reform.[45] The margin of only 19 votes was inspiring since it was much smaller than when a similar bill, introduced five years previously, was defeated by a margin of 114.

Lord Arran's bill continued in its passage through the House of Lords. Before the final vote on the bill was taken, Arran convinced the editor of *The Times* to commission a poll regarding public opinion on the bill. The survey found that 63 percent of the population (of England and Wales) favored decriminalization. This percentage represents a stunning shift from only two years previously when only 16 percent supported reform and 67 percent were against decriminalization.[46] Arran's bill passed its Third Reading on 28 October 1965 with a vote of 116 to 46.[47]

Conservative MP Humphrey Berkely introduced Lord Arran's Bill to the Commons in early 1966; it passed its Second Reading with a vote of 166 to 109 on 11 February 1966. Yet, it subsequently died when Prime Minister Wilson called for new elections on 31 March 1966. The elections returned a one-hundred MP Labour majority. At this point, the entire process had to start over. Arran reintroduced his bill in Lords, but after the Third Reading, on 16 June 1966, some MPs lobbied the Government to allow the Commons to consider in the issue. Abse introduced the bill which passed its Second Reading on 5 July 1966 by 264 votes to 102.[48]

The Home Secretary Roy Jenkins convinced the Prime Minister to abandon neutrality on the issue since both houses had supported reform. In marked contrast to the tediously slow passage of the bill to this point, the bill made it through a special debate on 19 December 1966 with remarkable speed. Due to some maneuvering by Abse, the Sexual Offences Bill, as it was now called, made it to the Third Reading without a vote.[49] The Bill came to the floor on 23 June 1967, and, despite a filibuster by anti-reformists, the Sexual Offenses Bill was passed on 4 July 1967 by 101 votes for and 16 against.[50] It became law on 27 July 1967 after receiving Royal Assent.[51]

The Sexual Offences Act of 1967 legalized private consensual homosexual sex between persons over the age of twenty-one. Yet, the law came with numerous restrictions. First, and perhaps most importantly given recent developments to be discussed below, the law legitimated a fundamental inequality in the age of consent: heterosexuals could consent to sex at the age of sixteen. Second, the law only applied to England and Wales and not to Scotland or Northern Ireland. Third, homosexuality was still illegal in the armed forces and the Merchant Navy. Fourth, the word "private" meant that no third person, even if consenting, could be present at any time during the sexual act. Finally, the charge for having sex with minors, i.e., anyone under twenty-one years old, was increased from two to five years imprisonment.[52]

After the Act was passed much of the impetus for reform died away. In no way did the Act achieve any measure of homosexual equality as later judicial rulings were to make clear. However, the Homosexual Law Reform Society was exhausted by its efforts. Furthermore, HLRS had permitted its allies in Parliament to direct reform; even at the early stages of bill development, Society members were excluded.[53] The

Sexual Offence Act of 1967 in no way struck at the root of institutional homophobia. A comparison with the United States illustrates that the situation in the United Kingdom is entirely paradoxical. In Britain, no homophile movement existed to the extent that it did in the United States. Yet, by 1967, consensual homosexual sex between individuals over the age of twenty-one was legal in the former country but not in the latter. *In one sense then, law reform occurred in the United Kingdom despite the lack of a mobilized social movement*; yet, the British activists had an enormous degree of opportunity not available to Americans since a majority of national representatives were amenable to reform. If anything, this example demonstrates that available resources, while important for the long-term sustainability of a social movement organization, do not determine the success or failure of a movement's agenda in the short term given the proper institutional and cultural milieu; policy change, especially in a closed-system like that in Britain, is dependent upon the degree of political opportunity and openness to change present at a given time. Whether MPs were responding to a cultural shift toward greater liberalism or whether the 1967 Sexual Offences Act passed due to the party discipline necessitated by the parliamentary structure is difficult to confirm. The Act was often referred to as a matter of conscience, and, in these cases, political parties do not necessarily enforce the official line. Most likely, the passage of the Act reflected both cultural and political factors. Either way, no similar degree of receptivity has ever existed in all three branches of the United States government at the national level.

In the United Kingdom, homosexual sex was legalized in a government-directed top-down manner rather than a grassroots bottom-up manner. The danger inherent in this circumstance, at least as it regarded the attainment of full legal equality, was that the government diffused the movement. The intransigence of the American government was at least part of the reason for the increasing militancy of the American gay and lesbian movement by the end of the 1960s. This militancy fostered the cognitive liberation so critical to social movement emergence. This psychological shift from a victimized mindset to one characterized by power and pride did not arise within the United Kingdom; it was imported from the United States. In other words, early government reforms, while seemingly demonstrating the British gay and lesbian movement to be more successful, revealed themselves as mere half-measures which jeopardized the strength of the movement in later decades.

Importing disco and radicalism: British gay liberation

so sit back and watch as they close all our clubs
arrest us for meeting and raid all our pubs
make sure your boyfriend's at least 21
so only your friends and your brothers get done
lie to your workmates, lie to your folks
put down the queens, tell anti-queer jokes
gay lib's ridiculous, join their laughter
"the buggers are legal now, what more are they After?" . . . tell them
sing if you're glad to be gay   "Glad to be Gay," Tom Robinson Band

NONE SO FIT TO BREAK THE CHAINS AS THOSE WHO WEAR
THEM ("Gay Liberation Front Supports Law Reform," South London GLF
Pamphlet)

Upon the passage of the 1967 Sexual Offenses Act, the Homosexual
Law Reform Society, exhausted from its campaign and having achieved
its primary aim, collapsed. Of all the local branches of the HLRS, only
the North Western Homosexual Law Reform Committee remained
active. Furthermore, Parliament demonstrated no signs of reevaluating
the anomalies of the reform such as the inequality between heterosexual
and homosexual age of consent or the curious definition of private
which contended that a locked hotel room was a public space. Yet, while
far from dismantling institutionalized homophobia and heterosexism,
the impact of law reform should not be underestimated. HLRS
mustered enough support at the Parliamentary level to decriminalize
homosexuality, at least in theory, throughout England and Wales.
Furthermore, the mere existence of the HLRS and the subsequent push
for law reform stimulated homosexual self-organization.

While the 1967 Act had absolutely no bearing on lesbianism – no law
in Britain to that point had even mentioned the concept of female
homosexuality – lesbian organizations did emerge in the late 1960s. The
gay subculture that had developed throughout the 1960s was dominated
by men, and lesbians and bisexual women had little means to contact
one another. Thus, the primary aim of lesbian organizations, including
the Minorities Research Group (MRG), founded in 1963, and later
Kenric, was to provide a social space for lesbians. Kenric's over five
hundred members were only known by their first name, further illustrating the strong stigma of homosexuality which necessitated such
secrecy.[54]

Individuals who remained politically active regarding homosexuality
after the 1967 reform often joined the North Western Homosexual Law
Reform Committee (NWHLRC) founded in October of 1964. Because

of its local standing and thus more indirect involvement in the passage
of reform, it could and tended to be more radical than the HLRS.
Whereas the HLRS was composed of straight allies and some homosexuals, members of NWHLRC, or the Committee for Homosexual
Equality (CHE), as it would be known after 1967, were homosexual.
Unlike the HLRS, it abandoned the medical model of homosexuality as
a sickness.[55] By June of 1967, CHE was calling not only for law reform,
but also for the establishment of social clubs for gay individuals. The
idea met an extraordinary degree of controversy. The Albany Trust,
wary of offending its Parliamentary supporters, rejected the idea. Lord
Arran claimed that the idea of such clubs represented "an open flaunting
of the new and legal freedom of outlet."[56] By making this statement,
Arran embodied a general feeling in Parliament that

with the passing of the new law the whole unsavoury matter [of homosexual law
reform] had been satisfactorily resolved and should now be removed from the
political agenda. The very idea of its practitioners attempting to move out of the
shadowy world to which they had been safely assigned to indulge their
unacceptable sexual habits in the strictest privacy was inevitably at odds with the
views of many of their staunchest supporters. In terms of public morality, all
manifestations of homosexuality were still deemed inadmissible.[57]

It was this type of institutionalized homophobia that CHE was attempting to confront and against which the existing law reform could
do nothing. A parallel rivalry to that which severed the Mattachine of
New York and that of Washington, DC, erupted. The more moderate
and gradually defunct HLRS and the Albany Trust were on the one side
and the more radical CHE, which understood the failings of law reform,
was on the other. Yet, this comparison is strained; even MSNY, which
was viewed as assimilationist by some gay Americans, was far more
radical than any group in the United Kingdom. This disparity led
Antony Grey, the director of the Albany Trust, to comment during the
late 1960s, "it's still inconceivable that such a group as the Mattachine
Society would exist here [in Britain]. I'd say it won't happen for at least
five years."[58]

Grey's prediction was completely off the mark since within a few short
years of the comment, a group far more radical than the Mattachine
Society, the Gay Liberation Front, held its first meeting in a basement
seminar room of the London School of Economics. Unlike the American Gay Liberation Front, the British version was not spawned by some
dramatic burst of reactionary activity such as the 1969 Stonewall riots;
rather, "it was the transmission of the American model which spurred
on the formation of the London GLF. There was no precipitating
occasion like Stonewall."[59] The concept that gay liberation was appro-

priated from the United States and was not indigenous to the United Kingdom is critical to understand the demise of the GLF detailed below.

The London GLF was founded on 13 November 1970 by Aubrey Walter and Bob Mellors who had both spent the previous summer active in GLF politics in the United States. The first meeting attracted less than twenty people, but within a few months, over two hundred people were attending meetings.[60] British gay liberation drew on the increasing European radicalism that characterized the Paris unrest of 1968, the Prague Spring of the same year, and numerous protests against American foreign policy excess especially in Vietnam.[61]

Similar to the American GLF and unlike the HLRS or CHE, the London GLF was not a single-issue reform group; rather, it perceived itself as a "people's movement." As one flyer, "Principles of the Gay Liberation Front," clearly asserts, GLF sought to align itself with the women's liberation movement, black and other racial minorities, the working-class, the youth movement, and all peoples oppressed by imperialism.[62]

Like its American counterpart, the London GLF did not necessarily reject law reform or, as was the case in the United States, the possibility of such reform. Instead, it suggested that legal changes were not enough. It had more revolutionary aims:

> Whilst appreciating the desire to reform the existing law, we believe that the law has no place in personal relationships. We do not believe that legal recognition alone will ever free gay people from oppression, anymore than it has freed women or blacks. Only by changing the sexist basis of our society can freedom for any of us be truly attained. This we can only achieve for ourselves.[63]

The above passage, besides detailing the revolutionary nature of GLF, gives insight into the organization's philosophy. By making reference to oppression of women and blacks as well as to sexism, it reiterates an implicit connection between gays and lesbians and other minority groups. The group's militancy and millennarian enthusiasm is clear as is its belief that revolution and not reform is its ultimate aim. Most importantly, the last sentence represents a dramatic departure from the tactics of earlier homosexual organizations. Gay people, the GLF contended, should not be reliant on the support of straight allies. Rather than pursuing government-directed tactics, GLF advocated a grassroots and particularly American methodology that emphasized the connection between the personal as political and that functioned as the theoretical basis for "coming out."

Coming out served much the same function for the London GLF as it did for its American counterpart, namely rejecting heterosexist definitions of an inherently victimized homosexual and the promotion of an affirmative identity. GLF turned coming out into a political act by utilizing it as a tool for collective identity formation. The seemingly disparate group of students, professionals, counterculturalists, artists, and social mainstream drop-outs created a sense of solidarity by being open about their sexual orientation. The London GLF went so far as to design buttons which proclaimed "Gay Power," "Avenge Oscar Wilde," "Lesbians Ignite," and "How Dare You Presume that I am a Heterosexual" as well as logos including the now popular pink triangle.[64]

This emphasis on cognitive liberation, pride, and personal power fueled GLF's rivalry with other gay organizations. The London GLF condemned the Albany Trust as an establishment body that was too assimilationist. It rejected the Committee for Homosexual Equality for similar reasons, although it further contended that by using the word "homosexual" CHE was tacitly accepting heterosexual society's notion of homosexuality as a disease. Like its American counterpart, GLF adopted the word "gay" because it represented homosexual self-definition.[65]

Yet, CHE's worries about losing its supporters to GLF were needless in retrospect; like the American version, British gay liberation was a fleeting phenomenon dying as an organization, if not as a philosophy, by 1972. Its lack of focus and diversity of supporters eventually produced insurmountable rifts on various fronts: between men and women, among activists, and between the revolutionary aims of GLF and the political realities of the United Kingdom in the 1970s. The British GLF, like the one across the Atlantic, was male-dominated and consequently gravitated towards issues concerning men. This tendency was exacerbated by the state of law reform: arrests of gay men increased after the passage of the 1967 Sexual Offences Act while lesbianism was not explicitly condemned under any existing law.[66] By the early 1970s, women tended to abandon gay liberation for the ultimately more inclusive women's liberation movement.[67]

Another rift, similar to that which spurred the Gay Activists Alliance in New York, developed in the United Kingdom. Numerous activists argued for a more structured organization. Structure, liberationists argued, undercut the core philosophy of liberation which emphasized spontaneity and direct participation. The disorganization which characterized GLF meetings ultimately repelled potential participants more than it attracted them.[68]

Another fundamental assumption of gay liberation was the need for revolution. Yet, as more people came out and as a larger subculture developed, the prospect or need for revolution seemed naive. GLF had succeeded in changing the consciousness of innumerable gay men and women, but, more importantly, it had accomplished this feat without revolution.[69]

The demise of the GLF was partly due to changes in society at large. GLF emerged out of the counterculturalist ideals of the late 1960s, and, by the early years of the next decade, these ideas had already fallen out of favor.[70] The same circumstances prevailed in the United States. Yet, the British GLF also collapsed for one uniquely British reason: homosexuality was legal in the England and Wales. No revolutionary outrage was native to Great Britain because earlier law reform pre-empted its development. The British had no Stonewall legend with which to incite anger, excitement, and energy.[71] Liberation was an American transplant which never firmly took hold and never could because the legal status of American gay men and women was fundamentally different from their British contemporaries.

While liberationism declined by the mid-1970s, it had had a profound impact on gay visibility in Britain not least through the development of the gay press. The most representative example is the publication of *Gay News*. Founded in 1972, the newspaper did not embrace the radical aim of the GLF to transform gay consciousness, but rather to serve individuals who were already out. By 1976, *Gay News* became a legitimate news source, with thirty-six pages of news articles, editorials, features, a three-page classified section, and a circulation of over 20,000, making it the most widely subscribed gay periodical to date in England. By the end of the decade, the newspaper was carried by such mainstream sellers as W. H. Smith. *Gay News*, like American periodicals such as the *Advocate*, did much to promote the gay community, foster gay consumerism, and target the gay individual as a viable market.[72]

The GLF's emphasis on coming out struck a chord in Britain much as it had in the United States. Paradoxically, the real beneficiary of liberationism was its unofficial rival, the Committee for Homosexual Equality, renamed the Campaign for Homosexual Equality in 1970. In November of 1970 – the month which coincided with the birth of the London GLF – CHE boasted five hundred members in fifteen local groups. By the end of 1971, CHE had nearly 1,800 members, and, by the end of the following year, it had approximately 2,800 members affiliated with sixty local divisions; thus, within two years – the same two years that coincided with the rise of the GLF – CHE membership increased by nearly 500 percent.[73]

Whereas GLF tended to be a much more personally oriented group, CHE targeted working out the anomalies of the 1967 Sexual Offences Act. In 1975, the group developed a bill for Parliamentary consideration

in coalition with the gay organization of Scotland, the Scottish Minorities Group, and that of Northern Ireland, the Union for Sexual
Freedom in Ireland. The bill called for an equal age of consent,
extending the 1967 law reform to Scotland and Northern Ireland,[74]
ability to display affection in public without threat of arrest, and the
removal of the military ban on gay men and lesbians. The Home
Secretary, Roy Jenkins, sidelined the bill by submitting it to the notor-
iously conservative Criminal Law Revision Committee. The CLRC
would not report on the issue for at least another two years.[75]

The CHE continued to support the gay community by backing three
gay men in their case against unfair employment dismissal based on
sexual orientation. CHE organized the first gay and lesbian trade union
conference in 1977.[76] It also encouraged political parties to establish
internal gay organizations. The Liberal Party was the first to do so; the
Labour Party followed with the Gay Labour Group created in 1975, and
the Conservatives founded a smaller group in 1976.[77] Local chapters of
CHE also established counseling arms such as Friend. A more radical
group called London Icebreakers which grew out of the Counter-
Psychiatry Group of the London GLF was established in 1973. It
provided a twenty-four-hour phone service for individuals questioning
and confronting their sexual orientation. Icebreakers was staffed by gay
men and women and was characterized by a decidedly affirmative
perspective on homosexual identity.[78]

These local developments throughout the 1970s did not amount to
any further reform of the 1967 Act. Yet, while gay politics may have
stagnated at the national level, the gay subculture and mainstream
integration of gay culture thrived during the 1970s. Gay liberation, with
its emphasis on gay pride and coming out, fostered the emergence of
this culture. Just as that decade was marked by the importation of the
American model of collective politics, it was also characterized by an
Americanization of gay culture. Gay men danced to American disco
music, and bars and clubs sported names of characteristically gay
American resorts such as Fire Island, Copacabana, and Key West.[79]
American influence was so pervasive because the American sexual
minorities movement was considered the pioneer of gay liberation. No
other nation could boast a catalyzing event such as the Stonewall riots:
"America seemed to represent a land of hope and freedom for European
gays. When the Stonewall queens hitched up their skirts and fought,
they had shown their European counterparts that it was possible to
resist and win."[80] Gay bars and clubs were no longer relegated to the
seedy dark urban underworld of previous decades; these clubs became
chic. Famous celebrities such as Andy Warhol, Rock Hudson, Rod

Stewart, and Elton John were all to be seen at the opening of Bang, a London gay club.[81]

British gay fashion also appropriated another American image: the gay clone. The clone image was characterized by Levi 501s, army surplus boots, and tight t-shirts. Yet, some gay fashion, most notably radical drag,[82] was indigenous to the United Kingdom. Radical drag had political roots in the London GLF, but by the late 1970s popular rock stars including David Bowie, Rod Stewart, and Mick Jagger were all experimenting with gender-bending outerwear.[83] British actor, Tim Curry, further demonstrated this fashion to the mainstream through his role as the transvestite hero of the 1975 film, *The Rocky Horror Picture Show*. Gay visibility began to flourish on television. In 1975, Thames Television produced the movie, *The Naked Civil Servant*, the autobiography of Quentin Crisp. A gay character was incorporated into the ITV series, *Rock Follies*, as well as into the situational comedy, *Agony*. In 1980, the television station, LWT, produced *Gay Life*, the first gay and lesbian show.[84] Not only was gay media visibility increasing, but the portrayal of these characters no longer relied on stereotypes prevalent in the films and television shows of the earlier decade.

In one sense, 1980 closed a decade in which it was wonderful to be gay in the United Kingdom, especially in London. Homosexuality, at least private consensual homosexual acts between men twenty-one years or older, was legal in England, Wales, and Scotland, and would be legalized within one year in Northern Ireland. Gay bars and discos were prevalent. The largest night-club in Europe, Heaven, was a London gay disco.[85] The news media began to use the word "gay" more often than homosexual when discussing relevant issues thereby signaling mainstream appropriation and tacit acceptance of gay self-definition.[86] Unlike the United States, where the 1970s was characterized by political gains and setbacks in major cities and the election of gay officials to sundry political posts, the 1970s in Britain were far more concerned with personal liberation and cultural development. The political status of the British gay male in 1980 was much as it had been in 1967; this was not the case of his American counterpart who witnessed the election of openly gay officials, the adoption of both city and state laws decriminalizing sodomy, the establishment of non-discrimination employment ordinances, and the rise of a vocal and highly organized conservative and religion-based countermovement.

The critical impact of the 1970s in the United Kingdom was not the fact that gay culture expanded and became more open, but rather that a *community* of gay people developed to promote this culture. The 1970s, in both the United Kingdom and the United States, were characterized by the transformation of homosexuality, which connoted a mere sexual act, to the idea of "gayness," which defined an affirmative identity. The gay community existed both in a physical sense, for example in Greenwich Village and parts of San Francisco and London, as well as an idea embodied in a variety of activities, for example, pride parades, which fostered this sense of commonality.[87] Through this common and collective identity, engendered by the political and cultural shifts of the decade, gay men and women were able to organize themselves without having to rely exclusively on allies.

These improvements of the 1970s did not occur without the development of some politico-cultural backlash. The emergence of the Moral Majority, Anita Bryant's "Save Our Children" campaign, and the election of Ronald Reagan have already been cited with regard to increasing opposition to the American gay and lesbian movement. Similar countermovements grew on the other side of the Atlantic. In 1971, Evangelical Christians established the Festival of Light to counter what they contended was increasing moral degeneration throughout Great Britain. In 1976, Mary Whitehouse had *Gay News* charged with blasphemy by utilizing a law that had been moribund since 1921. The editor received an eighteen-month suspended sentence and a five hundred pound fine. The newspaper was charged with a one thousand pound fine.[88] Although these groups did not muster the members and political strength of Bryant's and similar American countermovements, their development signaled a conservative shift in national British political culture, and they foreshadowed further assaults to be leveled on gay men and women after the election of the Conservative Thatcher government in May of 1979. Yet, as was the case in the United States, no backlash the Conservatives could mount could devastate the movement as much as AIDS.

Crisis and hope: conservative backlash and new labour

The association between AIDS and homosexuality, and its resultant effect on the way AIDS has been perceived and responded to by everyone from vocal minorities of the fundamentalist Christian Right to prison warders, theatrical staff, restauranteurs, refuse collectors, undertakers, laboratory technicians, government officials and ministers, is shaped by a living history, by what can best be described as an unfinished revolution in attitude to lesbian and gay lifestyle. (Jeffrey Weeks, *Against Nature*)

An assessment of the British gay and lesbian movement through the 1980s and 1990s is a complicated endeavor if only because the gay equal rights agenda becomes endlessly entangled with the AIDS crisis. The impact of both AIDS and the conservative governments that ruled throughout the first decade of the virus cannot be dismissed as entirely negative. As was true in the United States, AIDS fostered positive externalities such as increased visibility and self-organization for the gay and lesbian movement while also sidetracking the movement, fostering a reinvigorated conservative backlash, and ravaging the gay community. Such a complex and, indeed, double-edged impact led *Capital Gay*, a London gay newspaper, to conclude that

We have seen the coming of age of the gay and lesbian movement. Well-known figures, who have previously been quiet about their sexuality, have come out fighting, we have found support from across the political spectrum, ordinary homosexuals have written protest letters and taken to the streets in the biggest ever lesbian and gay demonstrations, the media coverage has been massive (and often sympathetic) and the visibility of our community has never been greater.[89]

Yet, while this assessment is accurate, the rise of the AIDS epidemic, the continuous re-election of a recalcitrant Conservative government, the passage of Section 28 of the 1988 Local Government Bill – all discussed in further detail below – engender a different interpretation of the decades provided by historian Jeffrey Weeks.

The New Right has been much more successful in capitalising on signs of social strain than the Old or New Left. A powerful wave of political and moral fundamentalism has tried to reshape the moral contours that many of us were beginning to take for granted in the 1960s and 1970s. In its context the new social movements have been thrown into the defensive. Most tragically of all, at this very moment of political challenge, the AIDS crisis has provided the excuse and justification for a moral onslaught on the lives of lesbian and gay people.[90]

Weeks perceives the two decades since the decline of gay liberation as characterized by a defensive gay movement battling, on one side, a growing conservatism and, on the other, a deadly disease. This evaluation does not necessarily contradict the interpretation provided by *Capital Gay*. As conservatives on both sides of the Atlantic attacked gays for their "unnatural" behavior and blamed them for the so-called gay plague of AIDS, they unwittingly also brought gay issues into the forefront of mainstream political debate and forced gays and lesbians to become more politically active than ever before. Tracing some critical events of the past to decades in the United Kingdom will further elucidate this point.

The explosive burst of open gay subculture that emerged throughout the 1970s fostered a hedonistic environment in which political activism for gay equality deteriorated. Many gay men misinterpreted the rise of this open urban gay subculture as representative of equality, and as long as this scene was available without too much interference from government authorities, then the further demands of activists did not seem particularly relevant. Questions of recriminalizing homosexuality were universally deemed ludicrous and infeasible, and with the extension of the 1967 reforms to Scotland and Northern Ireland by 1980 and 1981 respectively, gay men behaved as if they had attained full equality. Those individuals who attempted to reveal that the 1967 Sexual Offences Act had not provided legal equality nor had to any degree confronted institutionalized heterosexism, but had merely decriminalized sexual acts between some individuals in some places, were often drowned out by others who extolled the virtues of embracing the American gay scene with its fashion trends, heightened commercialism, and liberating sexual promiscuity.[91] The decline of political dynamism is clearly illustrated by the decline in CHE membership. It fell from a peak of five thousand in 1975 and fluctuated between three and four thousand for the remainder of the decade and the early years of the 1980s.[92]

British gays were, at first, also insulated from possibly the greatest rallying cry for collective mobilization of the American gay community: AIDS. The first cases of AIDS were diagnosed in the United States in 1981, and British gay men and women tended not to pay much attention to the illness. When a gay man, Terrence Higgins, became the first Briton diagnosed with AIDS, then known as the gay cancer or GRID, Gay Related Immune Deficiency, in January of 1982 and died on 4 July 1982, *Capital Gay* published an article entitled "US Disease Hits London." Hence, British gay men still were under the misguided understanding that AIDS was primarily an American disease. Perhaps more disturbing than this misconception was that the *Capital Gay* article was released five months after Higgins' death which was not reported at all in the mainstream press.[93]

The lack of coverage in the more widely circulated British newspapers such as *The Times* or *The Independent* as well as the national government's general indifference was paralleled in the United States. The reasons for such little national response to the crisis are twofold. First, in both the United States and the United Kingdom, conservative regimes had come to power promising to cut government spending; it could not therefore maintain this aim by increasing funding for AIDS research. Second, AIDS, at least during the early years of the crisis, seemed to affect politically marginal populations: hemophiliacs, intravenous drug users, and homosexuals.[94] Thus, much of the early response to AIDS in both the United Kingdom and the United States was organized by the gay community itself.[95] The Terrence Higgins Trust was established by Higgins' ex-partner, Martyn Butler, in 1982. A parallel Scottish organization, the Scottish AIDS Monitor, was established shortly thereafter.

Other organizations, such as Body Positive, were also established to disseminate safer-sex information and support HIV-positive individuals by providing them with meals or visiting them at the hospital.[96] The first British public seminar on AIDS was held on 21 May 1983 and was organized by the Gay Switchboard.[97] By March of 1983, six cases of AIDS had been diagnosed in England; by July of the same year the number increased to fourteen. By October of 1985, three hundred AIDS cases were documented with an estimated twenty thousand cases of undocumented infection.[98]

As noted in the previous chapter, the death of Rock Hudson marked the turning point in the American response to AIDS. After this event, the Republican-controlled White House increased funding for AIDS research and care by forty-eight percent to $126.3 million for the 1985–6 fiscal year. The British government did not follow the American lead; in March of 1985, the Conservative-dominated government granted the Terrence Higgins Trust only £25,000 and the Haemophilia Society only £15,000.[99] Following a Cabinet shuffle in September of 1985, the new Minister of Health, Barney Hayhoe, responded to increasing public outcry that the government more directly respond to the AIDS crisis by allocating an additional one million pounds to AIDS treatment. Yet, this amount was perceived as too little given that Americans were spending over one hundred million dollars to combat the disease. In December of 1985, the Social Services Secretary, Norman Fowler, announced that 6.3 million pounds would be spent to control the spread of AIDS. The distribution of these funds further illustrated the entrenched homophobia within the Conservative government; whereas £270,000 were allotted to six hemophiliac centers thereby raising government spending on HIV-positive hemophiliacs to £275 per capita, no additional funds were given to the Terrence Higgins Trust. The government spent approximately £1.75 per each homosexual infected with AIDS.[100]

One third of the 6.3 million pounds was devoted to a public awareness campaign. Yet, the campaign, "DON'T AID AIDS," was hindered by debates over whether it was too sexually explicit. In the end, the campaign went forward by March of 1986 with a moderated tone that tended to diminish its informative value.[101] It was horribly unsuccessful and counterproductive serving merely to compound existing confusion about the disease. A survey conducted by Southampton General Hospital found that only thirty-one percent of the population had seen the advertisements, and even more shocking, whereas five percent thought a vaccine to AIDS existed before the campaign, ten percent thought this was true after the campaign![102]

Another public information campaign, "AIDS: DON'T DIE OF IGNORANCE," was created a year later and entailed sending more explicit pamphlets to every household in the United Kingdom. While this campaign succeeded in making AIDS a household word, it tended to depict gay men as bearers of a modern plague. Thus, it both exacerbated some of the homophobia that had been latent since the 1970s and validated the homophobic frenzy which London tabloids had been whipping up since the early 1980s.[103]

Hence, AIDS had the same fundamental effects on the British gay and lesbian movement that it had on the American movement. It stimulated the growth of self-help organizations and repoliticized the movement. The "de-gaying" of the disease enabled straight allies to become more heavily involved in the movement. It promoted gay visibility and placed gay issues on the national agenda, though to a lesser extent than in the United States.[104] Yet, it also marginalized gays from AIDS and HIV work as the disease was recognized as a national public health concern regardless of sexual orientation.[105] AIDS often helped to bring lesbians back into the movement, although this consequence is more true in the United States than in Great Britain.[106] Finally, AIDS forced more public officials to come out in support of gay rights; Labour MP Chris Smith became the first openly gay MP when he outed himself at a gay rights rally in Warwickshire in 1984.[107] Yet, besides the death toll that AIDS inflicted on the gay community, it had other negative consequences. It reinvigorated the myth that homosexuality itself was a contagious disease because AIDS itself was so. It provided fodder for the Conservative Party, like the American Republican Party, with which to maintain a "family values" and subsequently anti-gay stance.

AIDS fostered increasing hostility towards the gay and lesbian community. The British Social Attitudes Survey found that the percentage of individuals who disapproved of homosexuality increased between 1983 and 1987. In 1983, sixty-two percent disapproved. Two years later, this number increased to sixty-nine percent, and by 1987, disapproval of homosexuality was up to seventy-four percent.[108] A London Weekend Television Poll, conducted on 24 January 1988, revealed that the proportion of individuals who supported legalization of homosexual relationships was forty-eight percent, a decrease of thirteen percent from 1985.[109] Margaret Thatcher captured the majority of public spirit and the stance of the Conservative Party when she stated at the 1987 party conference that "Children who need to be taught to respect traditional values are being taught that they have an inalienable right to be gay."[110] The statement clearly demonstrated that the Conservative Party had no intention of supporting further reform and gay men and lesbians were pushed to support either the Liberal or Labour Parties.

The Liberal Party was the earliest to support gay rights in Great Britain. Its 1987 Alliance Manifesto written in conjunction with the Social Democratic Party (SDP) claimed that the Alliance of these two parties would introduce a Bill of Rights to protect all citizens regardless of their sexual orientation, outlaw employment discrimination, and increase AIDS funding.[111] However, the Liberal party has never attained a working majority in Parliament since the end of the First World War.

While the Conservative Party was becoming increasingly hostile to the gay community, the other major party, the Labour Party, had abandoned its indifferent stance of the 1970s and began to support full gay equality from the beginning of the 1980s. This shift probably resulted, in part, from a change in strategy by gay rights groups from targeting MPs, after the Conservative landslide of 1979, to focusing on the local level.[112] Nowhere is this phenomenon more clear than in the case of the Greater London Council (GLC). Ken Livingstone, the leader of the Labour-controlled GLC, pledged to fight anti-gay discrimination. The GLC established a Gay Working Party in 1982. In 1984, it granted approximately £300,000 to various gay and lesbian groups as well as committing £750,000 for the creation of the London Lesbian and Gay Centre.[113] In 1985, the Labour-organized Trade Union Congress passed a motion condemning anti-gay employment discrimination. In 1986, the Labour Party Conference passed a motion supporting full gay and lesbian equality by a two-thirds majority.[114] When the 1987 elections approached, Labour became more timid. The party manifesto released in May of 1987 affirmed only that the party would attempt to ensure that gays and lesbians are not discriminated against.[115] Despite this downplaying of its gay rights agenda, Labour was branded as the "loony Left" during the 1987 campaign.

The Conservative Party Manifesto of 1987 did not mention any desire to promote gay equality; yet, Conservative antipathy towards homosexuality was not as extreme as the contemporary American version. Despite, or rather because of this, it was perhaps more insidious. Unlike far right Republicans who wanted to maintain criminal bans on homosexuality, the vast majority of the Conservative Party by no means wanted to reverse the reforms of the 1967 Sexual Offences Act. Homosexuality is not, and never was, in serious danger of re-criminalization in the United Kingdom. Rather the primary concern was the so-called "promotion" of homosexuality. Actions such as Section 28, known as Clause 28 before the passage of the 1988 Local

Government Bill, represented attempts to push homosexuality back into the private sphere leaving the public sphere clear of such "abnormalities" and reaffirming the findings of Wolfenden as implemented in the 1967 Sexual Offences Act.[116] Yet, the position of the Conservative Party is a clear instance of what Urvashi Vaid referred to as "virtual equality" alluded to in the previous chapter. Legal equality, which the 1967 Act only theoretically and never practically provided, will never successfully combat institutionalized homophobia; only a revolution in values would do so. Conservatives attempted to pre-empt this aim by relegating gay men and lesbians to the locked bedroom. What they failed to understand was that, unlike the notions that the homophiles presented in the 1960s, homosexuality was no longer a bedroom issue, but one which concerned basic human rights.

Once it was re-elected, the Conservative government began to attack the Left further through the introduction of Clause 28 of the 1988 Local Government Bill. Clause 28 prescribed that

(1) A local authority shall not
   (a) intentionally promote homosexuality or publish material with the intention of promoting homosexuality
   (b) promote the teaching in any maintained school of the acceptability of homosexuality as a pretended family relationship
(2) Nothing in subsection (1) above shall be taken to prohibit the doing of anything for the purpose of treating or preventing the spread of disease.[117]

The inclusion of Section Two marks the bill as quite distinct from the Helms Amendment that passed around the same time in the United States. The latter sought to prevent federal money from being used to provide AIDS education. Section 28 attempts no such restriction. However, both the Helms Amendment and Section 28 were grounded in the conservative notion that sexuality can be a form of contagion. As such, according to this rationale, its expression should be eliminated from the public sphere. The law was given royal consent and enacted on 28 May 1988 after it received a two to one majority in the House of Lords and a vote of 254 to 201 in the House of Commons.[118] Yet, the law itself, which turned out to be fairly toothless, is not so important as its effect on gay politics. The law was so vaguely worded that a multitude of texts, such as those written by Oscar Wilde or gay periodicals, could be condemned. Furthermore, any institution which needed a license from the local council, for example, a gay bar, a gay bookstore, or a gay club, could be shut down.[119] The prospect of Clause 28 becoming a law brought a new and unprecedented wave of collective action. On 8 January 1988, between eight thousand and ten thousand people gathered in London to march in protest of the clause.[120] On 1 February of that year, a full-page advertisement, signed by 281 prominent public figures from the arts, politics, and academia, appeared in *The Independent* condemning the clause.[121] A later anti-clause march in Manchester attracted 20,000 participants.[122] On 30 April a month before Clause 28 became law, a protest was held in London attracting almost 30,000 people.[123]

The battle against Clause 28 could be conceived of as Britain's version of the Stonewall riots. The large size of the protests, ranging between ten thousand and thirty thousand participants, demonstrated a degree of cognitive liberation which British gay liberation could not muster. While gay liberation suffered from being an appropriated American phenomenon, the potential passage of Clause 28 was portrayed as a national crisis, and the response to it was purely indigenous. The opposition which mobilized to protest against the clause represented unprecedented solidarity of the gay and lesbian community.[124] Lesbians, who had been on the outskirts of the gay and lesbian movement since the late 1970s may have felt compelled to participate since this was both the United Kingdom's first explicitly anti-gay law in the post-war period as well as the first not to concentrate exclusively on male homosexuality.[125] Furthermore, while the clause did become law, movement organizations and activists did manage to win the support of the Labour Party in denouncing the law.[126] Due to the nature of parliamentary politics (discussed in more detail in the following chapter), the law was passed because the Conservatives had a majority in Parliament and party discipline can insulate MPs from popular opinion.

Section 28 not only backfired in that it became a rather ineffective law, but it also unintentionally produced what it was attempting to legislate away: gay visibility in the public sphere. The crisis which the clause represented served as an impetus for collective mobilization on an unprecedented scale. The political opportunity which Section 28 provided led to the establishment of British ACT UP, OutRage (the British version of Queer Nation), and Stonewall in 1989. Unlike the two former organizations, Stonewall is a more moderate group that is not mass-membership based and, similar to the Homosexual Law Reform Society of the 1960s, serves primarily as a Parliamentary lobbying group.[127]

The 1990s, in both the United States and the United Kingdom, have brought further opportunity and possibility of gaining full gay equality. Gay visibility in the media has expanded although obviously having the potential disadvantages laid out in the previous chapter. British cinema has witnessed a veritable explosion of gay-themed cinema in recent years: *My Beautiful Launderette* (1988), *The Crying Game* (1993), *Beautiful Thing* (1996), *Different for Girls* (1997), *The Full Monty* (1997),

Alive and Kicking (1997), a film version of Martin Sherman's play *Bent* (1997), *Wilde* (1997), *Love and Death on Long Island* (1998), *Mrs. Dalloway* (1998), and *Get Real* (1999). British musicians and actors including Elton John, Boy George, Antony Sher, Simon Callow, Rupert Everett, and Sir Ian McKellan are all openly gay.[128] This appropriation of the gay subject by the heterosexual mainstream is paralleled by the commodification of gay subculture. Sociologist Ken Plummer notes that

To look at the 150-page, glossy, full-color catalogue of Gay Pride '96 is to enter an apolitical world of clubbing, Calvin Klein, Mr. Gay Britain, designer beers, body piercing, kitchen styles, dream houses, gay holidays, gay marriages, theme parties, suntan products, gyms for the body beautiful, antiques, flash cars, Internet, financial services, dance, video, and media of all forms – and all this sandwiched between ads for Benetton, Eyeworks, Virgin Vodka, Mercury, Buffalo Boots, and American Express.[129]

The British Left is critical of this commodification, marketing, and potential de-politicizing of the gay subculture. While this critique has also been present in the United States, it is far more potent in the United Kingdom as the Left is a far more unified voice in the Labour, Liberal, and Social Democratic Parties. Furthermore, British social movements have traditionally had a more socialist and class-based foundation rather than the ethnic/group identity politics common in the United States.[130]

On the political front, in 1994, Parliament finally implemented the 1981 recommendation of the Criminal Law Reform Committee and lowered the age of consent for homosexuals to eighteen after a failed attempt to place it on par with the heterosexual age of consent of sixteen.[131] However, most promising is the political opportunity established by the election of Tony Blair and a Labour-controlled government in May of 1997.[132] A political party potentially amenable to gay and lesbian aims, or, at least, historically more receptive than the Conservative Party, now holds a majority in Parliament. Parliament is currently considering lowering the age of consent to be on a par with heterosexuals, and the gay and lesbian organization, Stonewall, is so confident of the possibility of further reform that it has issued a pamphlet entitled "Equality 2000" which details its attempts to attain full gay equality – a repeal of Section 28, an equalization of the age of consent, a repeal of "gross indecency" laws, protection from employment discrimination, legal recognition of gay partnerships, and the legal right for gays to adopt children – by the turn of the millennium.[133] However, other gay organizations, such as OutRage, are more skeptical of New Labour's commitment to gay rights.[134] Noting similarities between Tony Blair and American President Bill Clinton, the organization was wary of repeating a political debacle similar to "don't ask, don't tell" in the United Kingdom. In January of 2000, some of this skepticism was overcome when, following a ruling by the European Court of Human Rights, the British government lifted its ban on openly gay men and lesbians from serving in the armed forces. (The circumstances surrounding this decision are discussed further in chapter 4.) Despite this outcome, cynics cite the less enthusiastic endorsement of gay rights in the 1996 Labour party manifesto as compared to that issued in 1992. Whereas the 1992 version stated "We will introduce a new law dealing with discrimination on the grounds of sexuality, repeal the unjust Clause 28 and allow a free vote in the House of Commons on the age of consent,"[135] the 1996 Labour manifesto stated only and noncommittally that "Attitudes about race, sex and sexuality have altered. We stand firm against prejudice."[136] Still, pointing to statistics such as a 1990 survey showing that 75 percent of Labour MPs wanted to repeal Section 28 compared with only 8 percent of Conservative MPs,[137] those organizations and individuals hopeful about the political opportunity, which this most recent electoral shift has created, emphasize that a Labour-led government provides more reason for optimism than any Conservative-dominated regime.

The two decades since the decline of British gay liberation have witnessed a fluctuating pattern of support for the British gay and lesbian movement extraordinarily similar to the circumstances experienced by the American counterpart. AIDS brought visibility and increased gay-community organizing as well as strengthening a conservative backlash in both countries. This backlash is represented by legislation in both nations: Section 28 in the United Kingdom and the Helms Amendment in the United States, although the former had a much greater impact on mobilizing the British gay community than the latter had on the American gay community. Both nations have seen the rise of direct-action organizations: ACT UP, Queer Nation, and OutRage. Both have witnessed the development and strengthening of more moderate and/or practical politically-mainstreamed interest groups: Stonewall in the United Kingdom and the National Gay and Lesbian Task Force and the Human Rights Campaign in the United States. Finally, each nation is now either led by parties and/or leaders that at least nominally endorse the concept of gay and lesbian equality. Only time will illustrate whether the increasingly positive media visibility of gay life and these receptive political administrations will profoundly affect the status of gay men and women in both countries.

Conclusion

This chapter has traced the development of a British gay and lesbian movement in the post-war period. Like its American counterpart, the emergence of this movement into its modern form was dependent on the interaction of changing opportunity, pre-existing organizations, and changes in collective identity. *As Figure 3.1 depicts, the British experience demonstrates far more opportunity and ironically, in a certain sense, far less development of the pre-existing organizations.* Opportunities which enabled a gay and lesbian movement to form included the circumstances of the Second World War, the outrage over the Montagu-Wildeblood trial of 1954, the creation and recommendations of the Wolfenden report, and the existence, though to a lesser extent than in the United States, of a movement culture and countercultural presence. Yet, from this enormous opportunity, only the Homosexual Law Reform Society and, later, the Committee for Homosexual Equality developed. The lack of a strong homophile movement may be attributed to both the prevalent British notion of sexuality confined to the private sphere and the lack of other domestic civil rights movement frames to emulate. The Mattachine Society had the original communist-influenced concepts of Hay and his followers to conceptualize homosexuals an oppressed minority class; thus, perhaps Americans were able to perceive homosexuality and gay rights as a public issue much earlier than their British counterparts.

Paradoxically, the less powerful British homophile movement was able to achieve formal legalization of homosexuality – with some notable restrictions – at the national level. This is a feat the American gay and lesbian has yet to accomplish. One cannot help but wonder why this seemingly strange difference occurred. Furthermore, the cognitive liberation of the 1970s, embodied in the new political connotation of "coming out" and initiated by the 1969 Stonewall riots in the United States, was not indigenous to Britain. Hence, while there was a measure of cognitive liberation, it was not nearly to the extent as that which occurred in the United States.

After the decline of gay liberation and the onset of AIDS, the development of the gay and lesbian movements in both nations more closely paralleled one another. Such similarities enable AIDS to be considered as an exogenous global shock that had little to do with national political structures. In this sense, AIDS is another type of critical opportunity in the way the Second World War was characterized in this chapter and in chapter 2, that is, both were international changing opportunities which fostered an environment ripe for gay mobilization. As Figure 3.2 illustrates, AIDS provides a similar type of crisis and opportunity in the United States and the United Kingdom. It

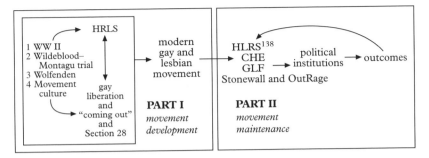

Figure 3.1 *Political process model applied to the British gay and lesbian movement*

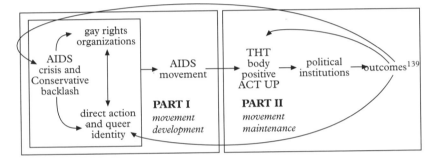

Figure 3.2 *Political process model applied to the British AIDS movement*

pressured pre-existing gay rights organizations such as the British CHE to foster the emergence of AIDS-oriented organizations such as the Terrence Higgins Trust and Body Positive. AIDS also fostered a continuation of cognitive liberation and coming out in both countries. The Conservative backlash, crystallized in the passage of Section 28, provided further opportunity for the British gay community to develop this psychological shift from victimized status to an assertion of pride and political power. Out of this change, more interest groups such as Stonewall developed.

While a formal separation of the gay and lesbian and AIDS movements is conceptually helpful, as was noted in the previous chapter, it is also potentially contrived; it may help isolate the distinctions between the two causes of public health and gay and lesbian civil rights, yet it may overstate the separation between these two movements. Far more dangerous and misleading is that these models, as they currently exist, demonstrate similarities of the emergence of the gay and lesbian movements, but gloss over and wrongly de-emphasize the distinctions. There was no American version of the Sexual Offences Act of 1967. Great Britain has a national law decriminalizing homosexuality and gays and lesbians are no longer banned from the British military while homosexuality is still illegal in approximately twenty states in the United States and the "don't ask, don't tell" policy has left the United States ban in a murky area of failing compromise. While differences in movement emergence are apparent from the developmental histories of the American and British gay and lesbian movements, they do follow essentially the same tri-factor interactive pattern. Yet, the differences in outcome seem to far outweigh any distinctions in the histories, and they do not seem to emanate from such differences alone. To address these paradoxical incongruities we must evaluate the second part of the political process model as it applies to the American and British gay and lesbian movements. These differences explicitly reflect movement maintenance or how the movements interact with the political institutional structures of nations. Chapter 4 examines the differences in these political institutions – the executive-legislative relationship, the party system, the judiciary, federalism, and so on – in order to understand why, despite similar developmental histories, the American and British gay and lesbian movements have experienced such disparate achievements.

4 Where and how it comes to pass: interest group interaction with political institutions

Reassessing and expanding the model

Interest group access in parliamentary systems is often more structured and executive-centered than in the United States. But this does not mean that interest groups are less influential. In many parliamentary systems, interest groups may be less well placed than their American counterparts to overturn government decisions that conflict with their goals, but they may be better placed to ensure that such decisions are never made to begin with.

> R. Kent Weaver and Bert A. Rockman, *Do Institutions Matter?*

The previous two chapters have traced the parallel developmental pattern of the British and American gay and lesbian movements: a changing opportunity – or multiple opportunities – was exploited by pre-existing organizations and coupled with cognitive liberation and subsequent collective affirmative identity formation to produce a social movement. This movement then spurred sundry interest groups at various levels of government. These histories are paradoxical; although the American movement emerged first, was recognized as the international leader, and maintained the largest mass constituency, it has been unable to secure any formalized national recognition of legal equality. Yet, its smaller British counterpart achieved this feat at a date when a movement – as defined by the political process model – had not yet fully formed.

Similar mobilization histories are told with regard to the AIDS crisis possibly because AIDS acts as an exogenous shock to the movement. In other words, AIDS was recognized as a global crisis fostering mobilization by gay organizations throughout the world. Second, both the United States and the United Kingdom were governed by conservative leaders at the beginning of the epidemic. By refusing to recognize the virus's dangers in its early years and failing to provide adequate funds to promote research and medical care, the recalcitrant governments spurred self-organization within the British and American gay communities themselves.

Table 4.1. *Summary of gay and lesbian movement development in the US and the UK*

	United States	United Kingdom
Political opportunity	1. World War II	1. World War II
		2. 1960s movement culture (to a
	2. 1960s movement culture	lesser degree than in the US)
		3. Wildeblood–Montagu Trial (1954)
		4. Wolfenden Report (1958)
		5. 1967 Sexual Offenses Act (both an opportunity and disopportunity – legalization hindered further mobilization)
	3. AIDS / lack of government response	**6. AIDS / lack of government response**
Pre-existing (homophile) organizations	1. Mattachine Society	1. Homosexual Law Reform Society (HLRS)
		2. North Western Homosexual Law
	2. Daughters of Bilitis (DOB)	Reform Committee (NWHLRC)
Cognitive liberation		1. Gay Liberation Theory – subsequent political redefinition of the "coming out" (appropriated from the American model)
	1. 1969 Stonewall Riots	
		2. Gay Liberation Organizations –
	2. Gay Liberation Theory – subsequent political redefinition of "coming out"	Gay Liberation Front (GLF) and Committee (later Campaign) for Homosexual Equality (CHE)
	3. Gay Liberation Organizations – Gay Liberation Front (GLD) and Gay Activist Alliance	**3. AIDS-related direct action to a lesser extent than the US)**
	4. AIDS-related direct action	4. Mobilization against Clause 28 of 1988 Local Government Bill
	5. Queer identity formation	**5. Queer identity formation (to a lesser degree than in the US)**
Interest groups	1. GLF	1. GLF (Died shortly after its American predecessor)
	2. GAA (Both GLF and GAA are dead by 1974)	2. Campaign for Homosexual Equality (CHE)
	3. National Gay and Lesbian Task Force (NGLTF)	3. Stonewall
	4. Human Rights Campaign	4. OutRage!
	5. Gay Men's Health Crisis	**5. Body positive**
	6. ACT UP	**6. ACT UP**
	7. Queer nation	
	8. Various state and local organizations	

Normal typeface – refers to development and organizations of the Gay, Lesbian, Bisexual, and Transgender (GLBT) movement

Bold typeface – refers to development and organizations of the AIDS movement considered as conceptually separate from the GLBT movement

Reductionism should be avoided and differences in movement development must be noted. For example, British homophile organizations were much less radical than their American contemporaries, and gay liberation and the subsequent cognitive liberation that it fostered were not indigenous to the United Kingdom, but appropriated from the American model. Britain's gay and lesbian movement is thus a "late bloomer" relative to its American counterpart since a prideful and politically empowered stance did not fully characterize the former until the 1988 anti-Clause 28 mobilization.

As Table 4.1 illustrates, despite slight differences in the early years of the gay and lesbian movement, the AIDS crisis, the conservative response or lack thereof, and both the organizational networks as well as further cognitive liberation which these circumstances have engendered, the gay and lesbian movements of the United States and the United Kingdom demonstrate relatively parallel historical development. This similarity is most dramatically seen in that the 1997 Pride Festival in London attracted 300,000 participants.[1] Given population differences between Great Britain and the United States, more Britons attended that celebration, proportionally speaking, than Americans attended the 1993 March on Washington for Lesbian, Gay, and Bisexual Rights.

Yet, to compare the movements only by tracing their respective developmental histories can be grossly misleading, both oversimplifying the similarities and belittling the potentially stark differences of these social movements. Part I of the political process model, while establishing an obviously useful conceptual framework with which to comprehend collective mobilization, cannot answer a series of vital questions. Why, for example, was the British gay and lesbian movement able to promote the passage of national legislation which decriminalized private consensual oral and anal intercourse within certain parameters at a date before which a fully developed movement – at least measured in terms of absence of cognitive liberation – even existed? Why is homosexuality still illegal in nearly twenty states in the United States[2] or, in other words, why is homosexuality not decriminalized on a national scale in the United States? Why are there so many more American gay, lesbian, bisexual, and transgender organizations than British ones? In short, how do the differences in the American and British political institutional structures affect the tactics and achievements of each nation's respective gay and lesbian movements?

Social movements do not exist in a political vacuum, and, as detailed in the previous chapters, their fundamental aim is political reform. Thus, the organizations which movements foster interact in a political institutional environment to promote change favorable to the move-

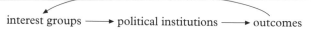

interest groups ⟶ political institutions ⟶ outcomes

Figure 4.1 *PPM part II – movement maintenance*

ment's demands. Political institutional structures include the executive–legislative relationship, the political party system, the existence of an independent judiciary, and the federalist design. This chapter aims to go beyond the insular development of the American and British gay and lesbian movements and examine the political structures with which they interact. Much of the exciting action of interest groups happens within the political institutional framework of a particular nation. Therefore, to attempt to answer the various questions raised above, we must refer to Part II of the political process model shown in Figure 4.1.

The schematic illustrates that the interest groups interact with the political institutions of a given nation to produce outcomes. A feedback loop exists between outcomes and interest groups: an outcome necessarily forces an organization to reorient itself to the new circumstances of the political environment. Regardless of whether the outcome is favorable or unfavorable to sexual minority interest groups, the groups must make adjustments to its tactics and agenda after each outcome.

This chapter will explore the distinct political institutions of the United States and the United Kingdom and assess how these differences influence the actions and achievements of gay and lesbian interest groups. First, a broad comparison of the British parliamentary and the American separation-of-powers structure will reveal how government systems represent a two-way process of input, that is, access and agenda setting, and output, that is, policy implementation. Then, the chapter will attempt more discrete comparisons of the executive–legislative relationship and the party systems as they relate to the level of interest group access and influence. Finally, the chapter will consider other institutional influences such as federalism, an American independent judiciary, and the European Commission and European Court of Human Rights. Comparing these different institutional levels in the British parliamentary and the American separation-of-powers system should provide some insight as to why the respective movements have had disparate achievements despite similar developments or, more specifically, why the British movement had more national level success despite the greater mobilization power of the American movement.

The power of interest groups: a transatlantic comparison

In no country in the world has the principle of association been more successfully used or applied to a greater multitude of objects than in America . . . There is no end which the human will despairs of attaining through the combined power of individuals united into a society. (Alexis de Tocqueville, *Democracy in America*)

Parliament is not a congress of ambassadors from different and hostile interests . . . but . . . a *deliberative* assembly of *one* nation, with *one* interest, that of the whole – where not local purposes, not local prejudices ought to guide, but general good, resulting from the general reason of the whole . . . You choose a member indeed; but when you have chosen him, he is not a member of Bristol, but a member of parliament. (Edmund Burke)

I   Political institutions as input-output structures

An evaluation of interest group interaction with political institutions necessarily explores the representative capacity of a government. It seeks to answer both to what degree that interest group can access and influence political leaders as well as how well the government can implement a policy which responds to interest group appeal. Political regimes can be classified in terms of input as either an open or closed system and output as either a strong or weak state. Various factors influence a government's degree of openness. First, openness is directly proportional to the level of independence existing between the executive and the legislative branch. The more ability the latter has to draft and control policies without regard to the power of the former, the more open a system will be. Second, the number of political parties and other political factions that exist to articulate popular interests effectively is also directly proportional to the level of institutional openness. Yet, the number of parties *per se* is not nearly as important as the extent of party discipline. In a nation where party discipline is strong, groups whose agendas do not conform to the platform of the party will not be represented. Hence, the American separation-of-powers system, characterized by its independent executive and legislative branches and the absence of political party discipline, is a much more open governing regime than its British parliamentary counterpart whose executive is dependent on power from the legislature and where party discipline reigns supreme.[3]

Yet, this characterization is one-sided. While the separation-of-powers structure, coupled with federalism and an independent judiciary, provides far more points for an interest group to achieve access, it also has a number of veto points which can stall and prevent policy implementation. State strength is thus determined by a government's output structures. National policies are more effectively implemented in a centralized state; American federal stratification can make policy implementation cumbersome and redundant. Furthermore, policy effectiveness is higher when branches act in concert and/or cannot be overruled by the other. In other words, the existence of judicial review often inhibits legislative policies from taking their intended effect.[4] *According to the characteristics discussed above, the United States is an open, weak state and the United Kingdom is a closed, strong state.*

Such classifications are still unsatisfactory. If they were true, how then did a relatively weak British homophile movement achieve nationwide homosexual decriminalization in a closed political system, while the much stronger American movement has still been unable to achieve this aim in an open system? How was the American government, which is deemed weak in terms of policy implementation able to confront the AIDS crisis with far more success, measured in terms of resources appropriated to medical research and care, than its far stronger British counterpart? Much of the answers to these questions lay in a far more detailed analysis of those institutions which make up that open or closed and weak or strong state as well as how interest groups interact with these institutions.

II   *The executive-legislative relationship and institutional venues*

As the political scientists, Frank Baumgartner and Bryan Jones, assert, governing power is characterized by a series of temporarily established policy monopolies of various groups. Such monopolies are constructed and destroyed as popular interest and, subsequently, political interest shifts. Often one group can achieve a policy monopoly by providing a new understanding or altering the previous conception of its demands; it must define the policy image in a new way.[5] Thus, the interaction of interest groups and political institutions is marked on the one side by the policy image established by the group and on the other by the receptivity of that institution to that image:

Issue definition, then, is the driving force in both stability and instability, primarily because issue definition has the potential for mobilizing the previously disinterested. The structure of political institutions offers more or fewer arenas for raising new issues or redefining old ones – opportunities to change understandings of political conflict. Issue definition and institutional control combine to make possible the alteration between stability and rapid change that characterizes political subsystems.[6]

This policy redefinition is what occurred in the early years of the AIDS epidemic. In order to achieve greater government response from a government that did not view homosexuals, heroin users, or hemophiliacs, as substantially beneficial or powerful electoral allies, gay organizations were forced to "de-gay" the disease. In other words, they shifted the common perception of the disease as one affecting primarily gay men to a disease that could be transmitted to anyone regardless of sexual orientation.[7] The movement essentially reoriented its focus from achieving gay and lesbian rights to preventing the spread of an epidemic. However, in terms of issue definition, the fundamental shift was the heterosexualization of the disease. Indeed, issue definition was profoundly reshaped by the media attention focused on Ryan White, a young white middle-class straight hemophiliac who had contracted AIDS. AIDS organizations were able to achieve the Ryan White Care Bill in 1990 through this reformulation of the policy image of AIDS.[8]

Yet, despite utilizing the same "de-gaying" strategy, British AIDS organizations were far less successful in achieving increased monetary allocation to their cause at a level proportional to their American contemporaries. Why then did this policy image reformulation of gay and lesbian rights attract more media attention and political response in the United States than in the United Kingdom? American institutional venues were not merely more receptive, more institutional venues *existed* to be receptive.

The clearest and most obvious difference between the parliamentary[9] and presidential or separation-of-powers system is the relationship between the executive and the legislature. In a separation-of-powers system, the executive and the legislative branches are elected independently of one another. The president serves a fixed term of office and his or her stay in that office is in no way contingent on the legislature. Conversely, the president does not have the power to dismiss congress nor call for new elections. Hence, each branch operates fairly independently of the other, and each one can be held by a different political party simultaneously.[10]

In a parliamentary system, the head of government comes from the majority party in the legislature; consequently, the executive and legislative branches are always held by the same party. The executive or prime minister is dependent on maintaining the confidence of the legislature to stay in office; yet, he or she also has the power to dismiss the legislature or Parliament and call for re-elections.[11] Furthermore, just as the prime minister is determined by the majority party, all other cabinet ministers are also drawn from that party. These ministers usually have a great degree of political experience from serving in Parliament and also tend to be policy generalists. The situation is radically different in the United States where the constitution bans legislative officers from holding executive posts; cabinet ministers tend to be specialists in their respective fields.[12]

Thus, at a most basic governmental level as the executive–legislative relationship, interest group access is already severely limited in Britain relative to the United States. American interest groups encounter multiple institutional venues. They can lobby either the president or members of Congress depending on which would be more receptive whereas in Britain, these bodies are always ruled by the same party. Furthermore, political theorist, Leon Epstein, contends that presidential support can be critical since it can potentially cut across political party lines.[13] Baumgartner and Jones echo this contention and note that "presidential involvement can be decisive. The personal involvement of the president can play a key role . . . no single actor can focus attention as clearly, or change the motivations of such a great number of other actors as the president."[14] This statement's veracity was demonstrated, in part, by the great stake gay and lesbian organizations put in the 1992 election of Bill Clinton. The prospect of a president receptive to gay, lesbian, and bisexual issues gave the movement an unprecedented national level of exposure.

Samuel Huntington explains the differences in the American and British political systems through a historical lens. The American government, Huntington contends, exhibits a kind of punctuated political development and thus, an antiquated government structure. By claiming indeed that "in institutional role, as well as in personality and talents, Lyndon Johnson far more closely resembled Elizabeth I than did Elizabeth II . . . Today America still has a king, Britain only the Crown,"[15] Huntington asserts that American democracy is reminiscent of Tudor England with its emphasis on divided sovereignty between the executive (king) and legislature (Parliament), intermingling of political and legal spheres, and the vitality of local government. The United Kingdom, on the other hand, experienced a rationalization of political rule resulting in a differentiation of function among the branches as well as a centralization of authority. Under the Tudor system and similar to American separation-of-powers, members of Parliament represented individual constituencies while the king was to represent the entire community. After the constitutional revolution of the seventeenth century, the king lost his representative function, and sovereignty became fully embodied in Parliament.[16]

The power of Parliament as wielding ultimate legislative power is still suspect. As will be further discussed below, Parliament does theoretically wield such legal supremacy since its acts are not subject to judicial review as is the case in the United States. However, it remains unclear whether the executive or the legislature has more power. One model suggests that supreme power lies with the Parliament since there is no constitutional restriction on its authority. While policy may be formed in the Cabinet, the ministers must answer to the Parliament, and the Parliament can always submit a vote of "no confidence" to force the prime minister and the cabinet to resign.[17] Yet, another model contends that Parliament is nothing more than a forum for debate. That it has no ability to control the administration is evidenced by the prime minister's power to dissolve the legislature.[18] This administrative capacity coupled with the extreme degree of party discipline in the United Kingdom – further discussed below – often yields a high potential for centralization of legislative power in the cabinet turning Parliament into nothing more than a rubber stamp for executive actions.[19]

Interest groups in Britain therefore tend to be more executive-focused than their American counterparts who often attempt simultaneous campaigns at the president and members of congress to mention nothing of local and state campaigns. This trend is even more true since 1867. Before that date, most bills were initiated by MPs and referred to as Private Member Bills. However, currently no more than twenty MPs can introduce bills per year; the particular MPs are decided by ballot. Only the first ten on this ballot stand any chance of a decent hearing. Thus, limited opportunity exists for the opposition party to introduce legislation.[20] For this reason, as well as others discussed above and below, British interest groups tend to focus attention at the administration. Those groups whose ideologies conform to that of the ruling party have a better chance of getting their demands on the agenda. In other words, the British gay and lesbian movement, as the circumstances of the 1980s demonstrated, were effectively shut out of government participation since the hostile Conservative Party held an overwhelming majority.

Yet, if British interest groups fare a better chance if they focus on the administration and not the Parliament, especially if a sympathetic party is in power, how then did the Homosexual Law Reform Society help to ensure the passage of the 1967 Sexual Offences Act? Given that HLRS aimed its reform campaign at MPs and not at the administration, the interest group's tactics do not seem to make any sense within the parameters of its political institutional environment. However, the Sexual Offences Act was an anomaly for a variety of reasons. First, we cannot contend that the passage of the Act is solely due to the actions of HLRS. A variety of socially liberalizing reforms were occurring during the late 1960s, such as divorce, which were dramatically transforming the traditional conceptions of family and gender roles. In this sense, the interest group does not necessarily need to be strong for its goals to be considered: "the right setting, timing, and circumstance can provide a political movement of only modest resources with an opportunity to exercise considerable influence on political outcomes. In other environments or at other times, social movement organizations need all the resources traditionally associated with interest group leverage."[21] In other words, reform was not due solely to the actions of the HLRS, but rather the interest group acted at a time when opportunity was ripe in the United Kingdom: cultural mores were relaxing and the current government administration was in favor of institutionalizing those more liberal attitudes. Second, it is sometimes contended that a British interest group embarks on a public campaign because it already failed to secure acceptance of its demands in Parliament; an antithetical supposition is applicable to the United States.[22] This maxim holds in the case of HLRS reform. The group attempted to secure the passage of the Wolfenden recommendations as early as 1958, but endured a conservative backlash. It then embarked on a successful near ten-year public education campaign. The passage of the act signals that in recent years, public campaigns have become almost as important as Parliamentary ones in securing change. Third, as the previous chapter noted, the Sexual Offences Bill was a Private Member's Bill introduced by Leo Abse. The government refused to issue a bill and, for most of the early 1960s, declared itself neutral with regard to homosexual decriminalization. As also noted above, only a limited number of Private Member Bills reach the floor for discussion and vote thereby testifying further to the anomalous nature of the Sexual Offences Bill. Fourth, homosexual decriminalization was deemed a matter of individual conscience; therefore, political party discipline did not hold, and MPs could vote as they wished regardless of the official party stance.

This last point is particularly important because it illustrates a feature of parliamentary government uncommon in the American separation-of-powers system: political party discipline. The notion that the passage of the 1967 Sexual Offences Act was an anomaly, in part, because party discipline was not enforced, should indicate the strength of such discipline.

III   Political party discipline

British political parties are quite different from their American counterparts. In both countries, parties serve to categorize candidates running for public office. Beyond this common function, the parties have distinct purposes. Given the heterogeneous population and the electoral bias of political parties, lack of party cohesion is common in the United States. This disunity is caused by the non-programmatic tendencies of American parties which, in turn, derive from the separation-of-powers system and federalism. This disunity hinders the ability of the party to represent policy demands within the government's institutional framework, but it does permit party members to break from party ideology thereby perhaps more accurately representing the interests of their constituents.[23] Furthermore, the central party organizations are far weaker in the United States than they are in the United Kingdom proportionally spending less energy and resources on candidate recruitment and campaign financing. Candidates concentrate on building a constituency by upholding popular interest over the party line.[24] Finally, unlike the situation in the United Kingdom, political advancement is usually not dependent on cooperation with party leaders; thus, party cohesion is further undermined.[25]

Political cleavages and diffuse interests are widespread in the United States and are reinforced both by the nation's geographic diversity on the one hand and the nature of the federal system on the other. Thus, consensus on party ideology is difficult to attain. The American population is sectionally diverse; little unity exists among various regions of the country. For example, Southern Democrats have different opinions and goals from their counterparts in Massachusetts. Although the government's power has gradually shifted away from the states and towards the national level, the United States party structure is still fragmented along regional as well as state lines.[26] In this diverse setting, and given that American political parties are electoral-based as opposed to mass membership parties, non-programmatic and flexible parties are advantageous; they need to be ideologically broad and represent a diffuse range of interests to win elections. Because the Republican and Democratic parties adhere only loosely to agendas, their programs overlap toward the ideological center to attract voters. As a result, individuals who do hold strong beliefs on either the right or left become effectively disenfranchised. Since these parties are non-programmatic and lack clear agendas, interest groups fill this representative niche and are able to influence elected officials.[27]

Unlike American political parties, British parties are mass membership parties. As of 1992, the Conservative Party had approximately one million members while the Labour had 280,000 members.[28] A more important distinction however is that strong party discipline is demanded by the nature of the parliamentary executive–legislative rela-

tionship. If party cohesion did not exist, the executive would always be
threatened with ouster from office, and the legislative would endure the
continuous instability of possible dissolution.[29] The MPs' and potential
candidates' dependence on the much stronger central party for official
endorsement and campaign financing helps to maintain this party
discipline.[30] Furthermore, since cabinet ministers are drawn from the
legislature, career advancement usually depends upon obeying the party
leadership.[31]

The cohesive and programmatic nature of British parties does not
necessarily mean that interest groups do not exist nor that they serve a
lesser function. Indeed interest groups such as HLRS and later CHE
existed because neither of the two main parties, Conservative nor
Labour, adequately represented the demands of the gay and lesbian
population. As political scientist Leon Epstein notes,

> even in Britain a major party is not so monolithic as always to be able to perform
> the policy-making function in the manner envisioned for a programmatic party
> . . . The most that might be said for the British party as a policy-maker, given its
> considerably greater cohesion in government, is that important interest groups
> may find it more advantageous to concentrate on winning a party, as such, over
> to its policy goals.[32]

This was the strategy that various British gay and lesbian organizations took on throughout the 1980s as it became increasingly apparent
that the Conservative-dominated government was not only going to
prevent further reform, but also attempt to roll back reforms already
made. The strong ties that the movement made to the Labour Party are
clearly stated by *Capital Gay*'s 1987 slogan that "A gay who votes
Conservative, is like a Turkey voting for Christmas."[33] The Labour-led
Greater London Council (GLC) supported lesbian and gay centers and
organizations, and Labour vocally opposed Section 28 of the 1988
Local Government Bill.

A greater degree of party cohesion does make it more difficult for an
interest group to have its agenda represented in the legislature. It
bolsters the already closed executive–legislative relationship thereby
further hindering agenda access by unrepresented groups. However, as
the experience of both the re-election of a Labour government in 1967
and the Labour-dominated GLC illustrate, party cohesion can be
advantageous if the party is supportive of the interest group. In 1967, for
example, the Labour government ended its official neutrality and
endorsed the Sexual Offences Act. Also, party cohesion can centralize
authority thereby making it more accountable and showing itself to be
an ally to a particular interest group. In the American separation-of-
powers system, lack of party cohesion makes the individual representa-

tive more accountable to his or her constituents; however, the structure diffuses power and responsibility to such an extent that it is often difficult for voters and interest groups to know who to hold accountable for a particular policy.[34] The President can blame Congress, and members of Congress can simultaneously blame the President. After the disastrous implementation of "don't ask, don't tell," gay and lesbian organizations did not know whom to blame for the institutionalization of the closet in the armed forces: a weak president, a recalcitrant congress, a disorganized interest group, or some combination of all of these factors?

The independence of the executive and legislative branches in the United States coupled with the little to no degree of political party discipline provides substantially more agenda access to interest groups than the British parliamentary structure. Two other characteristics of the American separation-of-powers system also provide more access by increasing the number of possibly receptive institutional venues: federalism and an independent judiciary.

IV   The impact of the federalist design and an independent judiciary

Federalism creates a variety of distinct venues to experiment with types of policies, and thus, its existence accounts for the great disparity of gay and lesbian law throughout the United States. More than 80,000 governments exist in the United States: one federal government, fifty semi-autonomous state governments, 40,000 municipalities, 26,000 special districts, and 15,000 school districts.[35] If gay rights legislation is unsuccessful at the national level, then such legislation can be tried at the state and local levels. The existence of more legislative venues means that more bills can be brought forth and potentially passed into law. The National Gay and Lesbian Task Force tracked 474 gay, lesbian, bisexual, transgender and HIV-related bills debated at the state level in 1999.[36] Besides the sheer volume that the federalist design promotes, it also provides the possibility that one state law might act as a model, experiment, or test case for other states. In other words, particular legislation may exhibit a certain degree of geographical and temporal diffusion. Marieka Klawitter and Brian Hammer utilize the growing prevalence of local antidiscrimination policies for sexual orientation in the United States to test this diffusion model. Their work suggests that diffusion is not a one-way dynamic of reform spreading outward from a nodal origin; rather, while one jurisdiction's adoption of an antidiscrimination policy may provide a model, it can also raise the salience of gay and lesbian politics in nearby jurisdictions. Heightened salience can spur

increased debate and potential for countermovement backlash. This
dual dynamic, referred to by Klawitter and Hammer as diffusion and
antidiffusion, is exhibited when issues can be framed from a moral
perspective as gay and lesbian rights often are. Morality issues as
opposed to economic ones, according to these political scientists,
involve less technical knowledge and tend to provoke strong opinions
and little room for compromise exists.[37] When potential legislative
innovation is removed from the control of political elites and interest
groups and subjected to popular opinion, conservative backlash can
often drown out minority political goals. This pattern may enable the
antidiffusion tendencies to counterbalance diffusion ones if the population of a certain jurisdiction is not persuaded by the arguments of the
group(s) seeking legislative change.[38]

Given the regional diversity of political ideology in the United States,
we can understand how federalism does indeed exacerbate the discre-
pancies of the legal and political status of American gay men and
lesbians. While British local governments can be more sympathetic to
the sexual minorities community as was the GLC of the 1980s, the
variety and range of diverse laws does not exist across the four sections
of the United Kingdom – England, Wales, Scotland, and Northern
Ireland – as it does across the fifty American states. Federalism accounts
not only for the diversity of legislation, but also for the greater success of
the American movement at the local as opposed to national level. The
gay community tends to be a powerful voting bloc where it is clustered
(most likely in urban areas); hence, these urban areas such as San
Francisco, Los Angeles, Chicago, and New York City tend to have
either more pro-gay laws or, at least, less anti-gay legislation introduced,
than more rural regions.[39]

The judicial branch and, more specifically, the tool of judicial review
represent another means not available to the British gay and lesbian
movement through which the American counterpart can attain reform.
In the United Kingdom, law consists of the common law as it is
interpreted by judges throughout history and Statute Law which is
enacted by Parliament. Unlike the United States, the United Kingdom
has no written constitution nor a written bill of rights.[40] Furthermore, no
British court can invalidate the laws passed by Parliament. Sir William
Blackstone asserted that providing the court with such power would "set
the judicial power above that of the legislature, which would be subver-
sive to all government."[41] Hence, no British counterpart to the American
Supreme Court exists. An interesting exercise might be to speculate on
the role of the European Court of Human Rights as an informal Supreme
Court of the United Kingdom and for the other member states of the

Council of Europe. Given that the United Kingdom has no written constitution, the European Convention on Human Rights and the Court provide a viable alternative venue for interest groups when reform via legislation is unlikely; with this understanding in mind legal theorist, Robert Wintemute, has characterized the European Convention as "the quasi-constitutional bill of rights of a nascent quasi-federal Europe."[42] In some sense, the relationship between the United Kingdom and the European Court of Human Rights is analogous to any of the United States' relationships to the Supreme Court.

As chapter 3 indicated, a variety of cases concerning gay rights in the United Kingdom have been heard before the European Commission on Human Rights and the Court itself including the case of Derek Ogg which resulted in the extension of the 1967 Sexual Offences Act to Scotland and that of Jeff Dudgeon which resulted in a similar extension of the law to Northern Ireland. Jeff Dudgeon submitted his case to the European Commission on Human Rights under the auspices of the Northern Ireland Gay Rights Association (NIGRA) in 1976. Dudgeon claimed that Northern Ireland's criminalization of homosexuality violated Article 8 of the European Convention on Human Rights.[43] The Article states that "Everyone has the right to respect for his private and family life, his home and his correspondence."[44] Section 2 of the Article states that

There shall be no interference by a public authority with the exercise of this right except such as is in accordance with the law and is necessary in a democratic society in the interests of national security, public safety or the economic well-being of the country, for the prevention of disorder or crime, for the protection of health or morals, or for the protection of the rights and freedoms of others.[45]

In short, the legal argument used to support Dudgeon's case rested on the right to privacy. A similar argument would be used in the United States in *Bowers v. Hardwick*, discussed below, without success. In 1981, the Court agreed with the Commission's finding that such a violation existed. This decision fostered a ripple effect throughout the United Kingdom and other members of the Council of Europe. Homosexuality was decriminalized in Northern Ireland in 1982. Other United Kingdom territories including Guernsey, Jersey, the Isle of Man, Gibraltar, and Bermuda decriminalized homosexuality by 1994. Indeed, with the fall of the Berlin Wall in 1989 and the expansion of the Council into the former Eastern Bloc, decriminalization of homosexuality has become a tacit but necessary step for admission into the Council. Of the ten Eastern European countries that joined the Council before 1993, all but Romania had decriminalized homosexuality either before admission or shortly thereafter. At least regarding sodomy reform and the right to privacy, the Dudgeon case behaved as a kind of watershed event.[46] It is of note that the judgment came down in 1981, five years before a similar case, *Bowers v. Hardwick*, would be argued before the United States Supreme Court and the states' right to maintain sodomy laws upheld.

A more recent appeal to the European Court of Human Rights illustrates how litigation can lead to a transformation of national policy in the United Kingdom. In a struggle lasting since 1995 and decided in September of 1999, four former members of the British armed forces, supported by British gay and lesbian rights organizations Stonewall and Liberty, charged that the British ban on gays and lesbians from serving in the military violated their human rights under the European Convention. In these cases – *Jeanette Smith v. the United Kingdom, Graeme Grady v. the United Kingdom, Duncan Lustig-Prean v. the United Kingdom*, and *John Beckett v. the United Kingdom* – the plaintiffs alleged that the ban and the intrusive investigations regarding their sexual behavior contradicted the fundamental right to privacy granted in Article 8 of the Convention. Two other plaintiffs – Jeanette Smith and Graeme Grady – contended that the ban and corresponding investigation transgressed Article 3, which bans degrading and inhumane treatment, Article 10, which guarantees freedom of expression, and Article 13, which demands that the member nation have an adequate domestic means to remedy the complaint.[47]

In a 27 September 1999 unanimous ruling (7–0), the Court declared that the military ban and subsequent investigations into the sexual behavior of the plaintiffs breached individual privacy as guaranteed in Article 8.[48] The Ministry of Defence contended that allowing openly gay men and lesbians to serve in the military would depress unit morale and negatively affect performance, an argument also utilized by the United States Department of Defense to maintain that nation's "don't ask, don't tell" policy and one that has historically been used to prevent racial integration of the armed services and the exclusion of women.[49] The Court found no merit in this argument contending that the Ministry of Defence's ban was "not based on a particular moral standpoint and the physical capability, courage, dependability and skills of homosexual personnel were not in question."[50] On 12 January 2000, despite assertions from the Ministry of Defence that no action would be taken regarding the Court decision until the Armed Forces Bill came up for review in 2001,[51] the defense secretary, Geoffrey Hoon, announced that the government had a new code of conduct effectively lifting the ban on gays and lesbians from openly serving. The new code lays out guidelines regarding proper and offensive social and sexual behavior regardless of sexual orientation.[52] The new policy brings the British military into accordance with most other countries in the European Union, except Turkey.[53] However, now that the precedent has been established, other such military bans on gays and lesbians throughout the Council of Europe could be perceived as violations of the Convention. The change in British policy also means that the United States and Turkey are the only members of NATO that maintain bans on gays and lesbians from serving openly in the armed forces.[54] The American "don't ask, don't tell" policy enables gays and lesbians to serve as long as they do not reveal their sexual orientation. However, opponents of the compromise claim that it has led to more discharges of gay military personnel, not less: 1,145 discharges for homosexuality in 1998 compared to nearly half that number in 1993. No arguments regarding the ban are scheduled to be heard at the United States Supreme Court, so no litigation equivalent of the European Court decision is expected in the near future in the United States. The "don't ask, don't tell" policy is law and, as such, it cannot be eliminated by a presidential executive order (as President Truman made racial integration of the military a reality).[55] Few signs exist that any change in the American compromise will come either through a legislative or litigation strategy.

As the Dudgeon case (decided during the Conservative Thatcher government) and the more recent ruling regarding gays and lesbians serving in the British military demonstrate, the European Court of Human Rights does function as an alternative venue in the relatively closed British parliamentary structure. If the government is controlled by a political party not amenable to a particular interest group's goals, that organization and the movement it represents can seek change through litigation and not legislation. Given that the British government is currently held by the Labour party, which has been open to gay and lesbian demands, and that certain gay-friendly precedents have been established by the European Court of Human Rights, the British gay and lesbian movement stands a high chance, institutionally speaking of achieving a good deal of reform.

The dual strategies of litigation versus legislation have always confronted the American gay and lesbian movement. Gay rights litigation dates as early as the immediate post-war period when gay bars fought for their right to serve homosexuals. Indeed, as chapter 2 notes, one of the earliest and most visible actions the Mattachine Society undertook was to defend one of its founding members against police entrapment. Gay-themed magazines such as *The Mattachine Review* utilized the First Amendment to maintain its right to be published. *One* fought for and won its ability to be published under the First Amendment as early as

1950 in *One, Inc. v. Olson.* Legal reform is embodied in the American Law Institute's Model Penal Code, released in the 1950s, which decriminalized sodomy. Gay men and lesbians have used the court system to challenge federal and private employment policies, discrimination in the military, anti-gay immigration laws, denial of the right to marry, and denial of the right to adopt children. Since state-level court decisions apply only to the specific state, disparate laws exacerbate the inequality which is engendered by the federalist structure. As Urvashi Vaid details, this system allows for Massachusetts to have a state-funded gay and lesbian youth program while Alabama law prohibits the "promotion" of homosexuality in public schools.[56]

The separation of the judiciary and the legislative branches leads to a multiplicity and redundancy in function and powers, and this pattern is mimicked in the movement itself. Vaid contends that

Legal groups pursue litigation, speak before legal and legislative bodies, and speak out in the media in a parallel world to political groups. Political organizations, too, rarely involve the legal groups in drafting legislation or in debating the merits of various approaches they are considering. This separation results in an awkward and counterproductive situation, where each organization pushes an institutional agenda that overlaps with others.[57]

Thus, movement tactics appear to conform to the institutional environment to such a degree that the movement actually mimics some of the institutional disadvantages and confusing variety of participatory arenas within the separation-of-powers system.

The theoretical advantage of the legal versus the political route is that while politicians may feel compelled to bow to potentially prejudiced popular opinion or expedient concerns regarding re-election, the courts must show written justification for their decisions that are to be consistent with previous decisions and established precedents. Members of minority groups who may find it difficult to compel legislators to change a law or create a new legal protection from discrimination (given the bimodal nature of gay and lesbian rights), may find it easier to persuade a court that an instance of discrimination violates an existing law.[58] The litigation strategy was taken most vividly in the United States in 1986. The state-by-state process of repealing anti-sodomy laws, after surging in the 1970s, slowed by the early 1980s. A Supreme Court case provided the potential for overriding state law, bypassing arduous and repetitive state-by-state legislative reform and litigation, and decriminalizing homosexuality throughout the United States in one motion.[59] Unfortunately, the case of *Bowers v. Hardwick* did not realize that potential.

Various individuals within the sexual minorities community have used litigation to promote reform. Michael Hardwick is probably the most famous of such individuals. In 1982, he was arrested for engaging in consensual sex with another adult male in his own bedroom. His sexual actions violated the Georgia sodomy law which states that

(a) A person commits the offense of sodomy when he performs or submits to any sexual act involving the sex organs of one person and the mouth or anus of another . . . [and] (b) A person convicted of the offense of sodomy shall be punished by imprisonment for not less than one nor more than 20 years.[60]

The district attorney dropped the charges against Hardwick, but Hardwick, in turn, brought a suit to federal district court claiming that Georgia's sodomy law violated his right to due process of the law as stated by the Fourteenth Amendment of the United States Constitution. The federal court dismissed the suit, but the Court of Appeals for the Eleventh Circuit overturned the previous ruling and secured a review by the United States Supreme Court. The decision, which was divided five justices to four (Justices Burger, O'Connor, Rehnquist, White, and Powell decided not to extend the right to privacy argument and uphold the state's right to criminalize oral and anal intercourse while Blackmun, Brennan, Marshall, and Stevens dissented), dismissed Hardwick's claim, and the states' right to legislate anti-sodomy law remained intact.[61] Once released the decision came under immediate attack by legal scholars; some evaluations suggested that the supposed unprejudiced character of the court system was compromised,[62] i.e., that the decision reflected the personal prejudice of the justices rather than conforming to use of right of privacy precedents laid out by *Roe v. Wade*, *Griswold v. Connecticut*, or *Loving v. Virginia*.[63] *Bowers v. Hardwick* was not a watershed event like the Dudgeon case across the Atlantic; however, it did inspire decriminalization litigation at other venues, namely the state court system.[64]

The state court structure has also been the venue for other issues involving gays and lesbians. The most recent and salient example involved the right of same-sex couples to marry, the issue being brought before the Supreme Courts of Hawaii and Vermont. The prospect of state sanctioned gay marriage arose in 1993 when the Hawaii Supreme Court ruled that the failure to recognize gay marriage constituted sex discrimination. Hawaii and thirty other states reacted by passing laws which defined marriage as a union only between members of the opposite sex. The federal government passed the Defense of Marriage Act (DOMA) to prevent national recognition if gay marriage came to pass in Hawaii. The Hawaii state legislature sought a constitutional amendment to give itself the power to define marriage as a union between a man and woman, thereby overriding the state supreme court ruling. That amendment was passed in the autumn of 1998 by a margin of nearly two to one. The lawsuit disputing this ban on gay marriage was dismissed by the state supreme court in late 1999 on the grounds that the constitutional amendment rendered the plaintiff's claim moot. Of note is that although the constitutional amendment gave the state legislature the power to ban same-sex marriages, that authority was not yet exercised by the court's 1999 decision.[65]

The circumstances in Vermont differed from those in Hawaii and a nation-wide backlash did not occur if only because same-sex marriage bans were already in place at the time of the Vermont Supreme Court ruling. On 20 December 1999, that state's supreme court, in the case of *Baker v. State of Vermont* ruled that the state must guarantee the same rights and privileges afforded to married couples to gay and lesbian couples as well; the court turned the implementation of this decision over to the state legislature. The result was an unprecedented judicial–legislative cooperative effort toward compromise. The state legislature and governor signed into law a bill that would create civil unions, that is, state recognized partnerships for same-sex couples that include the nearly three hundred state statutes that derive from marriage; the law went into effect in July 2000. At the state level, the civil unions provide all the rights and benefits of marriage – inheritance rights, tax breaks, health insurance – without the granting of a marriage license. The new recognition does not include any of the one thousand federal statutes that derive from marriage, and the union holds no power to be recognized outside of Vermont's borders.[66] The Vermont case is groundbreaking because it both fostered a law that goes well beyond existing piecemeal domestic partnership statutes in other states as well as established legal and political precedent. By offering state-sanctioned recognition of same-sex partnerships without using the term "marriage,"[67] the Vermont legislature provides a model for other states to consider and adopt without necessarily contradicting the existing bans on same-sex marriage or the federal Defense of Marriage Act.

Now that the decision regarding gay marriage has transferred from the judiciary to the legislature, the issue becomes subject to the whims of public opinion. A statewide poll in mid-January 2000 sponsored by *The Rutland Herald*, *The Barre-Montpelier Times Argus*, and WCAX Channel 3 found that 38 percent of the state supported the state supreme court's ruling while 52 percent disagreed, and 10 percent remained unsure.[68] When asked whether it was in favor of a constitutional amendment that would overturn the court ruling, that is, following the strategy taken by Hawaii, 49 percent of this cohort favored such action while 44 percent opposed an amendment to the state constitution.[69] These numbers bear out the observations of Klawitter and Hammer discussed above, namely that on morality issues such as gay and lesbian rights, public opinion is likely to impede innovation by political elites. If the prospect of gay marriage were offered in a referendum as opposed to brought through litigation, it is highly unlikely that any civil union law would have been devised. Furthermore, as both the entire state legislature and the governor are up for re-election in 2000, the battle over gay marriage and the creation of civil unions will undoubtedly impact the campaigns. Given these polling numbers, of concern for gay and lesbian activists and interest groups is protecting the new law against repeal if a backlashing legislature comes to power.

As the above discussion demonstrates, the separation-of-powers system exhibits more drawbacks than just a redundancy of function and responsibility. The multiplicity of access points also creates a variety of veto points. Hence, while an interest group can get its demands on the political agenda, implementing those demands is much more difficult than in the centralized parliamentary system of the United Kingdom. As Huntington indicated, the rationalization of the political system in the United Kingdom coupled with the alternative venue of the European Commission and European Court of Human Rights provide movement activists with a more open system (although much less open than the American structure) that also has a strong enforcement ability. The concentration of authority may result in a less representative government, but it also engenders a greater ability to impose losses on political actors as well as promote policy innovation by eliminating veto points. In the United States, a prospective policy is subject to so many veto points that not only is implementation process slow, but the process is marked by such continuous compromise that the implemented law may not at all resemble the proposal. Furthermore, the British centralization of authority in cabinet provides an active forum in which to debate issues with limited susceptibility to outside influences. A Parliamentarian might argue that Congress is so easily infiltrated by interest groups that the common good is always secondary to the aims of a particular group.[70]

Conclusion

Apparent from this analysis is not only that neither parliamentary nor the separation-of-powers system is clearly superior to the other, but also that each has structured the tactics and achievements of the gay and lesbian movement. In general the American system is better at representing diverse interests and providing the opportunity for agenda access. Baumgartner and Jones assert that

Failure in one venue can lead to resignation, but it can just as likely lead to a search for a new venue. If the state is unresponsive, what about the courts? Will a federal agency intervene on our behalf? Can we approach the school board as a potential ally? These sorts of calculations go on every day in America.[71]

The United Kingdom does not have this variety of institutional venues, but the cohesion and centralization of British parliamentary structure facilitates the targeting of resources, the coordination of conflicting objectives, and the implementation of policy decisions. This transatlantic comparison of political institutions engenders the following conclusions.

The independence of the American governmental branches promotes greater opportunity for access, but creates implementation problems. The American gay and lesbian movement has more institutional venues than its British counterpart in which to articulate its agenda, but these venues can work against each other thereby hindering agenda implementation.

An independent judiciary can enable reform, but it can also complicate policy implementation. The American movement has achieved many of its aims in a piecemeal fashion through the court system rather than securing a comprehensive piece of legislation through political channels.

Public education campaigns are an important means to achieve reform. Parliamentary campaigns are more effective in the United Kingdom, and the HLRS strategy of the mid-1960s tends to be considered a notable exception to this maxim.

Federalism accounts for the disparity and multiplicity of gay-themed legislation in the United States whereas centralization of power in the United Kingdom explains both the coherence and minimal amount of such legislation in that nation.

British interest groups are more likely to achieve their aims if a sympathetic party is in power. The political environment is so important relative to movement organizational resources that the resources do not appear as relevant when understanding British movement development. Hence, we see the 1967 Sexual Offences Act enacted under a Labour government even though the existing interest group mobilized few resources to lobby for its passage. Furthermore, the power of political opportunity – of timing and setting – as the determining factor in the United Kingdom to a far greater extent than in the United States is demonstrated by the failure to lower the age of consent for homosexuals (to have parity with the heterosexual majority) in 1994 despite a highly mobilized and wealthy coalition of sexual minority interest groups, support from parliamentary leaders, and the endorsement of popular celebrities.[72] We now witness the increasing saliency of gay and lesbian issues, including a reopening of the age of consent issue and the lifting of the ban on gays and lesbians in the British military with the election of Tony Blair and a Labour government.

Furthermore, in a distinct but related point, the European Court of Human Rights functions as an alternative venue for a British interest group or an individual acting as a member of a disenfranchized minority to seek reform. Given that the Labour party currently controls the government and that the European Court of Human Rights is more willing to perceive sexual orientation discrimination as a violation of Article 8 of the European Convention of Human Rights, the British gay and lesbian movement and its respective interest groups have an unprecedented opportunity to achieve gay-friendly legislation and litigation outcomes.

In the United States, the President is a powerful ally for an interest group since he or she can potentially mobilize support across party lines. As a result, the American movement targeted vast resources into the election of the potential supportive Democratic Presidential candidate, Bill Clinton, in 1992.

These findings suggest the general conclusion, illustrated in Figure 4.2, that the weaker British movement is better positioned (in terms of the receptivity of institutional venues) than its American counterpart if a receptive political party attains a Parliamentary majority. The American gay and lesbian movement will tend to be more successful than its British contemporary if an oppositional party holds a Parliamentary majority.

These characteristics are most clearly reflected in the circumstances of the AIDS crisis. Despite both movements encountering conservative and not necessarily amicable regimes, the American movement was able to attain more government resources by redefining the issue and approaching various venues. The British movement was not as successful because the Tories held one of the few institutional venues in the centralized government. In this case, without judicial review or the possibility of divided power, i.e., the prime ministership held by one party and the Parliament held by another, British sexual minority interest groups had few access points to have their agenda heard or implemented.

An overall evaluation suggests that neither the American system nor the British system is universally advantageous over the other with regard to gay and lesbian movement reforms. The United States government provides multiple points of access, but is unable to pass a national gay and lesbian equality law. Rather, reform will continue to move at

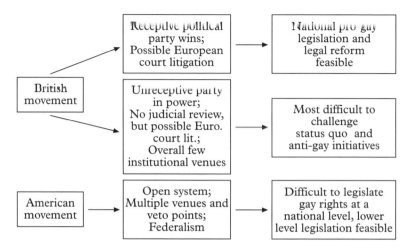

Figure 4.2 *How political institutions affect movement organizations' aims*

incremental steps in various states and through sundry legal decisions since the American institutional environment, marked by separated powers and federalism, prevents a nationally powerful movement from achieving national-level legislation. The United Kingdom has passed a national equality law, at least in theory if not in practice, and Stonewall and OutRage are examples of highly centralized and national-level British gay and lesbian parliamentary lobbies, but most MPs are shielded from public opinion and lobby action by party discipline. Even if gay issues, such as the age of consent, are treated as matters of conscience as opposed to regulated by party discipline, the level of unease about "promoting" homosexuality or demonstrating "approval" of homosexuality counters any overarching impulse for equality in even a potentially most supportive party like Labour.[73] Thus, in the United Kingdom, reform hinges on the receptivity of the ruling party, can occur through rational-comprehensive decision-making, as opposed to incrementalism, and thus, the status of British gays and lesbians can see-saw as Conservatives topple Labour and *vice versa*. Hence, each institutional environment excels in different areas fostering the respective movement to utilize distinct tactics. The differences in the political institutional environments can thus account for why the histories of the British and American gay and lesbian movements diverge at certain points only to appear similar and diverge again.

5   Asking the unasked question: grappling with the culture variable

Political culture . . . is an elusive concept that is difficult to capture empirically. But it is hard to avoid the impression – even if it is difficult to demonstrate – that the most far-reaching impacts of cycles of protest are found in slow and incremental changes in political culture.

Sidney Tarrow, *Power in Movement*

After the last paradigm shift to resource and structural analyses, social movement literature reacted by rehabilitating the social psychological study of movement participation. Let us not make the same mistake for the second time and turn our backs on those areas where social psychology, structural analyses, and rational choice might prove more powerful in favor of a totalizing theory that – ultimately – never can be.

Hank Johnston and Bert Klandermans, "The Cultural Analysis of Social Movements"

Structural bias: beyond the political process model

In reference to the 2000 election cycle in the United States, *Time* magazine columnist Margaret Carlson wrote

In 1992, not only would no one bring up gaydar, but also the subject of gays in the military was not nearly the preoccupation it is this time . . . With the exception of the novelty candidates, what this campaign shows is that the country has moved some distance in its acceptance of gays. Two years ago, gay bashing was a staple of the Republican right. Lately, Republicans have largely gone quiet since their pollsters warned them to knock it off. Spreading scare stories about gays just wasn't working. Too many people had come out, and too many blue-haired mothers in the heartland didn't like hearing that their gay son or daughter was worthless or immoral.[1]

Carlson succinctly isolates a shift in the national political culture in the United States. Unfortunately, given the variables and questions which come under the scope of the political process model, we have little leverage to figure out just what is going on here. What was it that made these "blue-haired mothers" come out in defense of their gay sons and daughters? Why has the party of "traditional family values" backed off its overt bashing of so-called sexual deviance? Why is the slang term "gaydar" suddenly becoming appropriated in national, if not international, discourse? Why is it normal for Gen Xers to joke that "all the good ones are gay"? The visibility and acceptance of gay men and lesbians in cultural and political media are higher now than they have ever been as discussions regarding gays in the military are re-opened, as the controversy over the possibility of gay marriage looms and civil unions become a reality, as gay characters are now prominently featured in prime-time television. Certainly, the reasons for this current circumstance cannot be, as the political process model would suggest, only due to the work of interest groups and legislation. Such an assessment does not mean that these groups – HRC, NGLTF, the Victory Fund, Lambda Legal Defense and Education Fund, countless state organizations, Stonewall, etc. – are not diligent and have not fought incredibly hard to secure a better and safer future for gays and lesbians. Yet, as past chapters have indicated, much of the comprehensive pro-gay legislation, despite the work of these organizations, such as ENDA or Hate Crimes legislation has failed, while anti-gay legislation such as DOMA, the Helms Amendment (or Section 28 in the United Kingdom) have passed and/or remained on the books. Certainly smaller achievements have been made such as the defeat of the Hefley Amendment in 1998, but Carlson's passage implies that something greater, more comprehensive, and, indeed, more difficult to define is at work here.

This book has sought to answer primarily two questions: First, how did the American and British gay and lesbian movements develop in the post-war period? This question leads to another: given relatively parallel developmental histories, why have these movements experienced such disparate levels of political achievement? Chapter 4, obeying the framework of the political process model, as laid out in chapter 1, has attempted to account for these differences by making reference to the political institutions of the United States and the United Kingdom. In other words, the reason why the British and the American gay and lesbian interest groups have attained distinct ends is because the separation-of-powers and parliamentary systems engender both different degrees of agenda access to interest groups as well as varying ability of the government to implement policy.

Yet, like the other social movement theories explored in chapter 1 and the appendix, the political process model has a certain bias; the theory continues unavoidably to reflect and/or portray a distorted interpretation of historical reality. PPM tends to emphasize the role of political institutions as environmental determinants of interest group action to such an extent that it disparages or avoids discussion of other factors. As

PPM is a structural theory, it, like its cousin, resource mobilization, desperately wants to interpret movement participants as rational actors, behaving in politically viable manners.[2] Hence, it overemphasizes the role of interest groups without giving due attention to other forms of politics. However, as has been hinted at in chapters 2 and 3, and as will be further discussed in this chapter, much of the action within the gay and lesbian movement has not been within the field of interest group politics.

Like any field of inquiry, social movement theories are not only complex, but continuously evolving as students of this discipline explore diverse aspects of movements. We have already witnessed some of this evolution in chapter 1 as theoretical explanations moved from the classical approach to resource mobilization to political opportunity structure and political process models in the structuralist schools, while students adhering to "new" social movement conceptions interrogated notions of collective identity, identity politics, and subculture development.

Another evolutionary stage in social movement theory is taking shape. As sociologists, anthropologists, and political scientists including Gamson, Melucci, Inglehart, Johnston, Klandermans, Swindler, Taylor, and Whittier suggest, this trend is not so much a paradigm shift as it is a paradigm *augmentation*. Recent scholarship is moving towards re-evaluating culture as a variable in social movement development and maintenance. In a sense, we are bringing culture back into the mix of variables under examination, but we are not merely shifting gears, wringing our hands and suggesting that structural models have gotten us this far, but will get us no farther. We are not, therefore, reverting to the culturally based models of the classical approach. Much of this more recent discussion of culture is fundamentally *reframing* the primary questions away from motivation for social movement behavior – the focus of classical theorists – and placing it in more observable and less subjective contexts to promote some level of empirical validity. Johnston and Klandermans suggest,

It is not enough to simply add culture to our list of independent variables. Unless we are able to construct theories that relate to culture's impact to variables that we already know to be of influence – such as resources, organizations, political opportunities, and perceived costs and benefits of participation – we will not get beyond the descriptive study of movements . . . in explaining the growth and trajectory of movements, and the careers of their participants, a decade of research on organizational strategies, networks, political opportunities, and participation makes it clear that cultural factors are not sufficient in themselves. Cultural analysis, then, ought to become embedded in and related to existing knowledge . . . theoretical advance comes from incorporating what we know about the role of organizations, material resources, and social structure with culture.[3]

This insight provides the purpose of this chapter. Through chapter 5, I will not complete a full cultural analysis of the American and British gay and lesbian movements; however, I will introduce the key concepts of debate and apply them to the case studies to produce a fuller and more robust understanding of movement strategies.

Cultural analysis suggests that individuals' decisions to engage in collective behavior are informed by subjective orientations that may vary across nations, and that these differences reflect a fundamentally distinct experience and socialization process.[4] Hence, the cultural approach demonstrates that actors and institutions do not exist in a vacuum and will unavoidably and unconsciously respond to social conditioning.

Yet the question remains as to why culture needs to be brought into the analysis or, put another way, what is the relationship between social movements and culture? As chapter 2 and chapter 3 have indicated, the gay and lesbian movement and social movements in general are producers of culture; a social movement community is identifiable by its own subculture whether that be demonstrated through dress or language for example. Taylor and Whittier noted that "to be gay in the contemporary context is not simply to state an individual sexual preference. Rather, it is a collective identity that conveys a distinct set of statuses and roles, relationships and meanings."[5] This notion has been alluded to with regard to the expansion of cultural spaces for gays and lesbians in the post-Stonewall period: bars, clubs, social organizations, coffeehouses, travel agencies, mass media, and the internet.[6] However, the relationship of culture and social movements is not merely one of production, but rather of power.

A social movement has been defined throughout this text as primarily a political phenomenon whose target is the power wielded by the state. Yet, with modernization and industrialization, the sites of power have proliferated and become de-centered. Power is held by the state, but it is also wielded by cultural institutions such as the medical field, schools, and the family.[7] These institutions condition our thinking and relational behavior, and, as such, function as contested terrain that a social movement might target for change. We can now understand why the gay and lesbian movement sought to remove homosexuality's listing as a mental illness, the proliferation of sexuality studies programs at universities, and the increased discussion about gay marriage. This multiplication of sites not only provides new ways to frame issues thereby bringing more people into the movement and helping others understand movement goals,[8] but demonstrates how power is dispersed and is no longer a purely political tool.

Michel Foucault's hypothesis about the creation of the homosexual, discussed in chapter 2, relates to the idea of culture as power and the proliferation of discourses (especially in the late nineteenth century) which sought to categorize and thereby control different behaviors. Power, then, is the deployment of knowledge and, more importantly, meaning, for meaning constitutes the cultural subject.[9] With regard to sexuality, Foucault comments that

The machinery of power that focused on this whole alien strain did not aim to suppress it, but rather to give it an analytical, visible, and permanent reality: it was implanted in bodies, slipped beneath modes of conduct, made into a principle of classification and intelligibility, established as a *raison d'être* and a natural order of disorder. Not the exclusion of these aberrant sexualities, but the specification, the regional solidification of each one of them. The strategy behind this dissemination was to strew reality with them and incorporate them into the individual.[10]

The last sentence in that passage indicates that naming the behavior was not the goal, rather it was naming it in such a manner that the behavior became convoluted with the individual. Classification and labeling thereby became a mechanism of power of one individual over the other – the namer and the named.

The power of labeling is exemplified in the evolution of labels in the gay and lesbian community: homosexual, homophile, gay, and queer. As indicated in chapter 2, homosexual was the term used by the hetero-sexual majority; homophile and, later, gay were identifications used within the community. Each connotes a specifically contextual meaning. "Queer" best expresses a response to this cultural power of labeling; the term embodied a backlash against pigeonholing identities. To some degree, queer identity is a non-identity transgressing labeling and inclusive of the entire community. As sociologist, Steven Epstein, notes, "the turn to 'queer' was an act of linguistic reclamation, in which a pejorative term was reappropriated to negate its power to wound."[11] In this sense, identifying as "queer" usurps that cultural power of naming from the dominant heterosexual majority and places power in the hands of the queer minority. The process of self-naming is an expression of cognitive liberation and collective identity formation; given the idea of culture as a mode of power, collective identity now serves both political and cultural ends.

In other words, culture must be brought into the analysis because the field on which a social movement plays out has widened beyond the power of the state; other institutions which have the power to support and/or suppress movement actors are included. These other discourses – medicine, science, education, family – fall outside of the political realm and inside the cultural realm. Given these circumstances, social movements can no longer be interpreted as simply sustained collective challenges against political elites, but they must also be perceived as "'communities of discourse' engaged in the enunciation of new cultural codes that very often contest dominant representations."[12] Even this expanded field of power dynamics, while not political institutions themselves, can be incorporated into the political process model. The other institutions – economy, law, religion, medicine, education – foster and reproduce inequality to the extent that they represent the ideas of the dominant cultural paradigm, and as such, create a more comprehensive array of opportunities and obstacles.[13]

The structuralist approach of the political process model must be embedded in a cultural context that identifies an increased number of discourses of power which, in turn, influences the movement's emergence and informs its methodology. The model of structure–agent interaction expands from political institutions–interest group interaction to political institutions/*culture*–interest group interaction. As Weaver and Rockman note,

Institutions reflect not just legal forms but also normative understandings and expectations. The legal forms, moreover, may not always be their most crucial aspects. Although it is likely that formalized structures affect the way interest groups form . . . they are not likely to fully determine them. Hence, such factors as the histories of programs, successful responses in the past, dominant beliefs among leaders, and the political culture of the society may be especially vital in determining how institutions function.[14]

The point is not that culture exhibits a deterministic quality which can thereby account for everything. Culture, specifically political culture, and the political institutions of a given nation interact; political culture establishes the political institutions, and the institutions reinforce and can shape changes in that culture. In other words, these two factors inform one another and, as such, both configure the political environment in which an interest group both acts and attempts to alter. As Figure 5.1 illustrates, unlike political institutions, culture does not necessarily insert itself as an identifiable factor at any particular stage in social movement development or maintenance, but rather remains as an invisible nebula which infiltrates every step. While this conception of culture helps us to bring culture to bear on our analysis, it is still fundamentally unsatisfying. As sociologist Ann Swindler notes, "if culture is relegated to a vague – if 'constitutive' – penumbra, we will sacrifice more incisive ways of thinking about its power."[15] In other

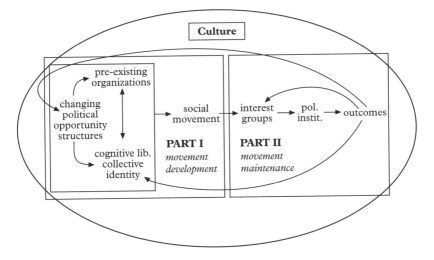

Figure 5.1 *Including culture in the political process model*

words, the notion of culture as an influencing nebula leaves any notion of it as merely descriptive, but analytically unattainable. Second, this conception relegates our thinking of culture as purely an environmental factor which impedes or enables movement actors. While culture can and is explored in this light, namely within the frame of cultural opportunity structures as explored by Gamson and Tarrow, culture also acts within a movement – as a characteristic of the movement itself – to give that movement internal structure and provide movement strategies and actions with internal meaning for participants.[16] Third, this notion of culture is still embedded as a variable within the political process model: it conjures up images of merely adding an ingredient and stirring, and it still privileges interest group politics over other forms of action. Feminist scholars, Taylor, Whittier, and Katzenstein, assert that within the feminist movement, two forms of politics have evolved: interest group activism, which is geared towards legislative change, and discursive politics, expressed in speech and text, and aimed at reshaping and reformulating fundamental norms and rules which underlie conceptions of society and the state.[17] Gay and lesbian interest group politics, as sociologist Ken Plummer has indicated, takes the form of "liberal and assimilationist voluntary pressure groups: often formally structured; usually middle-class, male, and even elitist; and primarily concerned with claims over rights and legal change . . . And there are the less formal, grass roots-based, and challenging radical activist collectives . . .

This is the classic divide of all gay movements – between those who seek legal change through lobbying and those who believe in a much more radical stance."[18] While Plummer makes this observation with respect to the movement in the United Kingdom, we have already witnessed that this cleavage is readily applicable to its American counterpart. Thus, PPM, which has structured the discussion around interest group formation, not only favors a specific type of political action, but, consequently, a specific type of political actor, an actor (most likely adhering to an essentialist framework)[19] who represents only a part of the movement. Discursive politics, on the other hand, is a *cultural* phenomenon whose goal is more in line with the far more revolutionary nature of gay liberation, lesbian feminism, Queer Nation, and social constructionists in general. By integrating the cultural realm into our discussion we will not only be able better to understand the movements' descriptive histories, but also better analyze its development.

Culture is an extraordinarily difficult concept to define. Culture, unfortunately for many of us, has an "I-know-it-when-I-see-it" quality; it is abstract, does not exist *a priori*, and is really only recognizable when it can be viewed in an objective and empirical sense. The goal then when defining culture, and its relationship to social movements and the communities that they spawn, is to isolate those activities which are the outward and empirical expression of culture.[20] Culture is made of those rules, values, and/or norms which code and give meaning to our everyday behavior; therefore, culture is expressed through interaction in the form of language and by extension speeches, text, literature, or art, through performance in the form of ritual, through collective identity as exemplified by dress, action, and speech, and through institutions or patterns of behavior that are reinforced by legal sanctions and benefits. Furthermore, as culture is given observable form through interaction and the development of institutions, it has an inherent power dynamic: heterosexual culture can be dominant whereas movement communities develop subcultures which are oppositional to and weaker than the dominant culture.[21] Indeed, the difficulty in analyzing culture is that many of these tangible and objective examples of a highly subjective concept are interrelated and thus, difficult to extrapolate from their context.

This chapter will sketch how American and British culture – and here, I will be discussing primarily political culture – has influenced the development and maintenance of the respective gay and lesbian movements. It will begin with an analysis of how culture spurs movement growth and promotes internal sustainability of a social movement community. This section will focus on three concepts. First, we will

explore how cultural opportunity structures, similar to political opportunity structures, provided an environment conducive to movement
formation. Second, we will examine the emergence of movement culture
focusing on how it is constructed and reinforced by ritual. Third, we will
look at the effects of the movement subculture on mainstream heteronormative culture and, indeed how the gay and lesbian movement has
shaped much of the political conversation in the United States and the
United Kingdom in the 1990s. Then, the discussion will turn to an
evaluation of those elements of American and British political culture
which have either hindered or enabled the maintenance of this movement. The analysis of the United States will concentrate on the influence, and indeed, conflation of religion and politics that promotes and
maintains a heterosexist, if not overtly homophobic, political culture.
British political culture is evaluated in terms of how the relationship of
homosexuality to historically Victorian and more recently Thatcherite
ideology of the family, the class structure, and the decline of the British
empire has fostered homophobia. These latter two discussions are not
intended to suggest that religious or class politics are the only or even
the prime cultural obstacle challenging the implementation of pro-gay
and lesbian legislation. Indeed, as other political scientists have often
discussed, numerous variables contribute to whether public opinion is
amenable to such legislation: education, affluence, ethnicity, population
size and heterogeneity, and religion. Various studies have concluded that
caucasian persons living in large urban cities with higher incomes,
higher levels of educational attainment, and who do not exhibit a high
degree of religious conservatism tend to be more amenable to legislation
ensuring lesbian and gay equal rights.[22] Rehashing the validity of these
studies is beyond the scope of this text; the point is that such studies
confirm that considerations other than those directly related to institutional venues and political structures must come into play when considering movement success and failure. This chapter concentrates on
the connection between religion and politics in the United States and
economic class-related morality in the United Kingdom to highlight
particular examples of how cultural influences external to the movement
may condition movement objectives.

Bringing culture back in

The concept of movement culture or subculture is not new to this text.
Both historical case studies have revealed the extent to which gay
subcultural development and mainstream cultural appropriation of gay
culture is integrally tied to the evolution of the political movement. In

chapters 2 and 3, culture has been considered as an environmental factor discussed in purely descriptive, and not evaluative, terms. We have seen how American gay liberation was enabled by the cultural opportunities set forth by the precedent-setting civil rights and feminist movements, and recent growth in popular cultural visibility has provided opportunity for movement actors to achieve political and legislative ends. Yet, as indicated in the previous section, this treatment of culture leaves it within the structurally biased political process model. By framing culture in this way we have merely shifted the focus from political opportunity structures to cultural opportunity structures, from political institutions to cultural institutions. We have created a springboard from which to dive into the discussion of the relation between movements and culture, but it is only a first step.

Expanding cultural opportunities include any not necessarily politico-economic event, e.g., industrialization, or a series of events that is likely to promote collective mobilization. Whereas political opportunity structures are far more tangible and exist as electoral realignments or party cleavages and thus have to do with the distribution of concrete power, cultural opportunity structures are much more abstract and deal with the distribution of meaning (and of power in a Foucauldian sense). Like political opportunity structures, cultural opportunity structures can facilitate the rise of new actors and new actions. Three general types of cultural opportunity structures can spur the growth of social insurgency: a contradiction between a social value and social practice, a suddenly imposed grievance, and the availability of "master frames" or examples which legitimize and foster protest activity.[23] The contradiction in value assertion and value practice is revealed in the discrepancy between the ideas and actions of the New Left. As was noted in chapter 2, despite espousing a belief in racial and gender equality, the New Left and student movements were rife with internal sexual and racial prejudice to mention nothing of discrimination based on sexual orientation. This discrepancy led to a splintering of the New Left into offshoot movements like the feminist and the later gay liberation movement.

Suddenly imposed grievances, defined as highly dramatic and unexpected occurrences that heighten popular awareness of and antagonism toward existing sociopolitical conditions, can also function as changing cultural opportunities.[24] For example, the assassination of San Francisco Supervisor Harvey Milk on 27 November 1978 by ex-Supervisor Dan White sparked an immediate collective response: a candlelight vigil through the streets of San Francisco that evening. The verdict from Dan White's trial also served as another opportunity for mobilization. After receiving what many gay activists considered a lenient sentence of only eight years, gay men and women erupted in riotous violence at San Francisco's City Hall.[25]

Finally, sociologists David Snow and Robert Benford have promoted the theory of "master protest frames" which function as another example of cultural opportunity for protest. As these theorists as well as sociologist Sidney Tarrow note, social movements are not isolated and discrete phenomena, but they occur in clusters or what Tarrow refers to as "cycles of protest."[26] Hence, we see a burst of collective mobilization initiated in the late 1950s and early 1960s by the civil rights and student movements followed by the feminist and the gay liberation movement. These instances of collective social insurgency are not independent; rather, all subsequent movements following the civil rights movement have utilized the "frame" established by the civil rights movement. In other words, other disenfranchised minorities that have collectively organized have appropriated the cultural symbols and language of the black struggle to inform their own mobilization efforts. In this sense, the concept of framing is inextricably tied to the political process model; the opportunities created by political and cultural institutions make a master frame, such as the civil rights strategy, so resilient and useful.[27]

Frame alignment then is simply when movement actors interpret their cause, goals, and agenda, in a way that already conforms to existing or well-known cultural concepts. For example, "Black is Beautiful," the phrase associated with casting off the negative stereotypes associated with African–Americans during the civil rights movement morphed into the slogan, "Gay is Good," which served the same purpose for the budding gay and lesbian movement.[28] The American gay and lesbian movement utilized the March on Washington model, popularized by the civil rights movement, in 1979, 1987, 1993, and 2000 precisely because it evoked a symbolized fight for equality that had cultural resonance stemming from Martin Luther King Jr.'s 1963 march.[29]

Frames, since they function as ways to interpret or give meaning to certain actions and develop through the course of collective action, can change over time, be utilized by movements as a recruiting tool, and can shape the way an interest group is organized.[30] For example, homosexuality can be framed as a private "bedroom" issue or as a more public political issue. Depending on which frame a person can align with his or her own beliefs affects which branch of the gay and lesbian movement he or she feels compelled to support. Hence, a frame shift occurred between the homophile movement, which downplayed sexual difference and viewed homosexuality as a private issue, to the concept of coming out as endorsed by gay liberation.[31] By framing gay identity as a public issue, gay liberation – as indicated in chapter 2 – utilized coming out as a way to increase supporters. In short, gay liberationists took the already popularized feminist frame of "the personal is political" and applied it to sexuality. Thus, homosexuality was fundamentally altered from a stigma to hide to an identity to celebrate.

Framing issues can affect not only the visibility of and participation in a movement, but how that movement is organized. Two frames that have predominated the gay and lesbian movements is the essentialist versus social constructionist debate as it relates to homosexual identity. The former theory suggests that homosexuality is an innate, perhaps biologic/genetic trait whereas the latter suggests that all sexuality is polymorphous, fluid, and chosen. Proponents of this latter view included the gay liberationists of the 1970s. By suggesting that homosexuality was a transgressive and radical choice, gay liberationists did not seek change in the existing political structure, but through coalitions with the anti-war movement, the environmental movement, the black power movement, and the feminist movement to bring about widespread cultural transformation. In other words, as described in the beginning of chapter 1, social movements are antagonists of the state, and, as such, they propose models of social interaction distinct from those already established. Movement participants often attempt to adopt the proposed model as an organizational style to demonstrate its viability. Since liberation theory, as detailed in chapter 2, is grounded in egalitarian notions of participatory democracy, a group which actuates this theory cannot employ any of the standard organizational techniques. There can be no hierarchy of responsibility. No officers or chairpersons can facilitate the meetings. The Gay Liberation Front served as the practical expression of liberation philosophy.

Framing sexuality as an immutable essentialist trait, responds to current public opinion regarding discrimination in the United States and the United Kingdom.[32] The straight population is less willing to support institutionalized discrimination when gays and lesbians are seen as a distinct minority; in this sense, homophobia becomes comparable to racism. Movement organizations that promote this frame of homosexuality respond to public opinion polls in both the United States and the United Kingdom suggesting that a majority of people feel that gays and lesbians should have equal employment and housing rights, despite a majority also contending that homosexuality is always wrong.[33] These numbers suggest that while homosexuality is deemed wrong, gays and lesbians themselves should not be punished. The presumed reason for this logic is that homosexuality is not a fault of the person, it is a trait which cannot be chosen, an orientation and not a preference. Hence, adopting an essentialist strategy may promote short-term legal change at the expense of widespread and revolutionary sociocultural transformation.

The adoption of the essentialist versus social constructionist theory of sexuality also indicates how movement tactics are responses to historical tendencies of political culture. Adam, Duyvendak, and Krouwel note that "the gay and lesbian movement is not only dependent on the solidarity of social movements . . . it also has to 'fit' in the emancipation model used by other groups in society and recognized by authorities as valid and justified."[34] In other words, American political culture greatly influences the tactics of the movement organization itself as it encourages the adoption of certain frames. In their discussion of American political party exceptionalism political scientists, G. William Domhoff and Leon Epstein, note that factors exist in the United States that provide for more glaring cleavages than those based on economic class. The heterogeneous population allows for the formation of ethnic, religious, and regional divisions, and parties divide accordingly.[35] The American working-class, for example, never formed a comprehensive class consciousness because the

primary producers in the United States . . . were more seriously divided among themselves than was the case in most other countries. The deepest and most important of these divisions was between whites and African–Americans . . . This black–white split in the working class was reinforced by later conflicts between craft workers . . . and industrial workers . . . [Craft workers'] sense of superiority as skilled workers was reinforced by the fact that they were of northern European, Protestant origin whereas the industrial workers tended to be Catholics and Jews from eastern and southern Europe.[36]

Race and religion divided the classes. No class consciousness could be developed which would be analogous to that of the homogeneous European working-class.

While this discussion refers to political parties, its insights can be diffused to cover American political culture in general. Race and religion have been the dominant cleavages in American society, and as such American political institutions have responded to groups which mobilize around this type of identity.[37] In this way, by demonstrating how and to whom it responds, American political culture has conditioned the gay and lesbian movement to present itself in a quasi-ethnic manner in order to achieve reform. Such self-perception is dependent on an essentialist view of sexual orientation. In legislative debates concerning the Defense of Marriage Act (DOMA) or the Employment Non-Discrimination Act (ENDA), pro-gay advocates represented sexuality as biologically determined, i.e., analogous to skin color, and, as such, gays, lesbians, and bisexuals should not be denied civil rights or loss of benefits on the basis

of an unchangeable trait such as sexual orientation. Political culture
conditioned the anti-gay response, which contended that homosexuality
was a preference, and the law has no responsibility to protect the rights
of individuals who *choose* to live in a certain fashion.[38] Anti-gay advocates used the social constructionist argument against the movement
thereby underlying one of the main problems why social constructionists
such as gay liberationists found it difficult to sustain mobilization. In
other words, American political culture has promoted a specific master
frame which can be utilized if groups can present themselves as unfairly
denied of basic civil rights.

A similar tactic cannot be used as readily by movement activists in the
United Kingdom. The appropriation of a quasi-ethnic collective identity
and then the use of this identity as a foundation for a rights-based
argument is wholly out of place in the United Kingdom given that
dominant cleavages in that country are not based on race, but on class.
Instead, the British have historically framed homosexuality as an issue of
conscience focusing on acceptable behavior in private and public
spheres as well as, more recently, creating legal parity with other nations
in Europe. The first argument suggests that homosexuality may be
tolerated as long as it is not given public voice; sexual behavior is a
personal, private domain in which the state has no reasonable authority
to legislate.[39] This frame was the foundational logic behind the
Wolfenden recommendations and the 1967 Sexual Offences Act as
discussed in chapter 3. Therefore, the theoretical purpose of 1988s
Section 28, from a Conservative perspective, was not to suppress or
promote identity, but rather to protect the public domain from a sexual
behavior that should be relegated to private sphere. Furthermore, this
frame conditioned language used in the 1994 debate concerning equalization of the age of consent. As political scientist, David Rayside,
observes, in her defense of equalization of the age of consent, Conservative MP Edwina Currie "lodged her argument in the laissez-faire tradition of defending the right to privacy against state intrusiveness into
'personal' lives; she also talked of British law being out of line with
Europe."[40] This second frame – comparison to other European states –
is particularly salient given the United Kingdom's status as a member of
the European Union and increased symbolic if not actual authority of
the European Court of Justice and the European Convention on
Human Rights (see chapter 3 and chapter 4). Furthermore, comparisons with laws in other countries generally hold less saliency in the
United States than the United Kingdom, and American movement
organizations generally pay less attention – relative to their British
counterparts – to their international contemporaries.[41]

Adoption of the basic rights-based frame is, however, gaining ground in the United Kingdom. Stonewall, the British organization established to organize sexual minority activists in the immediate aftermath of Section 28, released a pamphlet entitled "Equality 2000" states unequivocally that "lesbian and gay rights are human rights." The organization links this claim to the new Labour government's promise to incorporate the European Convention on Human Rights into British law and to establish a Human Rights Commission in the United Kingdom. While the Convention does not include sexual orientation as a category guarded from discrimination, its inclusion is a primary agenda item of Stonewall and similar organizations.[42]

Framing sexuality orientation as a human right, while not necessarily fitting within traditional British historical political cultural context, can be explained by some new research regarding the globalization of the gay and lesbian movement. Sociologists, David John Frank and Elizabeth McEneaney, have found that in the years since the end of the Second World War, a transformation has occurred in how society views sexual relations which corresponds to the growth of historically Western individualism as a culturally prioritized trait across the globe: "a pervasive redefinition of same-sex sexuality is under way . . . [and] has occurred within a wider transformation in the meaning and organization of sex more generally, involving a shift in the locus of sexuality from the family to the individual, and a shift in the purpose of sex from procreation to pleasure."[43] Frank and McEneaney purport that the rise of individualism corresponds to the depiction of same-sex sexuality being perceived as a human right "which as a matter of natural law accrues to all individual persons."[44] Furthermore, this redefinition of sex from purpose to individual pleasure has fostered a cultural opportunity structure enabling social movement organizations to push a gay and lesbian equal rights agenda.[45]

Historian Theodore Von Laue, while not speaking directly to transforming meanings of sex, also contends that the latter half of the twentieth century has witnessed a "world revolution of westernization" which corresponds to this rise of traditionally Western individualism throughout the world. Von Laue posits that

traditional culture and society in non-Western parts of the world were subverted . . . After World War I, and even more after World War II, Western democracy, with the United States as the lead, stood out as the universal model of power in the world, of good government, and of economic prosperity . . . Equality in political power, though deftly omitted from the Western-inspired inventory of human rights, certainly was claimed as an entitlement by proud non-Westerners.[46]

As the acceptance of human rights spread across the globe, so did the legitimacy of gay and lesbian rights if they could be framed in an essentialist perspective. An analysis of the globalization of the gay and lesbian movement is far beyond the scope of this book, and far more in-depth research has been undertaken than could be provided within the limits of this chapter. However, the point is that a certain degree of globalization has occurred, and it is not merely limited to the transference of strategy across national boundaries, but a wider cultural opportunity marked by the changing of fundamental social definitions toward a Western orientation in which same-sex relations is one part. National context is still vitally important when discussing political institutions and indeed cultural frames, but, in terms of the latter, the expansion and acceptance of Western and, specifically American, traditions, has provided non-Western gay and lesbian activists a means to legitimate their struggle beyond their national political cultural arsenal. Given that the United Kingdom and the United States are both Western countries, the expansion of Western political tradition fosters little change in movement strategy. However, given also that British political culture is more likely to perceive same-sex sexuality as a public/private issue, the growth of a human rights frame does provide a legitimate alternate conception which may be of use now that Labour holds power.

The creation of frames and the subsequent use of frame alignment as a persuasive tool on the part of movement leaders helps us to understand how cultural opportunities can be exploited to promote movement development; frames are useful as an interpretive schema and consequent strategic recruitment device. William Gamson suggests that collective action frames – as interpretative schema – consist of injustice, agency, and identity. Injustice supposes some level of moral indignation or grievance structure as mentioned above. Agency necessitates a level of cognitive liberation altering the victim status to one that can bring about change that is either reform-oriented or revolutionary. Identity refers to the formation of a "we" or an "us against them" motif which indicates collective identity formation. In other words, what frames enable is a way for movement actors and potential actors to perceive a problem and how to perceive themselves in relation to that problem.[47] Frames and frame analysis do not suggest how to solve that problem, or how the movement promotes change. In short, frame analysis does not demonstrate how movements can use culture as a tool to maintain themselves.

To gain a greater understanding of the role of culture and movement maintenance, we must move beyond culture as an external factor associated with cultural opportunity structures and investigate the ways culture is promoted by the movement. Put another way, how is a social movement community sustained? Sidney Tarrow has suggested that cycles of protest promote a movement culture, and Doug McAdam asserts,

social movements tend to become worlds unto themselves that are characterized by distinctive ideologies, collective identities, behavioral routines, and material cultures . . . Having dared to challenge a particular aspect of mainstream society, there is implicit pressure on insurgents to engage in a kind of social engineering to suggest remedies to the problem. The challenge is to actualize within the movement the kind of social arrangements deemed preferable to those the group is opposing.[48]

A clear example of how movements have challenged dominant social arrangements is the formation of alternative and "utopian" gay communes in the 1970s and the rise of lesbian feminist cultural institutions in the 1970s and 1980s. The 95th Street collective in New York City was one such gay collective. John Knoebel, one of the collective's members, has detailed that the collective's living situation attempted to parallel the openness espoused by liberation theory. Members sometimes switched beds, slept with each other, shared house chores, and valued the collective over personal desires.[49] The radical feminist movement, or what became lesbian feminism, fostered bookstores, music festivals, self-defense schools, publishing houses, and travel agencies. Through this network, lesbian feminists were able to provide the institutions necessary for sustaining everyday life within a subculture that protected a woman-identified woman against an increasingly oppressive culture giving greater voice to the New Right.[50] By evaluating how these cultural networks have maintained the members and, by extension, the political aspects of the movement, our focus has changed from the external constraints and opportunities to the internal promotion of subculture through ritual and collective identity formation.

A Weberian concept of culture suggests that culture is internalized by individuals and expressed in the actions of those individuals. Therefore, those actions are the observable and empirical embodiments of culture. One such action is ritual. Ritual was the key concept for Durkheim as it produced social solidarity and prevented the anomic breakdown of society; ritual brought individuals together and provided the group with meaning and purpose. Contemporary conceptions of ritual place it within the dramaturgical school where it is both performance and expression of social relations. Rituals are therefore "the cultural mechanisms through which collective actors express emotions – that is, the enthusiasm, pride, anger, hatred, fear, and sorrow – that mobilize and sustain conflict."[51] Rituals such as speeches, protests, or marches make the emotional dimension of movement actors observable – an idea that has been belittled in favor of viewing the movement actor as rational. Rituals act as the collective response to oppression, encourage redefinition of self, and express collective identity.[52] Examples of ritual in the gay and lesbian movement include Gay Pride parades or the National Marches on Washington for Gay and Lesbian Rights in 1979, 1987, 1993, and 2000.

National Coming Out Day, held every 11 October, celebrates and encourages men and women to come out of the closet, and is a ritual created to foster positive self-perception and collective identity as well as commemorate the collective action of the 1987 March on Washington for Gay and Lesbian Rights. This annual event is held at universities and college campuses, workplaces, is often discussed on the evening news, and has been the topic of numerous talk shows. This ritual then not only promotes internal cohesion of the sexual minorities community, but enables wider visibility of that community to the heterosexual majority.

As ritual is defined as the collective and symbolic expression of emotion, other examples would include demonstrations by Queer Nation activists. Such demonstrations have included: "queer night out" where queers would raid straight bars and clubs to kiss, dance, etc.; "queer shopping trips" where queers, readily identifiable by their dress, invade suburban shopping malls; and "queer be-ins," where queers would simply congregate in heavily trafficked public locales such as parks or beaches.[53] By participating in such ritual, queers claimed public space, validated their existence to the dominant heteronormative culture, and participated in a group exercise further strengthening their own collective bond.

The collective identity fostered by group participation in ritual is reinforced by symbols which identify members of a group to one another, but also indicate separation from the majority population. This collective difference can function as a source of pride, and underlies the politics of difference which sustained organizations like Queer Nation. Common symbols of the gay and lesbian movement have included the pink triangle, the rainbow flag, freedom rings, the red AIDS ribbon, and the Greek letter lambda. Other symbols, such as flags, represent specific identity *within* the gay and lesbian movement.[54] These symbols function as an outward expression of collective identity serving as identifiable connections among gays, lesbians, bisexuals, and transgenders as well as increasing the visible existence of this community to the general public.

As the case histories also demonstrate, movement culture is not stagnant; rituals and other forms of cultural expression, including symbols, change over time as new participants become active in the social movement.[55] The post-war American history of homosexual collective organization is riddled with such alterations. Recall that the movement culture of the homophile Mattachine Society dramatically shifted in 1953 when, after an influx of new members, new leadership gained control; the group abandoned its communist-influenced ideology, its promotion of a homosexual culture, and its aspiration to build a mass movement. By the end of the 1960s, the movement culture shifted again towards a more militant stance. This change actuated by the Stonewall riots of 1969, was engendered by a new type of movement participant. Whereas the homophiles were characterized as middle-aged professionals, these more militant activists, some of whom had participated in the New Left and would spearhead the Gay Liberation Front, were counterculturalists. They tended to be young, poor, antiestablishment, and into the drug scene. As liberation politicized and encouraged "coming out," the movement expanded and thus experienced another shift embodied in the formation of the Gay Activist Alliance, a more structured and single-issue counterpart to the GLF. Finally, as noted in chapter 2, the AIDS crisis brought an influx of upper middle-class white men into movement politics. This new activist cohort influenced movement reorientation towards a more conservative and elite stance which, in turn, fostered another movement shift to the participatory direct tactics of ACT UP and Queer Nation, reminiscent of liberation.

Similar movement cultural realignments occurred in the United Kingdom. The narrow political focus of the Homosexual Law Reform Society (HLRS) gave way to the more subculturally oriented Committee for Homosexual Equality (CHE). This latter group was forced to compete with the London Gay Liberation Front in much the same way that the Mattachine Society of New York clashed with the New York Gay Liberation Front. Liberation theory soon declined as more people came out of the closet thereby revitalizing CHE. The 1988 anti-Clause 28 mobilization fostered the development of another interest group, Stonewall, which has reestablished a movement culture similar to the parliamentary-oriented and decidedly not mass-membership stance of the HLRS.

The array of institutions which make up the gay and lesbian social movement community or subculture is dizzying. Bars, dance clubs, restaurants, travel agencies, libraries, publishing houses, gyms, choirs, theaters, film festivals, document archives, and switchboards have all proliferated since the Stonewall riots on both sides of the Atlantic. Support groups have been created by gay youth, gay elderly, the children of homosexual parents, and the parents of homosexual children. Since the dawning of the AIDS crisis, the gay community has also established sundry organizations for people with AIDS (PWAs), the partners and families of PWAs, and individuals who are HIV-negative.[56] *This sub-cultural community is important because it continues to thrive despite the political movement's potential inactivity.* Doug McAdam contends that "what is too often overlooked in structural accounts of movement emergence is the extent to which these established organizations/networks are themselves embedded in long-standing activist subcultures capable of sustaining the ideational traditions needed to revitalize activism following a period of political dormancy."[57] For example, in the United States, but especially in the United Kingdom, political activism decreased in the late 1970s among gay men and women relative to earlier in the decade. Yet, the maintenance and expansion of a gay subculture and "gay ghetto" throughout this "quiet period" enabled the community to mobilize actively and effectively in the early years of the AIDS epidemic despite lack of government support.

Finally, movement cultures can influence mainstream culture thereby creating further opportunities for mobilization as well as paradoxically potentially crippling the movement's sustainability. This concept was introduced in chapter 2, but it should be reiterated that social movements do have cultural consequences.[58] The most dramatic example is the explosion of gay visibility in cinema and television in recent years. As chapters 2 and 3 also demonstrate, gay subcultural notions of male, female, and even androgynous fashion have been appropriated by mainstream culture.

The new social movements have also led to a restructuring of higher education curriculum. Ethnic, gender, and gay and lesbian or queer studies programs have been established at numerous universities throughout the United States. Furthermore, social science and humanities courses not in these immediate fields tend to exemplify a degree of heightened awareness towards adequate and responsible minority representation.[59]

Furthermore, as noted by Chris Bull and John Gallagher, issues of pre-eminent concern to the gay and lesbian movement have structured much of the mainstream political conversation of the 1990s. The debate over gays in the military, discussed in chapter 2, was a key issue in the 1992 presidential election. Furthermore, issues such as gay marriage and gay parenting were overthrowing traditional conceptions of family which has become a benchmark of New Right philosophy. The Defense of Marriage Act (DOMA) is a clear example of the conservative response to the growth of untraditional family structures which have at least an indirect link to the increase in gay and lesbian visibility. DOMA was not only a response to the increased eligibility of gays and lesbians for domestic partner benefits, but to the looming "threat" of gay marriage given the Hawaiian Supreme Court decision that marriage licenses could not be denied to gay and lesbian couples. Realizing that, under the Constitution, other states would be forced to recognize a marriage license issued in any state, DOMA was introduced at the national level to define marriage as only possible between a man and a woman thereby defeating possible gay and lesbian "encroachment" on this heterosexual right.

Hence, political and popular culture help to determine the emergence of a social movement both by providing opportunities and through the development of movement subcultures. These subcultures are important because they help to maintain movement cohesion despite possible political dormancy thereby facilitating activist revitalization given the proper changing opportunity. Yet political and popular culture do not only influence whether or not a movement will emerge. Like political institutions, culture creates an environment in which social movement interest groups must act. Thus, similar to political institutions, culture in general, and political culture specifically, in part, determines how a movement maintains itself, what tactics it utilizes, and whether or not it achieves its ends.

The United States: religion, politics, and homophobia

Let me tell you something Andrew. When you're brought up the way I am – the way most people are in this country – there's not a whole lot of discussion about homosexuality or . . . what do you call it . . . "alternate lifestyles." As a kid, you're taught that queers are funny, queers are weird, queers dress up like their mother, that they're afraid to fight, that they . . . they're a danger to little kids, and that all they want to do is to get into your pants. And that pretty much sums up the general thinking out there if you want to know the truth about it. ("Joe Miller" (Denzel Washington), *Philadelphia*)

At first glance, the relationship between American politics and religion appears tenuous; such a conclusion is supported by both the complete separation of church and state and the tolerance of religious freedom as espoused within the Constitution. The United States thus becomes classified as a secular republic only in the sense that religion is relegated to the private sphere while politics occupies the public sphere. Yet, upon closer inspection, religion, especially Puritanism, has profoundly influenced the political culture and institutions of the United States. Theorists including Alexis de Tocqueville and Samuel Huntington have evaluated the effects of religion on American democracy concluding that this political ideology is strongly influenced by religious beliefs. Religious ideology and the political culture which it implies functions as the foundation for both American democratic political culture and institutions.

De Tocqueville notes that "Puritanism was not merely a religious doctrine, but corresponded in many points with the most absolute democratic and republican theories."[60] He thereby establishes a correlation between the religion and American democracy which is, in turn, revealed by the two roles which Puritans' prescribe to their followers in relation to their government. According to Puritanism two covenants exist: one between the people and God, and one among the people to establish a state which will enforce the will of God.[61] All people have the right to play an active role in the formation of that second covenant. Furthermore, Puritans also have the responsibility to ensure that the government continues to execute God's law:

> The institution of government, however, did not absolve the people from responsibility. As long as the government did its job, the people must give it all the assistance in their power. But if the governors failed in their task and fell prey to the evils they were supposed to suppress, then the people must rebel and replace the wicked rulers with better ones.[62]

To some degree, the maintenance of just governance was the responsibility of the Puritans as much as it is the responsibility of American citizens today. In order to facilitate the fulfillment of this duty, section 4 of Article II of the Constitution states that "the President, Vice-President, and all civil Officers of the United States shall be removed from Office on Impeachment for, and Conviction of, Treason, Bribery, or other high Crimes and Misdemeanors."[63] The Constitution also establishes a balance of power among the executive, legislative, and judicial branches in order to guard against political corruption.

Puritanism also influenced the American democratic mindset by imparting an emphasis on equality as a fundamental goal of American political institutions. Equality is one of the principal characteristics of the American democratic mindset. In reference to the importance of equality to Americans, de Tocqueville asserts that "liberty is not the chief and constant object of their desires; equality is their idol: they make rapid and sudden efforts to obtain liberty and, if they miss their aim, resign themselves to their disappointment; but nothing can satisfy them without equality, and they would rather perish than lose it."[64] This intense faith in equality is maintained in both the Declaration of Independence and the Constitution. Amendments XIII, XIV, XV, and XIX all affirm the importance of equality either by eliminating slavery or granting suffrage to African–Americans and women. The obsession with equality is embedded within American political culture, and it appeared throughout the late twentieth century via the civil rights, feminist, and the gay and lesbian movements.

De Tocqueville relates the primary importance of equality to the need for collective action in American politics: "If men living in democratic countries had no right and no inclination to associate for political purposes, their independence would be in great jeopardy . . . whereas if they never acquired the habit of forming associations in ordinary life, civilization itself would be endangered."[65] The communal spirit which collective action implies has its origins, like many other characteristics of American political culture, in Puritan ideas. For example, Puritan leader John Winthrop expressed grave reservations about traveling to the new world and therefore of being labeled a separatist. Separatists abandoned their fellow believers, and thus failed to uphold God's will. Hence, separatism contradicted Puritan belief and threatened the survival of the Puritan colony.[66] Winthrop's emphasis on eliminating separatists from Massachusetts indirectly influenced later American tendencies towards collective action.

The emphasis of Puritanism specifically and Protestantism in general on American political culture should not be overdrawn. De Tocqueville notes that other Christian religions – not to mention other non-religious factors such as geographic isolation, internal consensus, and external security – also affect the development of the democratic mindset in the United States.[67] Considered historically, the United States is not merely a Protestant nation, but a Christian republic. Christianity, regardless of the specific sect, pervades the development of democratic political culture. According to de Tocqueville,

it must not be forgotten that religion gave birth to Anglo-American society. In the United States, religion is therefore mingled with all the habits of the nation . . . in America religion has, as it were, laid down its own limits. Religious institutions have remained wholly distinct from political institutions, so that former laws have been easily changed while former belief has remained unshaken.[68]

By being relegated to the private sphere, religion recognizes civil society as a distinct world in which humans exercise their political will. The democratic state acknowledges religion as providing the basic source of its claims to equality and social responsibility. Religion enables democracy, and democracy allows for the existence of religion.

How then is this connection between religion and politics related to the appearance of the modern gay and lesbian movement in the post-war period and to the expression of homophobia and heterosexism in general? As Ronald Inglehart demonstrates, a strong positive correlation exists between religiosity and homophobia, and since American democ-

Table 5.1 *Belief in God in the US and Great Britain*[69] *by Age Cohort*[70]

Age group	United States %	Great Britain %
15–24	97	67
25–34	97	77
35–44	98	88
45–54	98	86
55–64	98	91
65+	98	92
Total	98	81

Table 5.2. *Religiosity in the US and Great Britain by Age Cohort*[71]

	%	%
15–24	75	34
25–34	79	47
35–44	85	64
45–54	89	64
55–64	92	72
65+	92	77
Total	83	55

racy is grounded, in part, in religion, the inherent anti-homosexual bias of religion is necessarily translated to American political culture.

Inglehart utilized the World Values Survey to support this conclusion. He isolated the degree of personal religiosity by asking two questions. First, do you believe in God? Second, would you describe yourself as a religious person? The percentages that answered "yes" to these questions are shown in Tables 5.1 and 5.2.

The statistics generate various conclusions. First, the United States tends to be a religious nation with eighty-three percent of the population describing itself as religious and holding an almost unanimous belief in God. This assertion is further justified upon comparison with other Western developed democracies. Only 81 percent of Great Britain's population believes in God, and only 55 percent of the general public would describe itself as religious. Only 65 percent of the French and 62 percent of the Japanese believe in God, and 53 percent of the French and merely 28 percent of the Japanese would characterize itself as religious.[72] Second, excluding the category of Americans' belief in God, the percentages answering these questions affirmatively tend to decrease as the age cohorts become younger. Inglehart links this finding with his

Table 5.3. *Rejection of homosexuality in the US and Great Britain by Age Cohort*[73]

Age cohort	United States %	Great Britain %
18–24	55	31
25–34	57	30
35–44	64	38
45–54	77	40
55–64	78	67
65+	78	72
Total	65	43

theory on post-materialist values. This theory suggests that individuals who established their value systems *before* the relative economic stability of the post-war period tend to exhibit a higher degree of social conservatism; this group of people, in general, were more concerned with economic survival than with quality-of-life or sociopolitical issues. Individuals who constructed their value systems during a period when economic concerns were not primary tended to reveal a greater level of social and political liberalism. Hence, we see the rise of new social movements throughout the 1960s and early 1970s while the United States was still experiencing unprecedented economic growth after the Second World War. People do not therefore simply become more conservative as they become older; rather, as their politico-economic environment shifted, so did their values.

If the level of religiosity is compared to toleration of homosexuality among the population, a positive correlation exists. Table 5.3 shows what percentage of the public believes that homosexuality can never be justified. In general, these data illustrate that the British population tends to be less homophobic than its American counterpart. The decrease in homophobia among younger age cohorts lends further credibility to Inglehart's post-materialist versus materialist values theory. More importantly for our purposes, the data reveal a positive correlation between religiosity and homophobia. We can say that, in general, the more religious an individual, the more likely he or she is to be homophobic.[74] A *US News and World Report* poll of one thousand voters asked what the top-ranking influence on voters was with regard to gay and lesbian rights. Twenty-nine percent of those polled indicated that their religious affiliation influenced their perspective on homosexuality. Indeed, this category was the highest of all possible influences which included gay and lesbian friends, media, and family. Even more telling, of that cohort indicating religion as the top-ranking influence,

70 percent of them opposed gay rights.[75] Indeed this relationship is noted by Alfred Kinsey himself in his studies on human sexuality. Kinsey noted that nothing had "more influence upon present-day patterns of sexual behavior than the religious backgrounds of that culture . . . Ancient religious codes are still the prime source of the attitudes, the ideas, the ideals, and the rationalizations by which most individuals pattern their sexual lives."[76] We *cannot* say that religious affiliation increases homophobia. *The statistics imply no causal relationship whatsoever; only a positive correlation is indicated.* A third unknown variable, such as political conservatism, may be influencing this relationship. Despite this possibility, statistics confirm that as the United States tends to be the most religious of all Western industrialized democracy, it also tends to have the most homophobic population.

The tri-part linkage between homophobia, religion, and politics is one of the foundations of the New Right and helps to explain that movement's tactics. The New Right is concerned primarily with the sanctity and maintenance of traditional family structure as it relates to gender and sexuality norms. Steven Epstein noted that this neo-conservatism "is a clear case in which the peculiarities of the United States affected the trajectory of the lesbian and gay movements: because the centrality of religion in general and fundamentalism in particular made such an opponent possible in the United States, gay men and lesbians here faced a set of challenges that their counterparts in most other countries escaped."[77] This passage not only illuminates the connection of religion and homophobia which underpinned Anita Bryant's campaign of the late 1970s as well as more recent conservative obsession with traditional family values and a corresponding anti-gay stance, but also indicates that this linkage is not prevalent in other Western democracies.

The most salient example of the effect of homophobia as it has been expressed in the religion-influenced American political culture is the decision delivered by Justice Burger in the 1986 Supreme Court Case *Bowers v. Hardwick*. The circumstances of this case, introduced in chapter 4, centered on the arrest of Michael Hardwick for engaging in homosexual sodomy with a consenting adult within the privacy of his own bedroom. Burger states that

Decisions of individuals relating to homosexual conduct have been subject to state intervention throughout the history of Western civilization. Condemnation of those practices is firmly rooted in Judeo-Christian moral and ethical standards . . . To hold that the act of homosexual sodomy is somehow protected as a fundamental right would be to cast aside millennia of moral teaching.[78]

Burger's decision blurs the separation of church and state asserting essentially that there is no constitutional basis to overturn religious and moral doctrine. Yet, as Justice Blackmun notes in his dissent, such religious doctrine should never had been used to support the law. In his attempt to counter the arguments suggested by the Court majority as well as by Bowers, the petitioner representing the state of Georgia, Blackmun avers that

The assertion that "traditional Judeo-Christian values proscribe" the conduct involved, Brief for Petitioner 20, cannot provide an adequate justification for §16-6-2. That certain, but by no means all, religious groups condemn the behavior at issue gives the State no license to impose their judgments on the entire citizenry. The legitimacy of secular legislation depends instead on whether the State can advance some justification for its law beyond its conformity to religious doctrine . . . Thus far from buttressing his case, the petitioner's invocation of Leviticus, Romans, St. Thomas Aquinas, and sodomy's heretical status in the Middle Ages undermines his suggestion that §16-6-2 represents a legitimate use of secular coercive power. A State can no more punish private behavior because of religious intolerance than it can punish such behavior because of racial animus . . . No matter how uncomfortable a certain group may make the majority of this Court, we have held that "[m]ere public intolerance or animosity cannot constitutionally justify the deprivation of a person's physical liberty." *O'Conner v. Donaldson*, 422 US 563, 575, 95 S.Ct. 2486, 2494, 45 L.Ed.2d 396 (1975).[79]

In this passage, Justice Blackmun identifies the conflation of religion and politics and how this combination leads to institutionalized homophobia. He claims that the Georgia statute banning sodomy is based on the religious beliefs of a particular group and therefore, they have no right to apply to the remainder of the population. He further cites that the petitioner's use of the Old and New Testaments merely testifies to the degree to which American political culture is influenced by religion as well as to the extent that this relationship undermines the theoretical separation of church and state as espoused by the United States Constitution. Yet, the connection between religion and political culture – thereby resulting in politically institutionalized homophobia and heterosexism – is so strong in the United States, that it accounts, at least in part, for reversing the decision of the Court of Appeals for the Eleventh Circuit. The state's right to pass laws criminalizing homosexual sex was upheld.

In the United States, therefore, religion is a major determinant of the extent to which homophobia infiltrates American democratic political culture. The statistics laid out above depicting the positive association between religion and homophobia are not as strong in the United Kingdom. The British population, in general, is less religious than its American counterpart: "in America, politicians are apt to be judged on moralistic grounds . . . In Britain, political and religious issues are ᴎᴏʀᴍally ʜᴇᴘᴛ ᴏᴏᴘᴀᴇᴀᴛᴏ ᴀnd the great majority of British voters neither know nor care what religious views (if any) are held by candidates for political office."[80] Furthermore, David Rayside confirms that "religious leaders [in the United Kingdom] have played much less a role in reinforcing homophobia than their counterparts in most of Western Europe and North America . . . in the twentieth century, religious participation has been at a relatively low level, and political intervention by religious leaders has also been low-key in comparison to Roman Catholic Europe, Canada, and especially the United States."[81] *This lower degree of religiosity in the United Kingdom corresponds to lower instances of institutional homophobia.* Yet, various surveys, taken throughout the post-war period, already discussed in chapter 3, bear witness to a steady undercurrent of homophobia and heterosexism in British culture. If religion does not function to bolster this prejudice, as it does in the United States, how then can this institutionalized homophobia be accounted for?

The United Kingdom: bourgeois morality, national threat, and aristocratic vice

It's only love. What's everyone so scared of? (Stephen Carter (Ben Silverstone), *Get Real*)

Institutionalized homophobia gained its most salient expression with the passage of the Labouchere Amendment in 1885; this amendment to the 1885 Criminal Law Amendment Act criminalized all homosexual acts – not merely sodomy – in private and public regardless of whether such acts were consensual. Yet, the impetus for this law, and, indeed, for most of the enduring heterosexism and homophobia in late twentieth-century British culture comes from three distinct but related concepts of Victorian ideology. This late nineteenth-century moral code was obsessed with maintaining boundaries between the city and the country, among the socioeconomic classes, between the genders, within the parent–child relationship, and between the civilized motherland and the "barbarian" colonies. In short, Victorian ideology focused on preventing infiltration by the "other," and the homosexual was conceived as one of many types of "others."[82] As such, he (the nineteenth-century popular concept of the homosexual tended to be limited to the male sex) presented an implicit threat to (1) the bourgeois familial ideal reflective of gender patriarchy, (2) to the stability of the British empire, and (3) to the "respectable" working-class; this threat has been appropriated, in part, to conform to the Conservative Thatcherite notion of homosexuality as a threat to traditional family norms.

The patriarchal dichotomy established between gender roles permeated Victorian culture via lectures including John Ruskin's *Sesame and Lilies*, popular literature such as Elizabeth Braddon's *Lady Audley's Secret* or Wilkie Collins' *The Moonstone*, and conduct books including Sarah Lewis' *Woman's Mission*. All of these texts were concerned with defining the proper model of the Victorian woman and family. They attempted to navigate through and account for two seemingly contradictory conceptions of feminine nature; hence, the nineteenth-century bourgeois notion that women represent the upholders of morality and domestic virtue is juxtaposed with the earlier idea that women are guided by emotion as opposed to reason and, as such, always demonstrate the potential to fall from grace.[83]

The paradox of the innately good and potentially fallen Victorian woman emerges in Ruskin's *Sesame and Lilies* precisely because Ruskin wishes to ally himself *with* women thereby protecting himself *from* women. If Ruskin can convince women that they are good and moreover, that they serve a powerful and fundamental role in maintaining social peace through the family, he can curtail women's latent threat to male dominance.[84] It follows that women will not desire to realize their sexuality because, in doing so, they will lose their "crucial" position as providers of domestic peace. Hence, the Victorian woman was relegated to the private sphere and her sexuality removed and replaced with maternal instinct.

This maternal instinct attributed to the Victorian woman not only allotted her power over her own children, but also over her husband.[85] This power is not exerted in the public sphere, but rather through moral influence over the husband within the private sphere. The husband then enters the public sphere cultivated by the virtue which the wife exhibits in the domestic sphere. Following this model, early Victorian writer Sarah Lewis claims that influence to be far more powerful than political power itself because influence shapes the expression of that power.[86] Through this creation of separate spheres articulated by Victorian gender roles "women become not some errant part of man, but his opposite, his moral hope and spiritual guide."[87]

Hence, the family home was perceived by Victorian ideology as a type of haven from the stress created by the moral vice which infused the external world. Within this conception, children, like their mothers, were idealized as innocent and feared as potentially lawless, savage, and susceptible to corruption if not properly restrained. This theme pervades such popular nineteenth-century British literature as Lewis Carroll's *Alice's Adventures in Wonderland* and Charles Dickens' *Oliver Twist*. Historian, Richard Davenport-Hines, notes that "in these efforts to characterize the family as a sexless sanctuary, and children as creatures without desires, the homosexual (perceived as an outsider from the family) increasingly became suspected of corrupting children. Precisely because they were so irrelevant to the causes of children's eroticism, they became irresistible for uses as scapegoats."[88] Children were conceived of as asexual beings, whose sexual awakening came from an external influence outside the family, from an "other," from the homosexual.

This Victorian notion of homosexuals as inherent corrupters of youth has outlived the Victorian era itself, and it is seen in Parliamentary debates concerning the implementation of the Wolfenden Report's recommendations. One member of Parliament, in reference to the potential passage of the 1967 Sexual Offences Act commented that "I envisage men walking down the street together arm in arm, possibly holding hands, and at dances perhaps wishing to dance together and even caressing in public places . . . it is a shocking example to young people."[89] The implied threat of homosexuality to the supposedly fragile sexual orientations of children is institutionalized by the inequality in the age of consent. Heterosexual sex can be consented to at age sixteen, but homosexual sex is illegal until age eighteen; young men must be "protected" as long as possible from "unnatural vice."

Homosexuality is thereby conceived as only existing as a threat to the heterosexual norm, and heterosexuality is perceived as under continuous siege by the predatory seduction of youth by older perverts. Yet, this idea is not limited to the Victorian era, or the mid-twentieth century, but resurfaces in the Parliamentary debates regarding the passage of Clause 28 of the 1988 Local Government Bill. The Earl of Halsbury contended that homosexuality is "one of the worst mischiefs corrupting the fibre of our children and ultimately of society itself."[90] Baroness Faithful goes even further to revive the Victorian supposition of children's sexuality as malleable, undetermined, and hence corruptible: ⌃

May I speak of adolescent boys and girls who, more often than not, go through a phase of experiencing deep feelings for older people of their own sex. It is a phase. If it is encouraged, if it is taught to be a way of life, there are some – and I say only some – who will not pass out of this stage, but will remain homosexuals and then follow the homosexual way of life to their lasting unhappiness.[91]

The ubiquitous nature of Victorian family ideology is further witnessed in Lord Campbell of Alloway's statement that "these positive images [of homosexuality], as implemented as a matter of policy, involve a direct attack on the heterosexual family life . . . they attack the paternalistic disciplines of an ordinary family as being totally wrong because children should be totally free."[92] In this statement, the Earl not only reiterates the notion that homosexuality is contagious and can infect children, but he revives the Victorian patriarchal family model which calls for the restraining of children. Youth is still perceived as sexually innocent and susceptible to the deviant influence from the "other" embodied in the homosexual.

Thatcherite anti-gay rhetoric, expressed through the Section 28 debates, is not merely moral conservatism, but is reflective of this nineteenth-century notion of family and the containment of sexual behavior within the private realm which the family occupied. As traditional patriarchal family structure eroded following the Second World War with the rise of divorce, at issue was not merely maintenance of a heteronormative family, but the relegation of sexual relations to the private sphere: "what persisted into the Thatcher era was the widely held belief in the importance of defending a respectable public space against sexual practices that challenge community norms."[93] Again, as indicated earlier in this chapter, at issue in Britain following the reforms of 1967 is not so much whether same-sex relations are a criminal act, but the ability to ensure that they do not spill into the public domain. If they are not in the public sphere, then the government has no right or responsibility to provide equal rights legislation or anti-gay legislation.

The homosexual "other" not only threatens the sanctity of the bourgeois family, but the stability of the entire British empire.[94] Homosexuality, often interpreted as symbolic of emasculation and effeminization of the male of the species – an image propounded by the popular press throughout and after the Oscar Wilde trials – carried with it an inherent destabilizing threat. If homosexuality was allowed to "spread," then the British population would be unable to defend itself. The historical fact that Great Britain, throughout Victoria's reign, was the pre-eminent global power, did not assuage this fear. Indeed, the nation's position as world leader paradoxically exacerbated such paranoia:

Nations are most apprehensive of ruin at the height of their power, and dread prostration when at their zenith. Increasing industrial competition from Germany and the United States, large territorial additions to the Empire in Africa and Asia, challenges to traditional naval invincibility, the splendid Jubilees but also the mortality of Queen Victoria, left the British aware not only of their triumphs but of their vulnerability . . . But it was this vitiation of male might at this critically insecure moment in the history of the empire that counted most. Homosexuals were a threat to imperial aggression and their proliferation was an augury of collapse: they were the rubble before the avalanche.[95]

In short, homosexuals symbolized weakness; their existence endangered the maintenance of the empire in an ever-increasingly competitive global environment.

This motif reappears with the defection to the Soviet Union of two British spies, Burgess and Maclean, in 1954,[96] and it is raised in Parliamentary debates as a justification to block the implementation of the Wolfenden Report. Conservative MP Cyril Black asserted that homosexual acts are "unnatural practices [which], if persisted in, spell death to the souls who indulge in them. Great nations have fallen and empires destroyed because corruption became widespread and socially acceptable."[97] Black, therefore, draws a link between the supposed contagious nature of homosexuality and the strength of the nation-state. Although this argument has lost most of its persuasive power in the United Kingdom, given that the nation has lost its colonial territories throughout the post-war period, a variant of it was used to justify banning homosexuals from civil service soon after the United States acquired superpower status and was confronted with another type of evil "other" – Soviet dictatorship. A similar justification is used to ban openly gay men and women from serving in the American military.

Besides its so-called power to destroy the bourgeois family structure, endanger British youth, and systematically dismantle the British empire, homosexuality was feared because it appeared to "infect" mostly the aristocracy and upper middle-classes. The upper classes appeared to tolerate a limited type of adolescent homosexuality that was prevalent in public boarding schools such as Eton or the Harrow School.[98] Indeed, as historian Jeffrey Weeks notes, the belief that homosexuality was prevalent among members of the ruling class further validated the inherent threat that such sexual behavior presented to the strength of the empire.[99] Furthermore, British working-class culture tended to perceive aristocratic homosexuals as predators on working-class youth, and exposure of homosexuals within the political and religious hierarchies throughout the century supported such a conclusion.[100] This perception continued to be strengthened in the immediate post-war period as the popular press focused on the homosexual sex scandals of members of Parliament and aristocrats such as William Field, Lord Montagu, and Peter Wildeblood.

This working-class conception of homosexuality has, in part, influenced how the Labour Party – the traditional party of the British working-class – has reacted to homosexual law reform. As was noted in chapter 3, Labour became increasingly supportive of such reform in the middle and late 1960s as economic stability and prosperity became a more secondary issue. However, Labour incurred severe national-level electoral cost after it supported gay and lesbian rights at the municipal level during the 1980s. Throughout the late 1970s and early 1980s, the United Kingdom experienced relative economic decline, and the

Labour Party had appeared to abandon its traditional constituency in favor of supporting "radical" minorities. Stuart Weir of the *New Statesman* has argued that the Conservatives were

> moving on from simply exploiting the unpopular attempts of a few Labour councils to promote equal opportunities and provide counseling and other services for gays and lesbians . . . Labour are indelibly seen as the gay party. The Conservatives are now positively coming out as the anti-gay party to milk for all it's worth the great and growing hostility towards homosexuals felt by the majority of people in this country.[101]

The Labour Party continued to lose working-class support as the AIDS epidemic became more visible and consequent right-wing moral backlash against homosexuality increased. Labour's support of gay and lesbian rights led the Conservatives to label the party as the "Loony Left." Since the middle of the 1980s, therefore, the Labour Party, has toned down its support of the British gay and lesbian movement. Thus, while the election of a Labour majority on 1 May 1997, after eighteen years of Tory rule, placed a party nominally receptive to gay and lesbian aims in power, the party's own agenda to rebuild trust with its traditional working-class constituency may run counter to and prevent the implementation of these movement goals.[102]

Homophobia has infiltrated British political culture and Parliamentary debate because it remains a persistent, if slowly diminishing, residue from Victorian ideology that has been appropriated to some degree during the Thatcherite era. British gay men and women, conceived as threats to the heteronormative family structure, national welfare, and the "respectable" lower classes, continue to endure a political society which treats them as second-class citizens. Hence, while statistical analysis in the previous section revealed that the British, in general, tend to be less homophobic than Americans, homophobia and heterosexism do nevertheless exist in the United Kingdom. A possible explanation for the lower degree of homophobia in the United Kingdom relative to the United States is that the sources of such prejudice have gradually disappeared in the former nation without being replaced by a strong evangelical religiously-based intolerance of gays and lesbians as occurred in the United States. Adherence to the bourgeois family model declined as divorce rates have increased in the post-war period; the British empire, as such, no longer exists; and, the vast majority of the population, regardless of socioeconomic class, supports the decriminalization of homosexuality as determined by the 1967 Sexual Offences Act. The circumstances are different in the United States because the primary influence on the level of homophobia, namely degree of religiosity, is still higher than in most, if not all, Western industrialized democracies.

Conclusion

The purpose of this chapter has been threefold. First, it has expanded our model of social movement analysis to include culture as an environmental factor providing opportunity and obstacle and as an internal factor fostering collective identity through symbol and ritual. In this sense, we have augmented our definition of a social movement from a purely political phenomenon to a network occupied with public policy change, transformation of cultural discourses, and formation of collective identity. Second, including culture in the analysis has demonstrated how movements introduce change to the dominant culture. Third, the chapter has sketched possible sources of homophobia and heterosexism in American and British culture in order to provide a fuller image of the political environment in which the gay and lesbian movement organizations act. It should reveal that each movement has and will continue to encounter cultural opposition to varying degrees as it attempts to push forward its agenda. The immediately apparent conclusion is that given that homophobia tends to be less culturally extensive in the United Kingdom than the United States, and given also the recent election of the Labour Party to Parliamentary majority, the British gay and lesbian movement now stands at the threshold of an unprecedented opportunity to achieve its aims. The British movement appears in a more advantageous position relative to its past as well as to its American counterpart.

However, perhaps this conclusion is immature. This chapter has noted that how homosexuality is framed – as an essentialist or socially constructed identity, as a private or public issue – profoundly affects whether or not the movement organizations are heard within their respective legislative forums. Thus, while a receptive political party may be in power in the United Kingdom, while the political machinery in place may now be able to push through policy with few veto points, while the culture may be overall less homophobic than American culture, the continued perception of homosexuality or sexuality in general as a private sphere issue is a considerable barrier to pro-gay legislation by the government at any level.

The American movement is facing a similar dilemma. Its degree of political access is better than it has ever been in the past, and the movement has far more resources than any other movement across the globe.[103] However, its goal of legislative reform, given the orientation of American political institutions, is dependent upon a quasi-ethnic approach which insists on an essentialist identity. Not only does this tactic alienate constituencies within the gay and lesbian movements, but it may not work given that a 1993 poll found that more Americans believe gays and lesbians choose their homosexuality than believe they are born that way.[104] In this sense, the tactics of these movements must differ, and at this point, there is no answer to that original question asked in the introduction: who wins? Or maybe the answer is an unsatisfying but evidentiary sound "No one wins."

If this chapter does nothing else, it should at least demonstrate that social movements respond to and act within a host of different culturally and institutionally induced stimuli. Moreover, it should further validate the notion, introduced in chapter 1, that no one theory is nearly comprehensive enough to account entirely for the emergence, maintenance, and possible decline of a social movement such as the gay and lesbian movements. This chapter introduces a variable which the political process model – the most encompassing of the theories evaluated in chapter 1 – does not adequately consider. Social movements respond to a variety of factors and emerge for reasons that can be accounted for by micro, meso, and macro analysis. In other words, the ability of the different theoretical frameworks – the political process model and the cultural model – to confront and respond to each other on issues where their analytical spheres overlap strengthens the validity of each perspective and demonstrates that no one theory of collective mobilization is absolutely superior to others.

Conclusion

A movement succeeds not when everything is perfect but when so much has changed that there's no going back. This is inarguably where we're at. Skirmishes will be won and lost, greater changes are to be anticipated, and the fight still needs everyone's best, but think of those women and men at the first Mattachine demonstration in 1965 and then watch a tape of Clinton's HRC speech.

Something's changed . . . We're still living in a world of shit, a lot of the shit is homophobic, all the shit's interrelated, and the fight is far from finished. But if we don't take an opportunity like a movie or a speech to mark that progress has been made, how are we going to remember, when we have cause to despair, that political action changes the world? Tony Kushner, "Gay Perestroika"

In 1969 some drag queens started a riot in Greenwich village sparking the gay liberation movement, and in 1997 the President of the United States of America delivered a speech to the Human Rights Campaign in Washington DC. In 1967, after Parliamentary debate ended on the Sexual Offences Act, the Act's primary architect, Lord Arran, contemptuously stated that "homosexuals must continue to remember that while there may be nothing bad in being homosexual, there is certainly nothing good."[1] Thirty years later, Labour Prime Minister Tony Blair proclaimed "I am eager to see a Labour government make significant progress towards ending discrimination and fostering a society free of homophobic prejudice."[2] In the mid-1980s few American mainstream films addressing gay themes or having gay characters were released. In 1998, three films with gay characters, themes, or sub-themes – *The Full Monty*, *L.A. Confidential*, and *As Good as it Gets* – were nominated as "Best Picture" by the Academy of Motion Picture Arts and Sciences. In 1996, the British film, *Beautiful Thing*, which confronted the inequality of the homosexual age of consent by portraying the budding relationship between two adolescent men, was a mainstream success. Tony Kushner's assessment of the gay and lesbian community and movement's status thus has relevance: the movement, though unfinished, has changed things; it has been successful.

Through this book, I have sought to understand how this success has occurred. In doing so, I have attempted to formulate some useful and potentially enlightening conclusions both about the nature of social movements, representative democratic political institutions, and cultural analysis on the one hand and the American and British gay and lesbian movements on the other. These are some of the major findings that emerge.

Social movements are fundamentally political phenomena; however, as power has become de-centered, contested fields expand beyond the state to the cultural realms of education, medicine, science, and the family. Social movements exhibit secondary goals of subcultural development which help to sustain the movement in times which lack political opportunity. The state is the ultimate arbiter of rights and resources. Social insurgency reflects a response by a disenfranchized minority group against the status quo perpetuated by existing ruling elites. While a movement may promote the development of a subculture – and indeed this subculture can be as destabilizing to mainstream cultural norms as overt political action – the primary aim of a social movement is to attain those resources and exploit any political or cultural opportunity in order to reorient the political culture and institutions of the state. Social movements view the state both as the antagonist and as the objective. Since control of or, at least, alteration of the state is a social movement's most fundamental purpose, a movement is inherently political. Yet, as chapter 5 detailed, modernization fostered the proliferation of sites of power beyond the state and/or economic structures to cultural discourses. Movement aims have adjusted accordingly seeking an alternative society through legislation and litigation but also at the cultural level through educational reform and the reshaping of underlying social norms.

Theoretical models of collective action are not mutually exclusive nor is any sufficient to explain social movements fully. As the first and last chapters of this book have demonstrated, each explanation of collective insurgency operates at distinct levels of analysis or at the juncture of two or more of these levels. Each level – micro, meso, or macro – is determined by the type and extent of inquiry into movement behavior. Micro-analysis seeks to explain individual participation. Meso-analysis explores how movements organize, mobilize resources, galvanize participants, and function through interest groups. Macro-analysis investigates the relationship between the state and the social movement focusing on how the latter is influenced by the politico-economic institutions of the former. The political process model, by operating at the intersection of these three evaluative spheres, answers a combination of these questions. PPM's focus on changing opportunities belies a macro-level tendency;

its concern with pre-existing organizations demonstrates its meso-level qualities; and, its explanation of cognitive liberation and the importance of collective identity are linked to individual motivations of movement participation so relevant to the micro-analyst. However, its structural bias leaves fundamental questions left unanswered, including the not so unimportant relationship of culture and social movements. By incorporating culture as an environmental condition as well as an internal characteristic of identity maintained through ritual or as a strategy tool such as framing, we more fully understand how movements and their sociopolitical environments interact and force each other to change.

Culture must be considered both as a tool manipulated by movement activists as well as an environmental variable that shapes the behavior of movement organizations. The American and British gay and lesbian movements have responded to cultural opportunities to promote their agendas, to foster the development of a movement subculture, and to engage in tactics such as Marches on Washington which utilize cultural resonance regarding the American value of equality and civil rights. British activists have framed arguments either as a matter of conscience and privacy or have capitalized on a frame of human rights (especially as regards a right of privacy) given the saliency of the European Convention on Human Rights (specifically Article 8). Culture also conditions the environment in which social movement organizations act. A sketch of British and American culture finds that they have homophobic roots in religion – as is the case in the United States – or vestiges of Victorian bourgeois ideology – as is the case in the United Kingdom. The discriminatory tendencies tend to be less pronounced in the United Kingdom relative to the United States signifying less cultural barrier to gay equality in the former nation. The introduction of culture as another variable which must be reckoned with further emphasizes the inability of one theoretical model to be truly all-encompassing.

The American and British gay and lesbian movements exhibit similar developmental histories emphasizing the role of changing opportunity, pre-existing organizations to manipulate this opportunity, and cognitive liberation leading to collective identity formation. The American movement developed in response to the opportunity provided by the Second World War and the publication of the Kinsey studies, the perseverance of the Mattachine Society and the Daughters of Bilitis in the 1950s and 1960s, and the cognitive liberation encapsulated in the Stonewall riots of late June of 1969. These factors are not as clearly identifiable in the United Kingdom, but they nevertheless exist. Opportunity was provided by the Second World War, but more so by the widely publicized 1954 Wildeblood–Montagu trial and the liberal recommendations made by the Wolfenden Committee in 1957. The Homosexual Law Reform Society formed to capitalize on these recommendations and lobby Parliament for their implementation into law, but it was also the liberal environment of the 1960s that enabled such a lobby even to act. Cognitive liberation and collective identity formation did not occur in the 1970s to the extent that it did in the United States for two reasons. First, the 1967 Sexual Offences Act, by nominally decriminalizing some homosexual behavior, deflated movement activism. Second, gay liberation was an American import like disco music and 1970s fashion; the British had no Stonewall to use as a prideful rallying cry. Indeed, the British "Stonewall" took shape in the anti-Clause 28 demonstrations of 1988. Hence, British prideful gay political agency, in general, lagged behind its American counterpart.

AIDS both promoted and derailed the American and British gay and lesbian movements. AIDS had a double-edged impact on the aims and tactics of the movement so much so that it can be broken into two parts: before AIDS and after AIDS. The epidemic created some positive externalities such as providing the gay and lesbian movement and community with greater political visibility, expanding movement membership, forcing it to act at the national level, renewing grassroots activism, and revitalizing direct action tactics. Yet, the virus has inflicted huge casualties on the community, forced the movement away from a long-term human rights agenda to a medical service provision and short-term survival orientation, fostered negative visibility, provided anti-gay fodder for the New Right, and spawned a separate but related movement that has competed with the civil rights aims of the gay and lesbian movement for popular and political support.

The American separation-of-powers system tends to provide more agenda access than the British parliamentary structure, but the governing cohesion inherent in the latter can be more successful within the realm of policy implementation. The separation-of-powers system is characterized by the independence of three branches of government: the executive, the legislature, and the judiciary. Coupled with the federalist design and minimal political party discipline, movement organizations have a multitude of venues in which to achieve their aims. If the legislature is not receptive, interest groups can turn to the executive or the court system. If a federal law does not appear feasible, maybe a local ordinance could suffice. The British parliamentary system, marked by the dependence of the executive on the legislature and *vice versa*, the strong degree of political party cohesion, the centralization of policy-making in the cabinet, and the absence of an independent judiciary, limits interest group access to governing officials. The European Court of Human

Rights provides an institutional venue outside the boundaries of the United Kingdom, and, as such, has opened the British government to further interest group influence. Even so, the American system remains a much more open system than its British counterpart. Yet, while the American system can better represent movement desires, the separation-of-powers also establishes numerous veto points that can hinder policy implementation and distort the policy intended for such implementation. Given the cohesion of the British ruling system, if a receptive party has the majority in Parliament, then the interest group will more likely see some or all of its agenda executed by the government.

Differences in the political and legal achievements of each movement can be partially accounted for by the distinctions between the American separation-of-powers system and the British parliamentary structure. As noted above, the differences in the governing institutions provide distinct degrees of interest group access and policy implementation. Hence, a Labour majority enabled the passage of the 1967 Sexual Offences Act while a Conservative majority passed Section 28 of the 1988 Local Government Bill despite public outcry. Most American gay-themed legislation has been passed at the state level, and, due to the nature of federalism, such legislation has varied from state to state.

While the existence of a global gay and lesbian movement cannot be definitively established, recent years have seen the movements in different countries utilizing similar strategies and cultural frames. With the emergence of gay liberation and especially after the dawning of the AIDS epidemic, we witness an internationalization and subsequent increased commonality between the aims and tactics of the American and British gay and lesbian movements. The AIDS epidemic, perceived as a global crisis, acts as an exogenous shock to gay and lesbian movements around the world. The epidemic engendered gay and lesbian community-based and grassroots organizing in the United States and the United Kingdom. Furthermore, similarities were also fostered by parallel conservative leadership in both nations. The recalcitrance of the Reagan and Thatcher regimes to respond to the AIDS crisis effectively provided further impetus for the development of community organizations such as Gay Men's Health Crisis in the United States and the Terrence Higgins Trust and Body Positive in the United Kingdom. Outrage at both governments' inability to promote sufficient research or medical care for HIV-positive and AIDS patients led to the establishment of direct action groups such as ACT UP in both nations. Although ACT UP builds on a substantial direct action political tradition in the United States, the expansive nature of the crisis appeared to counter the absence of such a tradition in the United Kingdom.

Globalization of the movement goes beyond similar reaction to a global crisis. As chapter 5 indicated, use of similar strategies and tactics results not merely from transnational diffusion, but signify common cultural responses to a world which is increasingly Western in its conception of human rights. National political cultures and institutions remain a crucial factor, but as diverse political cultures come to accept Western political traditions, the ability for movement organizations to use diverse frames expands proportionately.

This text has striven for two aims, one is a theoretical understanding and the other deals with practical application. Before continuing to adduce how the knowledge gained from this study may be made somehow applicable, that is, to bring our understanding out of the realm of theory to one of practice, there is an inherent underlying logic or illogic to this project which is profoundly unsettling, namely the use of models. Models or theories, that is, rational choice, resource mobilization, or the political process model, as elucidated in chapter 1 and the appendix are quite useful, but when we use them, we must be exceedingly aware not only of their limitations but cautious of their implications. This text has been written in a method that suggests a discursive frame commonly used in the hard social sciences of economics, political science, and some branches of sociology and which is critiqued extensively by cultural anthropologists and ethnographers, the softer social sciences, and the humanities. My uneasiness with this fact derives from the recognition that this text, in short, could be perceived as attempting an objective analysis, a "scientific" evaluation, when my own education suggests that any such endeavor is impossible. The use of flow charts and diagrams rings eerily of modernist attempts to understand and control both natural and social forces, and the reliance on such is, no doubt, bizarrely anachronistic in our own post-modern age. By employing a model, I have constructed a *representation*, a means by which to understand the historical phenomena which are the American and British gay and lesbian movements. My discomfort draws from my simultaneous recognition that inherent in representation is a power dynamic that the observer imposes upon the observed. A representation is a translation that distorts the object of study, and that reveals as much about the subject writing as it does about the object that is written about: "To represent means to have a kind of magical power over appearances . . . The true historical significance of writing is that it has increased our capacity to create totalist illusions with which to have power over things or over others as if they were things. The whole ideology of representational signification is an ideology of power."[3] This totalizing image, which this type of analysis could be misunderstood to be, is precisely what is to be avoided.

This point is the primary aim of chapter 1, was reiterated in chapter 5 and the appendix, and is a critical theme of this text. The aim was never to suggest a model by which we can fully understand the formation, development, and existence of a social movement. Such full and total comprehension is impossible. By introducing the variable of culture in chapter 5, by introducing a question that the political process model failed to ask, indeed was incapable of doing so, I was further attesting to this impossibility. As such, I have advocated investigating social movements from simultaneous multivariate perspectives in an effort to transcend the limitations and implications of a necessarily bounded theoretical model. Historical interpretation is highly dependent upon the framework adopted to investigate a particular phenomenon. Theory necessarily and inescapably conditions the evaluation by allowing only certain variables to come under the scope, only certain questions to be asked. The theoretical aim of this text was never to overcome this dilemma, but to recognize it as such.

The practical aim of this text is somewhat less cerebral. While the findings discussed above are important in and of themselves, the question remains how this knowledge is applicable or useful in any way. In other words, given these findings, can any predictions be made regarding the future of these gay and lesbian movements? The British gay and lesbian movement at the turn of the new millennium is advantageously positioned both in respect to its former status as well as relative to its American counterpart. A receptive political party is in power which has committed itself to equalizing the age of consent and lifting the ban on gays in the military as first steps toward full legal equality for lesbians and gay men.[4] The election of Labour coupled with both the nature of the parliamentary system as well as the precedents established by the European Court of Human Rights regarding Article 8 of the European Convention on Human Rights have heightened the probability that pro-gay legislation and litigation will at least be more actively debated if not passed. In a sense, limited agenda access and party discipline make the British governing structure far easier to maneuver; opportunities to act may be rare, but when they do present themselves, such action can be easily directed and the ruling party may only require a nudge by a movement organization. The British gay and lesbian movement, despite having fewer resources than its American contemporary, is not assaulted by a highly mobilized and powerful countermovement in the form of the Christian right. In real terms, the resources marshaled by the British movement can be devoted more towards pro-gay items rather than fighting anti-gay initiatives. The constituents of the British movement are more geographically centralized in London. This phenomenon not only facilitates rapid mobilization to capitalize on political opportunity, but targets social movement action at the national level since it is occurring in that nation's capital. Furthermore, British activists have a variety of cultural frames with which to legitimate their cause and fight for equal rights; while Americans have powerful frames as well, the continued persistence of the American public to view sexual orientation as a choice and not an inborn trait undermines the quasi-ethnic approach which has historical resonance and validity in the United States. These theoretical conclusions by no means suggest that the British movement will make any great strides while Labour holds power; it merely indicates that the political opportunity exists to make those leaps, leaps that given the peculiarities of the American political institutional environment are much more difficult in the United States

The American movement will most likely continue as it has been, promoting pro-gay and fighting anti-gay legislation at state, local, and national levels. The pace of change will be slow, and gains will be incremental. Indeed, all institutional access venues – the executive, the legislative, the judiciary, the party structure – have witnessed gains and setbacks throughout the 1990s ranging from the inclusion of sexual orientation in the 1990 Hate Crimes Bill to the failure of ENDA, the passage of DOMA, the banning of same-sex marriages in thirty states, and the creation of civil unions in Vermont. Furthermore, given that the gay and lesbian movement, while itself becoming more mainstreamed, has not yet achieved mainstream acceptability, the likelihood of an all-encompassing equal rights law passed at the national level is slim. The American movement will have far greater success at the local and state level preventing anti-gay legislation, promoting equal rights laws, and pursuing a simultaneous legislation–litigation strategy, but even this success will tend to occur in those states which tend to be the most urban, the most liberal, and the least susceptible to the influence of the Christian right.

The only thing that can be predicted for sure is that future years will continue to witness portrayals of gay characters and exploration of gay-related themes through cultural venues such as theater, film, television, and art. And, even at this level, British television tends to be more willing to air shows which contemplate themes and characters of far greater controversy than the innocuous and benign portrayals across the Atlantic.[5] Yet, as historical trends of the post-war period have confirmed, gay, lesbian, bisexual, and transgender political activism has sparked a revolution in values in both countries. No one can deny that the current status of the gay and lesbian community is better now than it was ten or twenty years ago in terms of cultural acceptance and political institutional power and maneuverability. Fewer still could contend that institutionalized homophobia is as insidious as in the past with homosexuality no longer treated as a psychological disorder, the growth of gay and lesbian studies and queer theory in the academy, the rise of anti-discrimination employment practices, the expansion of same-sex and domestic partner benefits in the corporate sector, and the increased discussion of gay marriage, gay service in the military, and other gay and lesbian issues in the national political, legal, and popular cultural discourse. While setbacks to movement aims will undoubtedly occur in a society that clings to the dying vestiges of homophobia, this movement will continue as celebratory as it has in the past, gaining strength from its diversity, and pulling itself along the political horizons in an ever-continuing struggle to make people realize that the differences between us exist only in closed minds and cold hearts.

Appendix: a survey of social movement theories

> If collective behavior was the theoretical response to the socio-political climate of the 1930s, and if the RM framework was the theoretical response to the socio-political climate of the 1960s, it remains to interpret the socio-political climate of the 1990s and to reformulate social movement theory in ways which will enlighten us about this new historical moment.   Steven M. Buechler, "Beyond Resource Mobilization"

To comprehend and appreciate more fully the robust quality of the political process model and the importance of multifaceted analysis, we must more carefully examine the utility and disadvantages of theories which remain confined to one evaluative sphere or to the overlap of only two such spheres. The field of social movement analysis is complex, and the language used to elucidate competing theories can be quite tangled and tricky. Therefore, as I evaluate the theories throughout this appendix, I will attempt to tie the theory with some concrete examples drawn from the civil rights movement and the gay and lesbian movement. However, before we apply these real-world examples, it might be easier to begin with a simplistic hypothetical model of collective action. Let's suggest that this particular instance of collective action is at a college campus where a group of students have mobilized in front of the administration building to protest against the distributor which supplies food to the dining hall. Perhaps the students are acting on behalf of migrant farm workers who supply produce to the distributor, but are underpaid, not offered health insurance, and are generally exploited. They may be demonstrating solidarity with university dining employees who contend that they are underpaid and subjected to poor working conditions. Perhaps the food distributor mandates a compulsory buy-in policy; in other words, each semester the students must pre-purchase meals without regard to their on or off-campus living status. Perhaps, the food is just entirely inedible. Whatever the motive, with this example of student protest, we may more easily navigate through the sometimes convoluted language of social movement theory. We begin with the classical approach.

Disorganized deviants

Since a body of rules is the definite form taken over time by the relationships established spontaneously between the social functions, we may say *a priori* that a state of *anomie* is impossible wherever organs solidly linked to one another are in sufficient contact, and in sufficiently lengthy contact. (Emile Durkheim, *The Division of Labor in Society*)

According to Emile Durkheim, modern industrial society is marked by the establishment of organic solidarity which results from the meshing of individual differences with the division of labor. With the advent of the division of labor each individual is given the opportunity to develop a specific role which, in turn, benefits the overall health of society. Society itself is not a conspicuous actor; rather, it merely declares the law which is no more than "a conciliator of private interests."[1] Hence, the individual is the foundation of society and contributes to the collective aims and purpose of that society. In this sense, Durkheim's philosophy is the basis of the modern pluralist perspective on state and social relations.

The pluralist perspective considers the individual to be an independent political actor. Society is composed of individuals who are bonded together through a set of common values. The state serves as a representative of these amalgamated values, and it functions properly when its interests are aligned with those held by society. Thus, two potentially contradictory notions underlie the pluralist perspective: participation and consensus.[2] The more participation there is, the higher the probability of conflict, and therefore, the more difficult it is to maintain consensus of political values.

The classical understanding of social movements is firmly grounded within a pluralist vision of state and society relations. Pluralism is a fundamentally dichotomous perspective which deems behavior rational if it acts within the existing institutional context and irrational if it acts outside of that context. This distinction relies on the assumption that in a democracy, particularly the United States, "groups may vary in the power they wield, but no group exercises sufficient power to bar others from entrance into the political arena."[3] Operating under this assumption, pluralists must not only consider mass movements to be extraordinarily rare and transitory phenomena indicative of an imbalance between participation and consensus, but also inherently *irrational* given the openness and responsiveness characteristic of institutionalized democracy. Collective protest is viewed as a pathological explosion of participation resulting from the breakdown of societal values characteristically attributed to rapid industrialization. A social movement represents the failure of existing political institutions; movement politics are discontinuous with, if not overtly contradictory to, conventional politics.[4] Furthermore, since collective behavior is perceived as an aberration of institutionalized politics, the development and survival of a given social movement is not seen as dependent on the internal dynamics of the movement, nor on the interaction between the movement and the existing political structure, but rather only as a reflection of the state's power to diffuse frustration and/or to suppress the challengers.[5]

While variants of the classical model including mass society theory, status inconsistency theory, relative deprivation theory, or rising expectations theory exist, they all propose similar general causal frameworks: some type of structural change fosters psychological disruption which, in turn, provides the impetus for a social movement.[6] Mass society theory contends that social movements result from a loss of structure. Hannah Arendt contends that movements capitalize on inclinations of hyper-loyalty resulting from social strain: "such loyalty can be expected only from the completely isolated human being who . . . derives his sense of having a place in the world only from his belonging to a movement."[7] People who cannot integrate themselves into existing sociopolitical life suffer from alienation and atomization; they engage in collective behavior as a means to mitigate these tensions.

Status inconsistency theory posits that when a discrepancy exists between an individual's perceived and actual status, cognitive dissonance inevitably results. As the discrepancy widens or lessens, the individual may engage in a range of dissonance-reducing behaviors. One common mechanism is to immerse oneself in a social movement that, in some way, relieves distress.[8]

Relative deprivation and rising expectation theory is most clearly explored by Samuel Huntington in his study, *Political Order in Changing Societies*. Huntington claims that socioeconomic changes, including industrialization, improved literacy, and the expansion of the media, undermine the political stability of developing countries. He concludes that "it is not the absence of modernity but the efforts to achieve it which produce political disorder. If poor countries appear to be unstable, it is not because they are poor, but because they are trying to become rich."[9] Huntington takes Durkheim's *anomie* from its sociological context and applies it in politico-economic terms. The modernization process leads to an increase in political consciousness and participation, but no corresponding rise in the level of political organization, that is, the party structure or interest group system. Essentially modernization increases participation without simultaneously establishing the tools or institutions needed to derive popular consensus This lag or gap creates a high level of political instability and embodies those very characteristics – excessive participation based on grievances and the state's inability to provide values consensus – that pluralists and classical theorists use to explain social movements.[10]

Embedded within the classical model is the notion that movement participants are psychologically impaired. Since pluralism takes its basic unit of political action to be the individual, the classical approach to social movements, despite its emphasis of social strain, is primarily concerned with the psychological strain at the individual level. As a result, according to classical theorists, a movement serves an ultimately psychological need; a political agenda, if it exists at all, is secondary.[11] Building on Durkheim's thesis that industrialization can create atomization, political theorist, Philip Selznick, notes that

> the need to belong is unfulfilled; insecurity follows and, with it, anxiety-laden efforts to find a way back to status and function and to some sense of relationship with society. But these efforts are compulsive: enforced by urgent psychological pressures, they result in distorted, pathological responses . . . "the substitute community," in which essentially unsatisfactory types of integration – most explicitly revealed in fascism – are leaned upon for sustenance.[12]

Movements are formed to aid individuals to cope with the psychological dissonance inflicted by social strain; in the classical model, they serve primarily therapeutic rather than political ends.

How would a classical theorist understand our simple example of student protest against the university's food distributor? In this metaphor, the role of the state is played by the university administration while the students would be perceived as the movement participants. Classical theorists would isolate the act of protest itself, interpreting it as an aberration; the students have behaved outside of structured political norms to achieve their ends. They could have acted through the established channels of the student governance system, that is, acted through elected representatives, petitioned their classmates, called for a vote, and presented their demands to the university dean, chancellor, or president. By rallying in front of the administration building, they are exhibiting irrational behavior and are exemplifying the breakdown of the political process as it is construed by pluralist-based classical theorists.

This hypothetical example, while providing a good foundation, is perhaps too simplistic as it lacks the chronological scope that a real-world example provides. In brief, a classical interpretation of the gay and lesbian movement in the United States since the Second World War would attempt to discover the structural strain and individual psychosis experienced by participants as well as the restorative services of the social movement itself. Utilizing the cognitive dissonance angle of status inconsistency theory, a classical theorist could claim that the Second World War represented a massive structural strain providing gay men and lesbians with an outlet to explore their sexual orientation in ways not permitted in peacetime. As demonstrated in Paul Fussel's *The Great War and Modern Memory*, and Randy Shilts' *Conduct Unbecoming*, the stress of war experience fosters intense bonding among soldiers often including a homoerotic element.[13] Classical theorists might argue that the aggressive nature of anti-homosexual rhetoric in the 1950s[14] represents an abrupt shift from opportunity – given the war emergency – to possibly one of the most repressive periods in American history. This change established a status inconsistency: gay men and lesbians who risked their lives for the preservation of United States were encountering severe discrimination. This discrepancy could lead to participation in a social movement.

Classical theorists would further suggest that the movement organizations established throughout the 1950s including the Mattachine Society and the Daughters of Bilitis had primarily therapeutic concerns.[15] Meetings of Mattachine often revolved around discussions regarding the causes of homosexuality and social hostility towards it. Few people returned to these sessions more than once hindering the development of long-term objectives and goals.[16] Hence, political objectives of the group were unavoidably secondary.

When applied to the Daughters of Bilitis (DOB), this line of argument is even more forceful. This lesbian organization, while maintaining close ties to Mattachine in its early years before the development of the feminist movement, was not as concerned with law reform as its predominantly male counterpart. DOB existed as "a haven where [lesbians] could experience a sense of belonging, put their lives in order, and then, strengthened and regenerated, venture forth into society."[17] DOB identified itself as primarily a self-help organization, and it existed to relieve the dissonance, the anxiety, and the alienation that resulted from an awareness of a same-sex attraction.

A classical theorist would focus on the Stonewall riots of June 1969 as the quintessential expression of a pathological explosion of irrational behavior. Rather than seeking reform against police entrapment and raids on gay bars through existing institutional channels, gays retaliated with violence when police raided the Stonewall Inn, a Greenwich Village gay bar. Selznick suggests that "the breakdown of normal restraints, including internalized standards of right conduct, and established channels of action . . . frees the mass to engage in direct, unmediated efforts to achieve its goals and to lay hands upon the most readily accessible

instruments of action."[18] Often, direct action can be violent, and this
tendency was expressed during the Stonewall riots: stones and bottles
thrown, police cars destroyed, and 400 police officers battled a crowd of
2,000 people.[19]

Yet to dismiss any stage of the gay and lesbian movement as primarily
therapeutic and peopled with individuals experiencing some form of
psychological disruption is to underestimate or ignore other factors.
First, the classical model presents movements within a political vacuum.
History has shown that movements develop as a response to environmental factors as well as individual desire; this larger context is missing
from the classical interpretation.[20] Second, a classical understanding
contends that movements are the expression of discontented *individuals*;
yet, they are unavoidably a group phenomenon. A logical inconsistency
exists. No explanation of this transformation from *individual* disorder to
collective behavior is given. Lastly, the dichotomy between institutionalized political behavior and social movements leads to a belittling of
movements as pathological and ignores the historical impact of movements. In terms of the gay and lesbian movement, discounting "coming
out" as therapeutic misses the point of gay liberation entirely. Gay
liberationists of the 1970s viewed coming out "as a profoundly political
act that could offer enormous benefits to the individual. The open
avowal of one's sexual identity . . . symbolized the shedding of the self-
hatred that gay men and women internalized . . . To come out of the
'closet' quintessentially expressed the fusion of the personal and the
political that the radicalism of the late 1960s exalted."[21] Furthermore,
this philosophy of coming out served political ends in expanding the
movement. By refusing to remain invisible, gay men and lesbians
became increasingly vulnerable, and, as a result, realized a heightened
investment in the success of the movement. These numerous inconsis-
tencies within the classical model are fundamentally unsatisfying and
propel us towards other means to make sense of social movements.

Beyond Olson's challenge: limitations of rational choice

When the number of participants is large, the typical participant will know that
his own efforts will probably not make much difference to the outcome, and that
he will be affected by the meeting's decision no matter how much or how little
effort he puts into studying the issue. (Mancur Olson, *The Logic of Collective
Action*)

In his treatise, *The Logic of Collective Action*, Mancur Olson provides an
economic interpretation of collective behavior. He agrees with the
classical understanding of participation as fundamentally irrational;

yet, in doing so, he also obliterates the basis of the pluralist perspective, namely political participation, itself. He suggests that any participation in a collective endeavor is economically irrational given the temptation of the free-rider problem. Thus, while concurring with the classical theorists' pluralist conclusion, Olson's analysis is decidedly anti-pluralist.

A collective action organization acts to attain a common objective that Olson views as a public good. Once a public good is available to anyone, it is available to everyone. One individual utilizing the product does not exclude anyone else from using that same product simultaneously. [22] Here the dilemma of collective action becomes apparent. If a rational individual is a member of a large group, he or she will realize that his or her own participation is negligible; if the group succeeds in achieving their objective, the individual will still receive the benefit regardless of his or her action or inaction. Or, in the case of our student protest, since a large number of students will protest, why should a particular student participate if he or she will receive the potential benefit of an altered meal plan policy regardless? Perhaps he or she has to study for a biology exam, go to athletic practice, or make a dance rehearsal and cannot afford to take time to protest. The costs of participation, derived from both the time lost to other pursuits and the monetary dues paid to cover organizational costs, will necessarily outweigh the benefits. Noncooperation is individually rational in this economic sense. A person will choose to avoid the cost, but enjoy the benefit; he or she will become a free rider.[23] Thus, rational choice is the basis for Olson's argument.[24]

Olson's theory demonstrates the general maxim that individual rationality can lead to collective disaster. His assertion that a group can rarely be mobilized around a collective material benefit coupled with his identification of the free-rider problem are both important insights in determining the motivations for participation in a collective movement. Yet, while it suggests this problem, it fails to offer a solution. Furthermore, while Olson's theory may apply to economic organizations such as unions, it does not explain the existence and success achieved by mass social movements characteristic of the 1960s and early 1970s. The limited applicability of Olson's theory reflects that individuals do not always act according to economic self-interested rationality; it attests to the difference between economic organizations and organizations which attempt to achieve social change. If Olson's hypothesis is true, then, in the extreme case, none of the mass demonstrations ranging from the Montgomery bus boycott of the civil rights movement to the 1993 march on Washington for Lesbian, Gay, and Bisexual Rights would have occurred.

Since Olson's theory does not reflect historical reality, at least since the upsurge of identity-based social movements, some other theory must be derived to explain why individuals do indeed participate in social movements. Political scientist, Dennis Chong, provides such a theory. He claims that Olson's notion that participation in social movements can only be deemed rational if selective incentives are offered is too narrow precisely because Olson conceives of benefits as *tangible*. Yet Chong theorizes that collective action offers a range beyond material inducements including both sociological and psychological incentives. He suggests that some people may engage in collective behavior because close friends and/or family members are participating; thus, he essentially describes a bandwagon effect. He also claims that involvement should not be conceived as susceptible to the free rider, but embedded in the norm of reciprocity. By participating, an individual is demonstrating concern for others; if and when that individual ever needs support he or she will have a network upon which to fall back.[25] Now participation in our student protest suddenly makes sense. Maybe one student is participating because her roommate truly believes in the cause, and she wants to show her support for her roommate. Students might defend the claims of the dining workers now so that when the students feel exploited, they can rely on the dining staff as allies.

Social movements also provide a means publicly to express and validate personal ethics. According to Chong social movements represent "tests [that] are administered in conjunction with the grand issues of our day involving the lives and fates of masses of people."[26] As such, cooperation and the promotion of the goals of a certain group reveal political, social, and moral beliefs in an extremely public forum. Perhaps the students want to use the protest to demonstrate their high degree of social concern. Or maybe one student is protesting to show his social concern in order to impress another student. Maybe he protests to improve his standing in the eyes of another student so he can later ask him or her on a date!

Psychological incentives also provide partial explanation for cooperating in a collective endeavor. Participation in a goal deemed beyond the scope of individual action encourages a feeling of self-importance and an increase in self-esteem. In this sense, the collective goal may be secondary to the degree of individual growth. This supposition is not a rejection of rational choice theory, but rather an extension of it beyond the boundaries of an economic sphere to a psychological one. In this case, perhaps the first-year student who is new to campus and does not know many other students participates in the protest to feel part of a community or to feel like he or she is contributing to something bigger than him or herself. The individual psychological benefit of participation may be more instrumental to a given individual than the collective goal; yet, despite this seeming inversion of priorities, the individual will nevertheless tend to participate.

What is crucial to understand about Chong's argument is first, that it operates at the micro-level of individual motivations for cooperation as do all the classical approaches. Second, and perhaps more important, Chong does not directly contradict the rational choice theory upon which Olson's argument is founded; rather, he expands upon it. He views the free-rider as a real problem to the possibility of collective behavior, and he overcomes it not by direct refutation of its existence, but through the exploration of other noneconomic justifications for cooperation.

Paradigm shift

Theory does not develop within the confines of a political vacuum; rather, since theory must explain historical events, it is forced to adapt to the circumstances of those events. The movements of the 1960s and 1970s confronted social movement analysts with a serious dilemma. The classical model did not seem to fit the reality in which they were living; its limited and unflattering depiction of movement participants as psychologically unbalanced was fundamentally unsatisfying. The concept of mass society breeding short bursts of inherently pathological collective behavior was neither congruous with the length of the movements nor the type of participants whom these movements attracted.[27] Some movements stretched between five and twenty years and appealed to mostly middle to upper middle-class individuals.[28] In other words, given their socioeconomic status, participants did not seem to suffer from relative deprivation, alienation, or atomization.

Resource mobilization (RM) theory developed to address these newly recognized blind spots. The theory abandons the problematic pluralist perspective and grounds itself in an elite-managerialist conception of democratic institutional relationships. Power and access to power are not evenly distributed to all rational actors, but rather they are wielded only by a few groups. Hence, collective action is perceived as the only mechanism seemingly powerless individuals have to voice their desires and influence the political system.[29]

Resource mobilization theory further contends that "there is always enough discontent in any society to supply grass-roots support for a movement if the movement is organized and has at its disposal the power and resources of some established elite group."[30] The notion that

grievances perpetually exist in any political system has numerous implications. First, grievances alone are deemed insufficient to instigate the
formation of social movements; the centrality of organizational needs
and resources, e.g., money, labor, office space, is established as a
primary factor in movement development. Here the primary research
question is altered from *why* individuals participate to *how* such participation is possible. Some theorists extend this notion of grievances to
claim that not only are they secondary to resource aggregation, but they
can be manipulated or even manufactured by movement entrepreneurs
so that a positive correlation exists between the grievance level and the
amount of resources amassed.[31] In other words, grievances will expand
and multiply as long as resources for that movement continue to
increase. Second, since grievances alone do not determine collective
action, but rather mobilization of resources must be taken into account,
collective behavior can be a long-term phenomenon rather than a
momentary expression of heightened strain.[32] Third, since the hypothe-
sized cause of movements has shifted from a fundamentally individual
psychological dilemma to an outgrowth of the political structure itself,
RM theorists view a movement as an extension rather than the antithesis
of institutional politics.[33] Building on the foundation laid by rational
choice theory, RM theory suggests that participation is determined
using a cost-benefit analysis which includes such noneconomic factors
as the benefits of group solidarity and values expression. Unlike some
rational choice theories, RM theory claims that collective behavior is
indeed rational, normal, and can be highly patterned and organized.[34]
Thus, it attempts to negate the classical model by blurring the distinction between conventional and movement politics.

As Figure A.1 demonstrates, the resource mobilization model seeks to
resolve Olson's dilemma by exploring the dynamics of formal social
movement organizations (SMOs). RM theorists explore the relationship
and strategy differences among various SMOs, as well as with "third
parties", such as media, which are indirectly related to the protest.
Media representation is a potential movement resource since it can shape
the movement's image thereby attracting or repelling participants.[35] RM
theory also explains the strength and longevity of certain movements by
exploring the changes in resources and internal dynamics of *pre-existing*
organizations thereby promoting further political opportunities.

The fundamental motivation for such a change is usually a crisis. For
example, during the civil rights movement, methods of protest including
bus boycotts, sit-ins, and freedom rides were employed according to
their ability to generate a crisis situation, thereby attracting media
attention.[36]

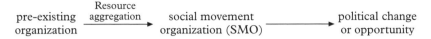

Figure A.1 *Resource mobilization*

Crisis inspires short-term and abrupt change as well as instigates further acts of protest. In the history of the black civil rights struggle in the United States, long-term alteration of the black community social structure had been occurring well before that movement became visible. Throughout the 1950s, blacks were increasingly becoming urbanized, attaining college-level education, and becoming members of the middle-class. These developments enabled the black community to establish a strong internal organization that could be utilized to subvert the oppressive remnants of the Jim Crow south as well as represent itself as a substantial voting bloc in national politics.[37] Early sit-ins emphasized the coherency of the internal organization and resource mobilization by the black community:

rational planning was evident in this early wave of sit-ins . . . [they] were sponsored by indigenous resources of the black community; the leadership was black, the strategies and tactics were formulated by blacks, and the finances came out of the pockets of blacks, while their serene spirituals echoed through the churches.[38]

The civil rights movement was well-organized around a core of black churches and colleges which served to finance the movement and advocate tactics of non-violence. This well-forged network of local movement centers spread throughout the border states and, later, into the deep south.[39]

The emphasis on organizations, or a meso-level analytical approach, can be used to evaluate the American gay and lesbian movement as well. Rather than focusing on the Stonewall riots as classicists might to demonstrate a pathological explosion of participation indicative of psychological dysfunction, RM theory would concentrate on the network of homophile organizations of the 1950s and 1960s – the Mattachine Society and the Daughters of Bilitis – to explain the massive mobilization which occurred in the 1970s. The gay liberation movement initiated by the riots would not have occurred, according to resource mobilization theorists, without the national network established by the homophile groups. As historian John D'Emilio notes,

gay liberation was able to give substance to the dreams of the Mattachine founders because of the work of the homophile activists in the intervening years . . . the pioneering activists of the 1950s and the 1960s had managed to disseminate throughout American culture information about homosexuality that reshaped the consciousness of gay men and women . . . Gay liberation propelled hundreds of thousands of men and women to act upon that belief, but two decades of work by homophile activists had made the individuals who were ready to respond.[40]

By publishing gay-themed magazines such as *One*, *Mattachine Review*, *The Ladder*, and *Vector*, by distributing educational pamphlets on homosexuality, by establishing the Committee on Religion and the Homosexual, and establishing ties with allies in the religious, legal, and medical communities, and by advancing a number of arguments for sodomy reform and anti-discrimination measures, the homophile groups established an organizational network upon which later organizations such as the Gay Liberation Front (GLF), the Gay Activist Alliance (GAA), or the National Gay Rights Lobby could draw. In other words, resource mobilization theorists view organizations as resource aggregates rather than therapeutic collectives emphasized by classical theorists.

RM theory might explore the AIDS epidemic as the necessary crisis to promote mobilization that was further stimulated by media coverage; RM theory might also focus on the increased visibility and political leverage of the gay minority in the 1992 election. Though no theorist would suggest that Bill Clinton owed his victory over George Bush to the decisive nature of the gay vote, the enormous visibility that the "gay issue" received is directly correlated to the degree of resource mobilization of various movement organizations including the National Gay and Lesbian Task Force (NGLTF), the Human Rights Campaign (HRC), and Gay Men's Health Crisis (GMHC).[41]

Despite the insights made by RM theory into the internal dynamics of social movement organizations, the extensive focus on the meso-level has left theoretical gaps in understanding exactly why individuals participate or how the greater political structural environment affects the development of the movement.[42] Resource mobilization promotes little understanding of individual involvement and commitment to collective behavior or of macro-structural determinants such as party systems, legislatures, demographics, or level of industrialization. This continuous stress on pre-existing and movement organizations indicates a bias against informal groups and gatherings that could promote the movement's objectives; to assume that formal structures are the primary engine of the movement is to negate or belittle the role of visibility, subculture development, or social movement community.[43] Also the presumption that resource aggregation can sufficiently overcome the free-rider problem ignores the role of collective identity and the formation of movement ideology.[44] RM theory is at a loss to explain the importance of consciousness-raising in both the feminist and the gay and lesbian movements. Overemphasis on the rational choice model which informs resource mobilization separates the individual from his or her environment producing a fictitious individual detached from *cultural* influence.[45] Given that the resource mobilization framework leaves many of the characteristics of social movements unexplored, another theory is needed to more fully comprehend the development and life of collective action.

Something new?

There is growing realization among scholars of social movements that the theoretical pendulum between classical and contemporary approaches to social movements has swung too far. Social psychological factors that were central to collective behavior theory have become the theoretical blind spots of resource mobilization theory. Ignoring the grievances or injustices that mobilize protest movements has . . . stripped social movements of their political significance. (Verta Taylor and Nancy E. Whittier, "Collective Identity in Social Movement Communities: Lesbian Feminist Mobilization")

In the late 1970s and throughout the 1980s, social movement theory reached somewhat of an impasse. Explanation of movements, until this point, exhibited a bipolarization which clustered around the stereo-typical American agency-based view or the structuralist orientation of traditional Marxism. Within the former paradigm, regardless of whether the individual is perceived as irrational according to the classical model or rational as resource mobilization purports, the emphasis is on the individual and his or her response to a crisis which disorients a political system usually at (a pluralist or elite-managerialist) equilibrium. Indeed, no reference is given to traditionally Marxist notions of solidarity, collective identity, or class consciousness. The American perspective also tends to lump all types of collective behavior together and differentiates them only by the degree of strain incurred; hence, a revolution is merely more extreme than a riot which is, in turn, only more extreme than a panic. Once tension is alleviated, the movement will cease to exist, and systemic equilibrium, whether it be pluralist or elite-managerialist, will be reestablished.[46]

The alternative to this perspective is a traditional Marxist interpretation of movement dynamics. Instead of analyzing the individual, Marxists tend to view movements as necessary outgrowths of politico-economic systems characterized by the ownership of the means of production. All history, according to Karl Marx, is a series of class struggles; class membership is determined by an individual's relationship to the means of production. Marx contends that history follows a definite pattern where

in the place of an earlier form of intercourse, which has become a fetter, a new one is put, corresponding to the more developed productive forces and, hence to the advanced mode of self-activity of individuals – a form which in its turn becomes a fetter and then is replaced by another. Since these conditions correspond at every stage to the simultaneous development of the evolving productive forces, their history is at the same time the history of the evolving productive forces taken over by each new generation, and is, therefore, the history of the development of the forces of the individuals themselves.[47]

Technological evolution recreates individuals' roles in societies and hence, their relationship to each other. Where there was once a tripartite division of serf–vassal–lord under feudalism, there remains after the industrial revolution and under capitalism only the dichotomy between the proletariat and the bourgeoisie, or between those who sell their labor power and those who can purchase it. Once this latter division exists, it becomes impossible, according to Marx, to liberate the oppressed class without overthrowing the entire structure of class exploitation. Hence, the proletariat revolution will unavoidably usher in a new social dynamic characterized by full equality of all citizens manifested in the total destruction of private property.[48]

Essentially, Marx asserts that the individual is purely a product of his or her socioeconomic circumstances: "it is not the consciousness of men that determines their being, but, on the contrary, their social being that determines their consciousness."[49] In doing so, Marx obliterates the notion of a free agent who can shape his or her own environment; rather, he or she becomes a mere passive receptor of that environment. A Marxist understanding underestimates the power of organization, mobilization, and leadership when accounting for the existence of a social movement. Since the ultimate aim of collective action according to Marxism is the conquest of the state, a movement that does not maintain this objective cannot be adequately understood.[50]

The aim of new social movement (NSM) theory is to explain the existence of movements of the post-1960 period which do not fit neatly into either the American or the Marxist paradigms. NSM theory attempts to expand traditional Marxist ideas of collective action by incorporating notions of the actors' collective identity. Yet, to consider NSM theory as a coherent framework, such as the classical model, the Marxist approach, or resource mobilization, would be a mistake. Rather NSM represents a group of theories each conceding that a linkage exists between structural changes characteristic of post-industrial society and the development of postmaterialist values on the one hand and problems regarding identity on the other.[51]

NSM theorists claim that, given the shift in the political and socio-economic environment, new or post-1960 social movements are fundamentally distinct from older movements. Proletarian unrest and labor movements were predominant in the nineteenth and early twentieth centuries given that the stage of capitalism was marked by materialist values. In other words, since the economy suffered from vast shocks and was inherently unstable, people were preoccupied with the maintenance of their socioeconomic status. Advanced capitalist societies have reached unprecedented levels of economic prosperity and, given the emergence of the welfare state, relative security. Hence, focus turned towards political or quality-of-life issues. According to sociologist, Ronald Inglehart, "whereas previous generations were relatively willing to make tradeoffs that sacrificed individual autonomy for the sake of economic and physical security, the publics of advanced industrial society are increasingly likely to take this kind of security for granted – and to accord a high priority to self-expression both in their work and in political life."[52] Thus, the new social movements do not conform to the economic determinism of Marxist theory since the motivating grievance is no longer economic but rather politically or identity-based.

NSM theory recognizes this cultural shift and attempts to place it within a variant of Marxist theory so as not to disregard completely the usefulness of Marxism itself. Advanced capitalism, according to NSM theorists, is no longer merely characterized by the production of goods, but also by the production of social relations and, by extension, of identity. The conflict over the reappropriation of the means of production characteristic of the traditional Marxist bourgeoisie-proletariat dichotomy, is now extended into the new territory of identity formation.[53] Hence, the defense and development of identity as a woman in the feminist movement or as gay or lesbian, in the gay and lesbian movement, is the aim of these new social movements.

Since these movements are identity and not necessarily class-oriented, they are not manifested in the actions of a single class. Group identities are derived from shared characteristics including gender, race, ethnicity, or sexual orientation. Furthermore, the new social movements tend to focus on a political value-based ideology rather than an instrumental economic interest. This shift demonstrates that deprivations attributed to postindustrial society tend to include issues regarding self-expression and therefore transcend class boundaries.[54]

New social movement theories differ from other models already explored above because in their responses to the inadequacies of the bipolar American and Marxist paradigms, they are forced to arrive at some linkage of a micro- and macro-level analysis of movements. In other words, NSM theories attempt to explain why individuals participate through reference to grievance articulation while also claiming that identity is shaped by the circumstances of advanced industrial society.[55] Yet, the new social movement framework is unsatisfactory for a number of reasons. First, NSM is not a unified theory like resource mobilization, but a group of theories that share some characteristics such as the role of post-materialist values and the construction of collective identities. As such it is still subsumed by internal debates regarding whether the movements are actually "new," whether they are class-based, and whether they are political, cultural, or both.[56] Second, but related to the first point, the new social movement framework underestimates the political origins of social movements by focusing on the apolitical objectives of the movement. New social movement theory tends to concentrate on the creation of movement subculture as it relates to the formation of collective identity to the point that the state, or reform of the state, is not just a secondary target, but it is not a target at all. The concept of "the personal is political" substituted movement politics aimed at reform and transformation with identity politics aimed at the creation of an autonomous subculture.[57] The movements are thus threatened by a loss of their political orientations. Without the involvement of the state, it is impossible to determine how the state affects the development of a movement; cross-national or historical comparison becomes extremely difficult.[58] (Since determining this exact point is the objective of the text, NSM theories do not suggest a paradigmatic fit.) Lastly NSM theory maintains some of the theoretical blind spots of the classical model: its emphasis on *why* a social movement is created ignores *how* a movement is able to sustain itself and adapt to a changing socioeconomic and political environment (with the possible exception of suggesting that a highly developed movement subculture can maintain the identity of a movement community).[59] This emphasis also hinders comparisons of similar movements because it prevents exploration of movement interaction with existing political institutions.

Timing is everything

People join in social movements in response to political opportunities and then, through collective action, create new ones. As a result, the "when" of social movement mobilization – when political opportunities are opening up – goes a long way towards explaining its "why." (Sidney Tarrow, *Power in Movement*)

The traditionally American approach to understanding collective action drew upon rational choice theory to inform both micro and meso-level interpretations. Little focus was given to a macro analysis, i.e., the interaction between the state and the social movement, within this paradigm. Rather, the only model that existed to explain the influence of the political and socioeconomic environment on movement development and tactics was either traditional Marxism or the neo-Marxist tendencies of new social movement theory. Yet, these theories were inherently incompatible with a reliance on a rational choice model that stressed the power of actors to determine structure as opposed to structure commanding agency. Political opportunity structure theory (POS) filled this theoretical gap.

Political opportunity structures refer to not necessarily permanent or formal configurations of political institutions and historical precedents for social mobilization which protesters can exploit to promote collective action.[60] This model differs from those explored above in various ways, but the major distinction is its ability to adopt a comparative approach which the other frameworks cannot. While the neo-Marxism of NSM theory can demonstrate links between the socioeconomic stage of development and the emergence of social movements, it cannot explain why similar movements might have dissimilar outcomes.[61] Resource mobilization concentrates primarily on internal variables of the movement including membership recruitment, goal formation, internal organization, and the establishment of alliances. POS, on the other hand, examines how the emergence and methodologies of the movements relate to *external* institutional constraints specific to distinct political systems.[62] POS seeks to understand how a given nation's political party, electoral, and representation systems influence a social movement. In other words, these elements, taken together, make up the political opportunity structure of a specific country and therefore imply "a country specific mix of facilitation/repression of the movement's mobilization, their chances of success, and the degree of reform/threat they have to reckon with. This specific mix defines the concrete opportunities of a given social movement."[63] This mix of institutions and opportunities helps the movement to conduct a cost-benefit analysis to determine the most efficient and strategic allocation of its resources; hence, the POS determines, in part, the extent of movement mobilization, movement sustainability, and the outcome of mobilization.[64]

Sidney Tarrow extends the macro-level orientation of the POS even further by arguing for a realignment in the current understanding of collective action beginning with a complete negation of Mancur Olson's depiction of the free-rider: "the theory of collective action must be extended from individual to collective decision making; from simple microeconomic models to social and historically embedded choices; and from single movements to the dynamics of the political struggle."[65] Olson's argument applies to economic interest groups such as trade unions, but not necessarily to social movements. Olson claimed that movement participation relied on marginal utility: does participation incur more benefits than costs? Yet, research has shown, and rational choice theorists, NSM theorists, and RM theorists concur, that people participate for a host of noneconomic reasons related to status, dissonance reduction, values expression, solidarity, and identity formation.[66] Second, Olson claimed that the strength of a movement could be illustrated by the proportion of organization members who participate in collective action; yet, new social movements such as the gay and lesbian movement cannot possibly fulfill this criterion if only because no one knows precisely the population of lesbians, bisexuals, and gays, and therefore cannot determine what proportion of this population is involved in acts such as the 1979, 1987, 1993, and 2000 National Marches on Washington for Gay and Lesbian Rights.[67] Lastly, the gay and lesbian movement is not an organization; rather, it is a social movement community which is composed of a variety of movement organizations each with potentially competing agendas. Tarrow asserts that ultimately the main problem social movements encounter is not the free-rider, but social coordination. How are disparate organizations to present themselves to political elites and potential supporters as integrated, goal-oriented, and rational?[68]

Tarrow posits that RM theory is fundamentally flawed since it takes Olson's challenge as given and attempts to resolve it via an emphasis on internal organization. Yet, since social movements are not groups *per se* and lack formal organization, they cannot solve the problem of coordination through internalization, but rather through externalization.[69] Social movements must utilize external resources including political opportunities and historical precedents to coordinate and maintain collective action. While internal resources are important, they do not ultimately determine the success of a social movement. Figure A.2 illustrates the dynamic of the political opportunity structure paradigm.

As this diagram indicates, two reciprocal dynamics occur in the POS model. Political institutions affect movement formation, and a movement acts through the existing political institutions to promote its goals. Tarrow suggests that these institutions could be separated into two distinct categories: changing political opportunity structures and stable political opportunity structures. The former category includes both short-term changes such as the opening up of access to participation,

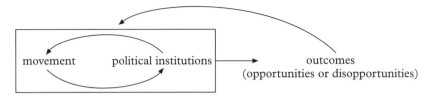

Figure A.2 *Political opportunity structure*

shifts in ruling alignments through elections, availability of influential allies, and splits among elites as well as long-term shifts such as industrialization or war.[70] The latter category refers to the party system, the executive–legislative relationship, and the concept of state strength as related to a parliamentary or separation-of-powers structure.[71] Some opportunity or crisis such as war occurs which allows the movement to emerge. Once the movement is developed, its tactics are shaped by the institutional environment. This interaction produces further opportunities or disopportunities. Disopportunities include countermovement development or the achievement of reform to a level that ultimately undermines the movement's sustainability.[72]

In our example of student protest, let's posit that one of the dining workers suffered an episode of respiratory failure due to a combination of steam, heat, and poor ventilation in the kitchen. This incident functioned as that initial crisis which sparked mobilization. The students' tactics of direct action may result from a perceived slowness or inaccessibility of established channels such as the student government. The protest may not only alter the dining policy at the university, but cause the student government to reassess its own structure thereby effecting potential change in the institutional environment. Even through this simple example, the danger of this approach is readily apparent; its emphasis on structural forces tends to diminish the power accorded to the movement actors themselves.

Conclusion

Each of the theories presented above responds to different questions circulating in the field of social movements. Classical and rational choice theories seek to discover why people participate. The resource mobilization model attempts to answer how people participate. Political opportunity structure locates its emphasis on when people participate as an explanation of why and how. New social movement theories address the why and when of such participation in a neo-Marxist analysis that shifts emphasis from economic class consciousness to collective identity formation and corresponding identity politics. By asking particular questions – the why, how, and/or when of participation – the conclusions, or at least how they are emphasized, are, to some degree always already preconditioned. The political process model, which answers the why, when, and how of movement formation and participation, avoids the privileging of one research question over another; it thereby enables a richer and more multi-faceted analysis. Yet, as pointed out in chapter 5, PPM's overemphasis on political institutions leaves the role of culture in movement formation and maintenance undecided. This observation does not imply that a wider net must be cast to create a more-encompassing theory; rather, it suggests that no such totalizing social movement theory is possible.

When beginning her text, *Ghostly Matters: Haunting and the Sociological Imagination*, sociologist Avery Gordon quotes Patricia Williams' observation: "That life is complicated is a fact of great analytical importance."[73] While this statement seems at once obvious and too trivial to waste ink upon it, the attempts to reduce our understandings of social movements to the interaction of certain variables will forever oversimplify the complicated nature of human interaction that sociologists and other social analysts attempt to grasp. Models such as those detailed above will always be, to some degree, blindingly reductive. The import of Williams' statement within the context of social movement theory should now be obvious. The aim of social movement analysts, then, should not be to abandon these models, but rather, with a better sense of their gaps, engage multiple theoretical explanations simultaneously. Social movements are like the people who comprise them . . . complex and multi-dimensional.

Notes

PREFACE

1 Dan Hawes, *1999 Capital Gains and Losses: A State by State Review of Gay, Lesbian, Bisexual, Transgender, and HIV/AIDS-Related Legislation in 1999* (Washington, DC: National Gay and Lesbian Task Force, 1999). http://www.ngltf.org/issues/pubs.cfm?issueID=18, 6 May 2000.

INTRODUCTION

1 Various works have begun to accomplish the task of analyzing the gay and lesbian movement according to a sociological, specifically social movement, frame. Numerous of these functioned as the foundation of this text and include works by Adam, Altman, Epstein, Escoffier, Rayside, Seidman, Tarrow, Taylor, and Whittier among others.

2 Indeed, the awesome power of only two major parties in both countries is where the similarities between these two-party systems end. British political parties tend to be nationally oriented and strongly disciplined. American parties are more locally focused and have displayed an immense inability to encourage ideological uniformity.

3 In their chapter, "Analytical Approaches to Social Movement Culture: The Culture of the Women's Movement," Taylor and Whittier contend that "emotion and reason are not irreconcilable, and social movement participants, like all other social actors, are not only thinking but also feeling actors" (180). Discussion of emotion is at the heart of understanding social movements, and to leave emotion out of this analysis is only to pretend that a purely rational unenculturated individual exists.

4 I use the characterization of the American movement as the "leader" cautiously. Certainly, modern gay liberation ideology developed in the United States first in the immediate aftermath of the 1969 Stonewall riots, and this ideology was then transplanted across the Atlantic. Furthermore, popular images of gay identity which pervade the subculture such as the "clone" developed in the United States before the United Kingdom. Finally, the more confrontational tactics utilized by ACT UP, Queer Nation, and similar groups in the late 1980s and 1990s in both countries, developed first (although the difference in time span is small) in the United States. (See Plummer, "The Lesbian and Gay Movement in Britain: Schisms, Solidarities, and Social Worlds" in *The Global Emergence of Gay and Lesbian Politics:*

National Imprints of a Worldwide Movement, eds. Barry D. Adam, Jan Willem Duyvendak, and Andre Krouwel (Philadelphia: Temple University Press, 1999), 147 and David M. Rayside, *On the Fringe: Gays and Lesbians in Politics* (Ithaca: Cornell University Press, 1998, 281–314).) However, in terms of official legal status, gay male (lesbians are not addressed in British law) sexual relations have been legal in England and Wales since the late 1960s. Furthermore, openly gay men and lesbians are no longer banned from the British military as they are from its American counterpart, and the Canadian parliament has considered extending to same-sex couples the same legal benefits as those enjoyed by heterosexual married couples. If only in these few instances where other nations seem vastly more progressive than the United States, it is difficult to characterize the American movement as the universal leader when it has not even attained this national status as late as 2000.

5 Plummer, "The Lesbian and Gay Movement," 137.
6 Ibid., 137–41.

I ASKED AND ANSWERED: HOW QUESTIONS CAN CONDITION
CONCLUSIONS IN SOCIAL MOVEMENT THEORY

1 For more detailed application and analysis of the classical approach, rational choice, resource mobilization, new social movement theory, and political opportunity structure, please see the appendix. The coverage given to these theories is not so much a literature review as it is a survey of historically commonly used models; some theories such as the dramaturgical approach or the social interactionist approach are not discussed. The six theories discussed in this chapter were selected because they represent the common genres of social movement theory as well as providing a tidy chronology of the field of social movement analysis itself. Discussion of other theories was deemed extraneous and detracted from the ultimate purpose of understanding the American and British gay and lesbian movements within the framework of the political process model.

2 McCarthy and Zald explain the growth of social movements throughout the 1960s and 1970s by suggesting a theoretical dissection of social movements into the social movement (SM), the social movement organization (SMO), the social movement industry (SMI), and the social movement sector (SMS). These authors contend that the separation between an SM and an SMO demonstrates that the mere existence of a social movement, as representing a set of beliefs aimed at altering the existing socio-political system, does not imply full mobilization. The use of SMOs as a theoretical tool emphasizes the organizational and meso-level focus of resource mobilization theory. The concept of SMIs demonstrates that social movements are represented by more than one SMO. Finally, such distinctions allow an explanation of the growth and decline of a social movement without relying solely on the size of the movement, but rather on how well the organization can mobilize resources. See John D. McCarthy and Mayer N. Zald, "Resource Mobilization and Social Movements: A Partial Theory," *American Journal of Sociology* 82 (6), 1977, 1212–41.

3 This idea is taken up in chapter 5.

4 The promotion of a sub- or alternative culture is demonstrated in the radical tendencies of lesbian feminist organizations such as the Furies to establish separatist collectives as well as in the gay and lesbian movement to maintain a bar culture or, as some radicals suggest, a queer counterculture which shuns gender roles as well as the hetero/homo binary division.

5 Max Weber, "Politics as a Vocation" in *From Max Weber: Essays in Sociology*, eds. H. H. Gerth and C. Wright Mills (New York: Oxford University Press, 1958), 78.

6 J. Craig Jenkins and Bert Klandermans, "The Politics of Social Protest" in *The Politics of Social Protest*, eds. J. Craig Jenkins and Bert Klandermans (Minneapolis: University of Minnesota Press, 1995), 3.

7 Sidney Tarrow, *Power in Movement* (New York: Cambridge University Press, 1994), 2, 4.

8 For more detailed synopsis of the classical approach see Doug McAdam, "The Classical Model of Social Movements Examined" in *Social Movements: Perspectives and Issues*, eds. Steven M. Buechler and F. Kurt Cylke, Jr. (Mountain View, California: Mayfield Publishing Company, 1997) 135–48; William Kornhouser, "The Politics of Mass Society" in *Social Movements: Perspectives and Issues*, eds. Steven M. Buechler and F. Kurt Cylke, Jr. (Mountain View, California: Mayfield Publishing Company, 1997), 91–7; Mancur Olson, *The Logic of Collective Action* (Cambridge, Mass.: Harvard University Press, 1965); John Elster, *Nuts and Bolts for the Social Sciences* (New York: Cambridge University Press, 1989), 22–42, 124–73.

9 Turner and Killian, 251, quoted in McCarthy and Zald, "Resource Mobilization and Social Movements," 1215.

10 Steven M. Buechler, "Beyond Resource Mobilization? Emerging Trends in Social Movement Theory," *The Sociological Quarterly* 34 (2) 1993, 218.

11 Hank Johnston, Enrique Larana, and Joseph Gusfield, "Identities, Grievances, and New Social Movements" in *Social Movements: Perspectives and Issues*, eds. Steven M. Buechler and F. Kurt Cylke, Jr. (Mountain View, California: Mayfield Publishing Company, 1997), 274–94. Alberto Melucci, "The New Social Movements: A Theoretical Approach," *Social Science Information* 19 (2) 1980, 119–26.

12 Herbert Kitschelt, "Political Opportunity Structures and Political Protest: Anti-Nuclear Movements in Four Democracies" in *American Society and Politics*, eds. Theda Skocpol and John L. Campbell (New York: McGraw-Hill, Inc., 1995), 321. Tarrow, *Power in Movement*, 85.

13 Ibid., 17.

14 Ronald J. Hrebenar, *Interest Group Politics in America* (Armonk, NY: M. E. Sharpe, 1997), 9.

15 Ibid.

16 Tarrow, *Power in Movement*, 178–82.

17 Ibid., 183.

18 Ibid., 182–3.

19 Ibid., 184.

20 Ibid., 186–90.

21 As chapters 2 and 3 will illustrate, the gay and lesbian movement expanded extensively in the 1970s because it fostered collective identity formation enabling the emergence of new interest groups.

2 TRACING THE RAINBOW: AN HISTORICAL SKETCH OF THE AMERICAN GAY AND LESBIAN MOVEMENT

1 Margaret Cruikshank, *The Gay and Lesbian Liberation Movement* (New York: Routledge, 1992), 69.

2 John D'Emilio, *Sexual Politics, Sexual Communities: The Making of a Homosexual Minority in the United States* (Chicago: University of Chicago Press, 1983), 232.

3 Ibid., 1–2.

4 Ibid., 2.

5 Michel Foucault, *The History of Sexuality: An Introduction: Volume I* (New York: Vintage Books, 1978), 43.

6 Ibid., 47–9.

7 D'Emilio, *Sexual Politics*, 24.

8 Ibid.

9 Allan Berube, *Coming Out Under Fire: The History of Gay Men and Women in World War Two* (New York: The Free Press, 1990), 33.

10 D'Emilio, *Sexual Politics*, 25. Note also that Dr. William Menninger, who assessed military social environment, claimed that "for every homosexual who was referred to or came to the Medical Department, there were five or ten who never were detected." Allan Berube claims that of the eighteen million men drafted and examined, only four to five thousand were rejected as homosexual (33). Given Kinsey's estimates that approximately ten percent of the population is gay, one would expect to find 1.8 million gay men among the population examined.

11 Berube, *Coming Out*, 37.

12 Howard Brotz and Everett Wilson, "Characteristics of Military Society," *American Journal of Sociology* 51 (March 1946), 371–5. quoted in Berube, *Coming Out*, 38.

13 Ibid.

14 *Gone for a Soldier* (Kineton, England, 1972) 102–103. quoted in Paul Fussel, *The Great War and Modern Memory* (New York: Oxford University Press, 1975), 274.

15 Urvashi Vaid, *Virtual Equality: The Mainstreaming of Gay and Lesbian Liberation* (New York: Anchor Books, Doubleday, 1995), 48.

16 D'Emilio, *Sexual Politics*, 25–6.

17 Ibid., 29.

18 Ibid., 27.

19 Ibid., 28.

20 Ibid., 31.

21 Ibid., 32.

22 Ibid.

23 Donald Webster Cory is a pseudonym. Cory's real name was Edward Sagarin.

24 Donald Webster Cory, "The Society We Envisage" in *The Homosexual in America: A Subjective Approach* (1951) in *We are Everywhere* eds. Mark Blasius and Shane Phelan (New York: Routledge, 1997), 277–81.

25 Ibid., 280–1.

26 For more information regarding both queer theory and the role of the homosexual as liberationist leader see Cindy Patton's "Tremble, Hetero Swine" in *Fear of a Queer Planet*, ed. Michael Warner (Minneapolis: University of Minnesota Press, 1993) and Craig Owens's "Outlaws: Gay Men in Feminism" in *Men in Feminism*, eds. Alice Jardine and Paul Smith (New York: Routledge, 1987).

27 Cory, "The Society We Envisage," 279.

28 Ibid., 280.

29 The consequences of gay and lesbian visibility in the media are further discussed in the last section of this chapter.

30 Cory, "The Society We Envisage," 271.

31 D'Emilio, *Sexual Politics*, 32–3.

32 Berube, *Coming Out Under Fire*, 271.

33 Vaid, *Virtual Equality*, 48.

34 Denunciation of homosexuality within the Judeo-Christian tradition was explicit during this time period. In recent years, Western religious attitudes toward same-sex attraction have become more liberal and variegated depending on the particular sect. A 1999 Human Rights Campaign report, *Mixed Blessings: Organized Religion and Gay and Lesbian Americans in 1998*, found that "there are, in short, no clear answers about gay and lesbian people within American faith communities at present . . . There are, instead, growing questions, controversies, and uncertainties – in other words, much soul-searching within the leadership of most of the denominations examined here . . . " (5). The religious denominations evaluated in the report include: Roman Catholicism, Southern Baptist Convention, United Methodist Church, National Baptist Convention USA Inc., Church of God in Christ, the Evangelical Lutheran Church in America, Church of Jesus Christ of Latter-day Saints, Presbyterian Church (USA), African Methodist Episcopal Church, Orthodox Judaism, Conservative Judaism, and Reform Judaism.

35 D'Emilio, *Sexual Politics*, 12.

36 Ibid., 18–21.

37 Ibid., 35.

38 Afred C. Kinsey, Wardell B. Pomeroy, and Clyde E. Martin, *Sexual Behavior in the Human Male* (Bloomington: Indiana University Press, 1998) (originally published in 1948 by W. B. Saunders Company), 636–41, 650.

39 Ibid., 627.

40 Barry Adam, *The Rise of the Gay and Lesbian Movement* (New York: Twayne Publishers, 1995), 61.

41 Ibid., 61–2.

42 Ibid., 62 and D'Emilio, *Sexual Politics*, 41.

43 Ibid., 42.

44 Note that even in the senate report, homosexuality is no longer an act to be avoided, but an ingrained and descriptive personality that infused and tainted every aspect of an individual.

45 United States Subcommittee of the Committee on Expenditures in the Executive Department, "Employment of Homosexuals and Other Sex Perverts in the U.S. Government" (1951) in *We are Everywhere*, eds. Mark Blasius and Shane Phelan (New York: Routledge, 1997), 241–51.

46 Ibid., 244.

47 Ibid., 244–5.

48 Ibid., 244.

49 D'Emilio, *Sexual Politics*, 44 and Adam, *Rise of the Gay and Lesbian Movement*, 62.

50 D'Emilio, *Sexual Politics*, 44.

51 Adam, *Rise of the Gay and Lesbian Movement*, 62–3.

52 D'Emilio, *Sexual Politics*, 50–1.

53 Adam, *Rise of the Gay and Lesbian Movement*, 63.

54 American Civil Liberties Union, "Homosexuality and Civil Liberties: A Policy Statement" (1957) in *We are Everywhere*, eds. Mark Blasius and Shane Phelan (New York: Routledge, 1997), 274–5.

55 Barry D. Adam, Jan Willem Duyvendak, and Andre Krouwel, "Gay and Lesbian Movements beyond Borders? National Imprints of a Worldwide Movement" in *The Global Emergence of Gay and Lesbian Politics*, eds. Barry, Adam, Jan Willem Duyvendak, and Andre Krouwel (Philadelphia: Temple University Press, 1999), 344.

56 D'Emilio, *Sexual Politics*, 52.

57 Ibid., 53.

58 Adam, *Rise of the Gay and Lesbian Movement*, 67–8.

59 D'Emilio, *Sexual Politics*, 65–6.

60 Mattachine, under Hay's direction, whether intentionally by or not, was capitalizing on a master frame which has had a great deal of cultural resonance in the United States: minority demands for civil rights. Indeed, Hay's theoretical foundation for this approach is a pre-cursor to the quasi-ethnic approach so prevalent today and which is further discussed in chapter 5.

61 "Statement of Purpose of the Mattachine Society" (1951) in *We are Everywhere*, eds. Mark Blasius and Shane Phelan (New York: Routledge, 1997), 283–4.

62 The concept of self-naming as it relates to collective identity formation and social movement cultural development is further discussed in chapter 5.

63 Vaid, *Virtual Equality*, 52.

64 D'Emilio, *Sexual Politics*, 65–8.

65 Police entrapment usually revolved around the activity of "cruising." Plainclothes police officers would stake themselves at rumored or known "cruising areas" such as parks or public restrooms. The officer would make overtures to have sex with an individual believed to be homosexual. If that individual accepted the offer, he would be arrested.

66 D'Emilio, *Sexual Politics*, 71–8.

67 Ibid., 71.

68 Vaid, *Virtual Equality*, 50.

69 Ibid., 77.

70 Marilyn Reiger, "Delegates of the Convention," 23 May 1953, Kepner papers quoted in Vaid, *Virtual Equality*, 53–4.

71 D'Emilio, *Sexual Politics*, 80.

72 Ibid., 85.

73 Ibid., 87–9.

74 Ibid., 89, 102.

75 Daughters of Bilitis, "Statement of Purpose" (1955) in *We are Everywhere*, eds. Mark Blasius and Shane Phelan (New York: Routledge, 1997), 328.

76 "What Is DOB?" DOB file, Lesbian Herstory Archives, New York quoted in D'Emilio, *Sexual Politics*, 104.

77 Frank Kameny quoted in Toby Marotta, *The Politics of Homosexuality* (Boston: Houghton Mifflin Company, 1981), 24.

78 Ibid., 48–9.

79 Shirley Willer, "What Concrete Steps Can be Taken to Further the Homophile Movement?" in *The Ladder* II (November 1966) 17–20, quoted in Marotta, *Politics of Homosexuality*, 51.

80 Marotta, *Politics of Homosexuality*, 52–3.

81 Willer, "Concrete Steps", 344.

82 Marotta, *Politics of Homosexuality*, 55.

83 Letter from Dick Lietsch to Frank Kameny, 19 June 1968, quoted in Marotta, *Politics of Homosexuality*, 61.

84 Ibid., 62–3.

85 D'Emilio, *Sexual Politics*, 134–9.

86 Adam, *Rise of the Gay and Lesbian Movement*, 75.

87 D'Emilio, *Sexual Politics*, 211–13.

88 Ibid., 214–15. The role of the church in the decriminalization of homosexuality by the Sexual Offences Act of 1967 in the United Kingdom is more extensively discussed in chapter 3.

89 Ibid., 215–17.

90 Ibid., 124–5, 147.

91 Marotta, *Politics of Homosexuality*, 68.

92 Dudley Clendinen and Adam Nagourney, *Out for Good: The Struggle to Build a Gay Rights Movement in America* (New York: Simon and Schuster, 1999), 408.

93 Ibid., 445.

94 Martin Duberman, *Stonewall* (New York: Penguin Books USA, Inc., 1993), 181–90.

95 Marotta, *Politics of Homosexuality*, 74.

96 The term "chicken hawks" refers to older men that sought sexual relations with young men in their mid to late teens.

97 *Village Voice*, 3 July 1969, 18 quoted in D'Emilio, *Sexual Politics*, 232.

98 D'Emilio, *Sexual Politics*, 232.

99 Duberman, *Stonewall*, 202.

100 Ibid., 207.

101 D'Emilio, *Sexual Politics*, 224–5.

102 Ibid., 224–8; John D'Emilio and Estelle B. Freedman, *Intimate Matters: A History of Sexuality in America* (New York: Harper and Row, 1988), 321–2;

Alice Echols, *Daring to be Bad: Radical Feminism in America 1967–1975* (Minneapolis: University of Minnesota Press, 1989), 6–11, 15–18.

103 Vaid, *Virtual Equality*, 56.
104 Stokely Carmichael quoted in Adam, *Rise of the Gay and Lesbian Movement*, 79.
105 Stokely Carmichael quoted in Marotta, *Politics of Homosexuality*, 135.
106 Steven Seidman, "Identity and Politics in a 'Postmodern' Gay Culture: Some Historical and Conceptual Notes" in *Fear of a Queer Planet*, ed. Michael Warner (Minnesota: University of Minneapolis, 1994), 109–13.
107 Ibid., 115.
108 GLF Statement of Purpose, 31 July 1969 quoted in D'Emilio and Freedman, *Intimate Matters*, 322.
109 Marotta, *Politics of Homosexuality*, 88–91.
110 Adam, *Rise of the Gay and Lesbian Movement*, 83; A Gay Male Group, "Notes on Gay Male Consciousness-Raising", *Out of the Closets: Voices of Gay Liberation*, eds. Karla Jay and Allen Young (New York: New York University Press, 1992), 293–97.
111 Marotta, *Politics of Homosexuality*, 91.
112 D'Emilio and Freedman, *Intimate Matters*, 322–3.
113 D'Emilio, *Sexual Politics*, 236.
114 Adam, *Rise of the Gay and Lesbian Movement*, 86–7; Marotta, *Politics of Homosexuality*, 140–7.
115 Clendinen and Nagourney, *Out For Good*, 50–6.
116 Adam, *Rise of the Gay and Lesbian Movement*, 99–103.
117 Ibid., 99.
118 D'Emilio and Freedman, *Intimate Matters*, 324.
119 Vaid, *Virtual Equality*, 66.
120 D'Emilio and Freedman, *Intimate Matters*, 324 and Randy Shilts, *And the Band Played On: Politics, People, and the AIDS Epidemic* (New York: Penguin Books USA, 1988), 32.
121 Clendinen and Nagourney, *Out For Good*, 405, 426.
122 Dennis Altman, *Homosexual Oppression and Liberation* (New York: Outerbridge and Dienstfrey, 1971), 52 quoted in Adam, *Rise of the Gay and Lesbian Movement*, 106.
123 Duberman, *Stonewall*, 209; Vaid, *Virtual Equality*, 67.
124 Clendinen and Nagourney, *Out For Good*, 290–330.
125 Ibid., 377–90.
126 Vaid, *Virtual Equality*, 72, 81.
127 D'Emilio and Freedman, *Intimate Matters*, 354.
128 Cruikshank, *Gay and Lesbian Liberation Movement*, 182.
129 Adam, *Rise of the Gay and Lesbian Movement*, 157–8.
130 Robert McFarlane quoted in Vaid, *Virtual Equality*, 90.
131 Vaid, *Virtual Equality*, 91 and D'Emilio and Freedman, *Intimate Matters*, 356.
132 Ibid., 357.
133 Leo Bersani, *Homos* (Cambridge: Harvard University Press, 1995), 17–19.
134 Vaid, *Virtual Equality*, 81.
135 Ibid., 74

136 Ibid., 89.
137 Eric E. Rofes, "Gay Lib vs. AIDS: Averting Civil War in the 1990s," *Out/Look* (1990) in *We Are Everywhere*, eds. Mark Blasius and Shane Phelan (New York: Routledge, 1997), 654.
138 Vaid, *Virtual Equality*, 94–102.
139 Newt Gingrich in ibid., 69.
140 Patrick Buchanan in *The Gay Almanac*, compiled by the National Museum and Archive of Lesbian and Gay History, A Program of the Lesbian and Gay Community Services Center – New York (New York: Berkeley Books, 1996), 77.
141 D'Emilio and Freedman, *Intimate Matters*, 354 and Adam, *Rise of the Gay and Lesbian Movement*, 155.
142 133 Congressional Record, 14 October 1987, S14216 quoted in Carl F. Stychin, *Law's Desire: Sexuality and the Limits of Justice* (New York: Routledge, 1995), 50.
143 Bersani, L. *Homos*, 21.
144 Vaid, *Virtual Equality*, 76–7.
145 Rofes, "Gay Lib," 654–5.
146 Vaid, *Virtual Equality*, 91.
147 Clendinen and Nagourney, *Out For Good*, 478.
148 Ibid., 88.
149 Rayside, *On the Fringe*, 285.
150 I use the term competitor not in a direct resources sense. Rather, AIDS presented such an immense public health crisis and fostered such a negative public image on the gay community, that pro-active civil rights legislation was forced to take a back-seat to defensive tactics and the more immediate needs of securing funds for continued research, medication, and services for PWAs.
151 Clendinen and Nagourney, *Out For Good*, 544.
152 Ibid., 546.
153 Stychin, *Law's Desire*, 53.
154 Vaid, *Virtual Equality*, 90; Rayside, *On the Fringe*, 286.
155 Michael R. Fraser, "Identity and Representation as Challenges to Social Movement Theory: A Case Study of Queer Nation" in *Mainstream(s) and Margins: Cultural Politics in the 90s*, eds. Michael Morgan and Susan Leggett (Westport, CT: Greenwood Press, 1996), 32–5; Steven Epstein, "Gay and Lesbian Movements in the United States: Dilemmas of Identity, Diversity, and Political Strategy" in *The Global Emergence of Gay and Lesbian Politics*, eds. Barry Adam, Jan Willem Duyvendak, and Andre Krouwel (Philadelphia: Temple University Press, 1999), 60–4.
156 Anonymous, "Queers Read This: I Hate Straights" (1990) in *We Are Everywhere*, eds. Mark Blasius and Shane Phelan (New York: Routledge, 1997), 774.
157 Ibid., 773.
158 Seidman, "Identity and Politics," 133.
159 Marlon T. Riggs, "Ruminations of a Snap! Queen: What Time Is It?!" in *Outlook*, Spring 1991, 15.
160 Vaid, *Virtual Equality*, 236–7.

161 Andrew Kopkind, "The Gay Moment," *The Nation*, 3 May 1993, 1.
162 Clendinen and Nagourney, *Out For Good*, 135–8.
163 Rayside, "Homophobia," 289–91.
164 John Gallagher and Chris Bull, *Perfect Enemies: The Religious Right, the Gay Movement, and the Politics of the 1990s* (New York: Crown Publishers, Inc., 1996), 69–79.
165 Ann Stockwell, "Yep, She Rules," *Advocate*. 20 January 1998, 92.
166 Susan Faludi, *Backlash: the Undeclared War against American Women* (New York: Doubleday, Inc., 1991), XVIII.
167 Martin, 140 in Rosemary Hennessy. "Queer Visibility in Commodity Culture" (Publisher information unavailable).
168 Barbara Smith, "Across the Kitchen Table: A Sister-to-Sister Dialogue" in *This Bridge Called My Back*, eds. Cherrie Moraga and Gloria Anzaldua (New York: Kitchen Table: Women of Color Press, 1981), 121.
169 Joseph Beam, "Introduction: Leaving the Shadows Behind" in *In the Life*, 14 quoted in Seidman, "Identity and Politics," 119.
170 Further discussion of the advantages and disadvantages of visibility in political and popular culture will be explored in chapters 2 and 3.
171 Rayside, *On the Fringe*, 301–2. Rayside notes that HRC has a female Executive Director, Elizabeth Birch, that the Victory Fund endorsed Sherry Harris, an African American Woman, running for Seattle City Council, the National Gay and Lesbian Task Force has had two women of color in senior staff positions including Urvashi Vaid as Executive Director, has had gender parity on its board since the early 1990s, and currently, one-fourth of the board is made of people of color.
172 Hennessy, *Queer Visibility*, 69.
173 Bersani, *Homos*, 17–18.
174 Vaid, *Virtual Equality*, 157.
175 Ibid., 159–61.
176 Ibid., 163.
177 Ibid., 166–7.
178 Rayside, *On the Fringe*, 242–3.
179 Vaid, *Virtual Equality*, 170–1; Gallagher and Bull, *Perfect Enemies*, 151–60.
180 This idea will be addressed further in chapter 4.
181 Vaid, *Virtual Equality*, 1–18.
182 Rayside, *On the Fringe*, 310–11.
183 The outcomes include such positive events as lifting of the ban on gays in the Civil Service in 1974, the removal by the APA of homosexuality as a mental illness in 1974, or the election of openly gay individuals to political office as well as countermovements such as Anita Bryant's "Save Our Children Campaign" and the rise of the Moral Majority and later the Christian Coalition.

3 TRACING THE RAINBOW: AN HISTORICAL SKETCH OF THE BRITISH GAY AND LESBIAN MOVEMENT

1 The number of illegitimate births increased from 26,574 in 1940 to 64,174 in 1945 while the instance of sexually transmitted diseases rose seventy

percent from 1939 to 1942. Alkarim Jivani, *It's Not Unusual: A History of Lesbian and Gay Britain in the Twentieth Century* (Bloomington: University of Indiana Press, 1997), 55–6.

2 One popular anecdote recalls how member of Parliament, Tom Driberg, engaged in oral sex with a Norwegian sailor in a London air raid shelter. When discovered by a police officer, Driberg was not charged after disclosing that he was the celebrated gossip columnist, William Hickey, of the *Daily Express*. Stephen Jeffery-Poulter, *Peers, Queers, and Commons* (London: Routledge, 1991), 1–2.

3 Jeffery-Poulter, *Peers, Queers*, 13.

4 David Rayside, *On the Fringe* (Ithaca: Cornell University Press, 1998), 24–6.

5 Colin Spencer, *Homosexuality in History* (Harcourt Brace and Company, 1995), 355.

6 Section 11 of the 1885 Criminal Law Amendment Act, commonly known as the Labouchere Amendment, was introduced by MP Henry Labouchere. It criminalized all homosexual acts, including sodomy (termed "buggery") as well as any other kind of homosexual intimate contact (termed "gross indecency") between two or more men committed in public or private. Oscar Wilde was imprisoned under this law in 1898. Jeffrey Weeks, *Coming Out: Homosexual Politics in Britain from the Nineteenth Century to the Present* (London, Quartet Books, 1979), 14.

7 Jeffery-Poulter, *Peers, Queers*, 14; Weeks, *Coming Out*, 160.

8 A chain prosecution refers to a situation where one individual is arrested and confesses to homosexual acts with other individuals. Those others are subsequently arrested who then cite further more, and so on. Chain prosecutions in Britain during the 1950s resulted in as many as twenty arrests at one time.

9 Jeffery-Poulter, *Peers, Queers*, 15–16.

10 Spencer, *Homosexuality*, 359–60.

11 Spencer, *Homosexuality*, 288; Weeks, *Coming Out*, 161.

12 Peter Wildeblood, *Against the Law* (London: Weidenfeld and Nicolson, 1955) quoted in Jeffery-Poulter, *Peers, Queers*,17.

13 Jeffery-Poulter, *Peers, Queers*, 18. Hence, a Christian-based rightist counter-movement is not nearly as strong in the United Kingdom as it is in the United States.

14 Jivani, *It's Not Unusual*, 129–33.

15 Jeffery-Poulter, *Peers, Queers*, 24.

16 Wildeblood quoted in ibid., 27.

17 Ibid., 19–21.

18 While the coupling of prostitution and homosexuality may seem odd, it stems from a Victorian notion that both of these issues represented a form of moral vice that threatened to undermine the empire.

19 *Report of the Committee on Homosexual Offenses and Prostitution (The Wolfenden Report)*. Sir John Wolfenden, Chairman (New York: Stein and Day, 1963), 48.

20 Wolfenden, 54–5.

21 Jeffery-Poulter, *Peers, Queers*, 33–7.

22 Julian Huxley to A. E. Dyson, 17 February 1958. Archive of Gay Organiza-

tions and Activists. British Library of Political and Economic Science (London School of Economics).

23 Jeffery-Poulter, *Peers, Queers*, 40.

24 Ibid., 46.

25 Weeks, *Coming Out*, 170.

26 Jeffery-Poulter, *Peers, Queers*, 49–50.

27 Of the 99 votes that favored reform, 22 were registered by Conservatives, and one of these was cast by Margaret Thatcher.

28 Jeffery-Poulter, *Peers, Queers*, 53.

29 Jivani, *It's Not Unusual*, 138.

30 Ibid., 139–40.

31 Ibid., 140.

32 Cultural opportunities such as the movement subculture and more liberal attitudes of the 1960s are discussed in further detail in chapter 5.

33 Jivani, *It's Not Unusual*, 141.

34 Jeffery-Poulter, *Peers, Queers*, 63.

35 Weeks, *Coming Out*, 178.

36 Bogarde quoted in Jivani, *It's Not Unusual*, 144.

37 Weeks, *Coming Out*, 178.

38 Jeffery-Poulter, *Peers, Queers*, 63–4.

39 Ibid.

40 Weeks, *Coming Out*, 181.

41 Ibid., 175.

42 Ibid., 176.

43 Jeffery-Poulter, *Peers, Queers*, 70.

44 Three ways exist to introduce a Private Member Bill in the House of Commons. First, an MP can win a place in the yearly ballot. Second, the bill can be introduced under the Ten-Minute Rule which allows for two ten-minute speeches – one by the sponsor and one by the opposition – and an immediate vote. Third, the bill can be suggested after the end of the main debate on a Friday, and the bill can only be considered if it received an unopposed Second Reading. This reading can be prevented as easily as one MP shouting "Object!" Jeffery-Poulter, *Peers, Queers*, 71.

45 Ibid., 71–2.

46 Ibid., 65, 73.

47 Ibid., 73.

48 Ibid., 74–8.

49 Abse originally wanted to decriminalize homosexuality in the Merchant Navy. However, he agreed to hear amendments that would maintain its misdemeanor status. In so doing, he was able to get the bill to the next stage without a vote by exploiting a technicality of parliamentary procedure. Jeffery-Poulter, *Peers, Queers*, 79.

50 Ibid., 80.

51 Weeks, *Coming Out*, 176.

52 Ibid.; Jeffery-Poulter, *Peers, Queers*, 82–4.

53 Ibid., 87.

54 Weeks, *Coming Out*, 177–9.

55 Ibid., 181.

56 Lord Arran, April 9, 1968 quoted in Jeffery-Poulter, *Peers, Queers*, 95
57 Ibid., 93.
58 Quoted in Arno Karlen, *Sexuality and Homosexuality* (London, 1971), 539 and subsequently quoted in Weeks, *Coming Out*, 182.
59 Ibid., 189.
60 Ibid. Jeffery-Poulter, *Peers, Queers*, 100.
61 Weeks, *Coming Out*, 186.
62 "Principles of the Gay Liberation Front," flyer published by South London Gay Liberation Front. Archive of Gay Organizations and Activists (British Library of Political and Economic Science. London School of Economics).
63 "Gay Liberation Supports Law Reform," flyer published by South London Gay Liberation Front. Archive of Gay Organizations and Activists (British Library of Political and Economic Science. London School of Economics).
64 Weeks, *Coming Out*, 191.
65 Jivani, *It's Not Unusual*, 162.
66 "Gay Liberation Front Supports Law Reform," South London Gay Liberation Front, Archive of Gay Organizations and Activists (British Library of Political and Economic Science. London School of Economics).
67 Jivani, *It's Not Unusual*, 169; Weeks, *Coming Out*, 200–1.
68 Ibid., 201–2.
69 Ibid., 205.
70 Jivani, *It's Not Unusual*, 170.
71 Jeffery-Poulter, *Peers, Queers*, 107.
72 Weeks, *Coming Out*, 221–2.
73 Ibid., 210.
74 The 1967 Sexual Offences Act only applied to England and Wales. In 1979, three Scottish gay rights activists challenged the illegality of homosexuality in Scotland at the European Court of Human Rights. Since the court only accepts cases on behalf of one individual, Derek Ogg, a gay lawyer from Edinburgh, submitted the case. Once the case passed through the preliminary stages, the British government decided to concede to reform rather than encounter a long and expensive court battle. The reform, which mirrored the 1967 Act, came as an amendment to the Criminal Justice Bill of 1979. Jeffery-Poulter, *Peers, Queers*, 145–7, Jivani, *It's Not Unusual*, 177. See chapter 4 for more detail regarding this case.

The situation in Northern Ireland was more complex due to the continuous fighting between Protestants and Catholics and the suspension of the Ulster Parliament. In 1976, the Northern Ireland Gay Rights Association (NIGRA) brought a case before the European Court of Human Rights submitted by Jeff Dudgeon claiming that the illegality of homosexuality contradicted Articles Eight and Fourteen of the European Convention on Human Rights. By February of 1979 various reforms to legalize homosexuality along the lines of the 1967 Act had been shelved to maintain government stability. The Callaghan government still fell on 3 May 1979 after a general election brought Margaret Thatcher to power. Thatcher's government informed the European Human Rights Commission that it could not legalize homosexuality due to the controversial nature of the issue as well as the peculiarities of direct rule of Ulster. By April 1980, Dudgeon had won his case with the Commission, but Parliament refused to act until the ruling of the European Court was given. On 23 April 1981, the Court, with twenty-one judges (as opposed to the usual seven), decided to hear the case. On 22 October of that year, Dudgeon won by a vote of fifteen to four. Ulster Secretary James Prior introduced an amendment to the Criminal Justice Bill which extended the 1967 reform to Ulster. The bill passed by a free vote on 25 October 1981 with a majority vote of 168 to 21. Jeffery-Poulter, *Peers, Queers*, 147–54.

75 Jeffery-Poulter, *Peers, Queers*, 113; Jivani, *It's Not Unusual*, 177.
76 Ibid., 179.
77 Weeks, *Coming Out*, 217; Rayside, *On the Fringe*, 60–7.
78 Ibid., 215–16.
79 Jivani, *It's Not Unusual*, 174.
80 Ibid.
81 Ibid., 172.
82 Radical drag differs from conventional drag in that an individual who dresses in the former makes no pretense to disguise his biological sex.
83 Ibid., 175. Punk music of the late 1970s also became a forum for gay visibility. Punk, which was at its core anti-establishment, likened homosexuality to the ultimate means of sexual rebellion. Tim Robinson, the first openly gay male rock star, had been a member of GLF and his song lyrics overflowed with overtly gay themes such as "Glad to be Gay." Jivani, *It's Not Unusual*, 180–1.
84 Ibid., 181–2.
85 Ibid., 183.
86 Ibid., 181.
87 Jeffrey Weeks, *Against Nature: Essays on History, Sexuality, and Identity* (London: Rivers Oram Press, 1991), 106.
88 Adam, *Rise of the Gay and Lesbian Movement*, 124.
89 Jivani, *It's Not Unusual*, 199.
90 Weeks, *Against Nature*, 97.
91 Spencer, *Homosexuality*, 377.
92 Jeffery-Poulter, *Peers, Queers*, 157.
93 Jivani, *It's Not Unusual*, 185
94 Weeks, *Against Nature*, 118.
95 Ken Plummer, "The Lesbian and Gay Movement in Britain: Schisms, Solidarities, and Social Worlds" in *The Global Emergence of Gay and Lesbian Politics*, eds. Barry D. Adam, Jan Willem Duyvendak, and Andre Krouwel (Philadelphia: Temple University Press, 1999), 133–4, 142–3.
96 Jivani, *It's Not Unusual*, 190.
97 Jeffery-Poulter, *Peers, Queers*, 179.
98 Jivani, *It's Not Unusual*, 186.
99 Jeffery-Poulter, *Peers, Queers*, 186; Weeks, *Against Nature*, 120.
100 Jeffery-Poulter, *Peers, Queers*, 186–9.
101 Ibid., 190. Jivani, *It's Not Unusual*, 186.
102 Ibid., 187.
103 Ibid., 188–9; Jeffery-Poulter, *Peers, Queers*, 194–8.
104 Weeks, *Against Nature*, 121.

105 Plummer, "Lesbian and Gay Movement," 143.
106 Jivani, *It's Not Unusual*, 190–2.
107 Jeffery-Poulter, *Peers, Queers*, 174.
108 Weeks, *Against Nature*, 137.
109 Ibid., 101.
110 Thatcher quoted in Jivani, *It's Not Unusual*, 195.
111 Jeffery-Poulter, *Peers, Queers*, 211.
112 Ibid., 203.
113 Ibid., 162, 203.
114 David M. Rayside, "Homophobia, Class and Party in England", *Canadian Journal of Political Science* 25 (March 1992): 134.   .
115 Jeffery-Poulter, *Peers, Queers*, 204.
116 Rayside, "Homophobia," 124; Stychin, *Law's Desire*, 40; Weeks, *Against Nature*, 138–9.
117 Section 28 quoted in Stychin, *Law's Desire*, 38–9.
118 Jeffery-Poulter, *Peers, Queers*, 229, 232.
119 Jivani, *It's Not Unusual*, 196.
120 Jeffery-Poulter, *Peers, Queers*, 223.
121 Ibid., 227.
122 Jivani, *It's Not Unusual*, 197.
123 Jeffery-Poulter, *Peers, Queers*, 233.
124 Plummer, "Lesbian and Gay Movement," 143–4; Rayside, "Homophobia,"19–20, 23, 30.
125 Ibid., 234.
126 At a Labour Party Conference in October 1988, party officials voted an overwhelming majority of 5,091,000 to 997,000 to repeal Section 28 through the sponsor of a Private Member's Bill, support anyone victimized by Section 28, and urge local councils to continue support for gay and lesbian-oriented programs. Peter Tatchel, "Labour Landslide Against Section 28," *Capital Gay*, 14 October 1988.
127 Jeffery-Poulter, *Peers, Queers*, 245–6, 251, 256. Jivani, *It's Not Unusual*, 198.
128 Edward Guthman, "The British are Coming," *The Advocate*, 3 March 1998, 51–3.
129 Plummer, "Lesbian and Gay Movement," 149.
130 Barry D. Adam, Jan Willem Duyvendak, and Andre Krouwel, "Gay and Lesbian Movements beyond Borders? National Imprints of a Worldwide Movement" in *The Global Emergence of Gay and Lesbian Politics*, eds. Barry D. Adam, Jan Willem Duyvendak, and Andre Krouwel (Philadelphia: Temple University Press, 1999), 366–7.
131 Jivani, *It's Not Unusual*, 206. Rayside, "Homophobia," 45–75.
132 Samuel Beer, "The Roots of New Labour," *The Economist*, 7–13 February 1998, 25.
133 Angela Mason and Mark Watson, "Equality 2000," produced by the Stonewall Lobby Group Ltd., June 1997; David Smith, "Government Promises Equal Age of Consent within Two Years," *Gay Times*, November 1997, 39.
134 "Labour Ditching Gay Rights, Say OutRage!," *Thud*, 5 July 1996.

135 1992 Labour Manifesto quoted by Vicky Powell, "No Promises in Labour's Manifesto," *Gay Times*, August 1996, page number not listed.
136 *The Road to the Manifesto* quoted in ibid.
137 Rayside, "Homophobia," 134.
138 The Homosexual Law Reform Society (HLRS) appears in the model as both a pre-existing organization and an interest group spawned by the movement. The latter classification is somewhat misleading since HLRS was more a homophile and not a gay and lesbian movement organization. Nevertheless, I have included it as an interest group to emphasize its interaction with the political institutions, i.e., Parliament. As the model notes, the most important outcome, the 1967 Sexual Offences Act, influenced the movement organizations: it destroyed HLRS while spurring the development of the Committee (later Campaign) for Homosexual Equality (CHE) and the Gay Liberation Front (GLF).
139 The most notorious outcome is the passage of Section 28 of the 1988 Local Government Bill. While AIDS spurred the Terrence Higgins Trust and Body Positive, the effect of Section 28 was, as the model depicts, to cycle back and foster the development of ACT UP, OutRage!, and Stonewall. More importantly, the passage of Section 28 finalized the development of collective identity and cognitive liberation. We could therefore add an arrow from "outcomes" to the cognitive liberation section detailed as "direct action and queer identity" to depict how outcomes have affected this psychological transformation.

4 WHERE AND HOW IT COMES TO PASS: INTEREST GROUP INTERACTION
WITH POLITICAL INSTITUTIONS

1 Simon Edge, "Proudly, Openly, Equally Gay," *New Statesman*, 18 July 1997, 22.
2 As of December of 1999, thirty-two states and the District of Columbia have either repealed their anti-sodomy law or such legislation has been deemed unconstitutional or unenforceable by the state court system. Five states (Arkansas, Kansas, Missouri, Oklahoma, and Texas) ban same-sex oral and anal intercourse. Thirteen states (Alabama, Arizona, Florida, Idaho, Louisiana, Massachusetts, Michigan, Minnesota, Mississippi, North Carolina, South Carolina, Utah, and Virginia) ban anal and oral intercourse between same-sex and opposite-sex partners. Dan Hawes, *1999 Capital Gains and Losses: A State by State Review of Gay, Lesbian, Bisexual, Transgender, and HIV/AIDS-Related Legislation in 1999* (Washington, DC: National Gay and Lesbian Task Force, 1999), 10, 151.
3 Herbert P. Kitschelt, "Political Opportunity Structures and Political Protest: Anti-Nuclear Movements in Four Democracies," *American Society and Politics*, eds. Theda Skocpol and John L. Campbell (New York: McGraw-Hill, Inc, 1995), 225; David Rayside, *On the Fringe* (Ithaca: Cornell University Press, 1998), 11–15.
4 Kitschelt, "Political Opportunity," 225–6.
5 Frank R. Baumgartner and Bryan D. Jones, *Agendas and Instability in American Politics* (Chicago: University of Chicago Press, 1993), 5–8.

6 Ibid., 16.
7 The redefinition of AIDS from a gay disease to sexually transmitted disease that could be contracted by anyone is not a falsehood. In global terms, more heterosexuals have AIDS than homosexuals. De-gaying also had negative consequences which are laid out in chapter 2.
8 Vaid, *Virtual Equality*, 88–90.
9 While the United States is the only separation-of-powers system in the world, no typical parliamentary system exists. Rather, parliamentarist governments fall into two categories: either the single-member-district plurality two-party system of Westminster or the proportional representational multiparty system more common of Germany or Japan. Since my thesis is limited to a comparison of the United States and the United Kingdom, I will not be discussing this second category; therefore, when I use the term "parliament," I will be referring to the Westminster model.
10 R. Kent Weaver and Bert A. Rockman, "Assessing the Effects of Institutions" in *Do Institutions Matter?*, eds. R. Kent Weaver and Bert A. Rockman (Washington, DC: The Brookings Institution, 1993), 12.
11 Ibid.
12 Ibid., 14–15.
13 Leon Epstein, *Political Parties in Western Democracy* (New Brunswick, NJ: Transaction Publishers, 1993), 347.
14 Baumgartner and Jones, *Agendas*, 241.
15 Samuel P. Huntington, *Political Order in Changing Societies* (New Haven: Yale University Press, 1968), 115.
16 Ibid., 96–108.
17 Anthony H. Birch, *The British System of Government* (New York: Routledge, 1993), 24–7.
18 Ibid., 27–31.
19 Ibid., 112. Weaver and Rockman, "Assessing the Effect of Institutions," 14.
20 Birch, *British System of Government*, 112, 183.
21 David Rayside, *On the Fringe: Gays and Lesbians in Politics* (Ithaca: Cornell University Press, 1998), 10.
22 Birch, *British System of Government*, 114.
23 Epstein, *Political Parties*, 341.
24 Birch, *British System of Government*, 64.
25 Epstein, *Political Parties*, 321–2.
26 Ibid., 31–3.
27 Ibid., 278.
28 Birch, *British System of Government*, 66.
29 Epstein, *Political Parties*, 320–5; Weaver and Rockman, "Assessing the Effects of Institutions," 15.
30 Epstein, *Political Parties*, 321.
31 Ibid., 322.
32 Ibid., 282.
33 Jeffery-Poulter, *Peers, Queers*, 213.
34 Weaver and Rockman, "Assessing the Effects of Institutions," 16.
35 Baumgartner and Jones, *Agendas*, 217.
36 Hawes, *Capital Gains and Losses*, 4.

37 In his analysis of public opinion theory, John Dorris suggests that issues are either unimodal or bimodal. Unimodal issues exhibit mild disagreement with a wide expanse for potential compromise. Bimodal issues are often hotly debated and dichotomous offering no room for a middle position. Historically, gay and lesbian rights has been perceived as a bimodal issue. John Dorris, "Antidiscrimination Laws in Local Government: A Public Policy Analysis of Municipal Lesbian and Gay Public Employment Protection" in *Gays and Lesbians in the Democratic Process: Public Policy, Public Opinion, and Political Representation*, eds. Ellen D. B. Riggle and Barry Tadlock (New York: Columbia University Press, 1999), 40–1.

38 Marieka Klawitter and Brian Hammer, "Spatial and Temporal Diffusion of Local Antidiscrimination Policies for Sexual Orientation" in *Gays and Lesbians in the Democratic Process: Public Policy, Public Opinion, and Political Representation*, eds. Ellen D. B. Riggle and Barry Tadlock (New York: Columbia University Press, 1999), 25–35.

39 Randy Shilts, *And the Band Played On: Politics, People, and the AIDS Epidemic* (New York: Penguin Books USA, 1988), 15, 45. Klawitter and Hammer note that local antidiscrimination policies for sexual orientation cluster along the east coast, the west coast, and urban centers of the midwest. Many to most jurisdictions of the midwest and portions of the south have no such antidiscrimination laws; these are also the areas that, historically speaking, high populations of gays and lesbians do not concentrate, 30–1.

40 Birch, *British System of Government*, 181.

41 Sir William Blackstone, *Commentaries on the Laws of England*, ed. Thomas M. Cooley (Chicago: Callaghan, 1876), I, 90 quoted in Huntington, *Political Order*, 112.

42 Robert Wintemute, *Sexual Orientation and Human Rights: The United States Constitution, the European Convention, and the Canadian Charter* (New York and Oxford: Clarendon Press, 1995), 4.

43 Jeffery-Poulter, *Peers, Queers*, 133.

44 Eur. T.S. 5, 213 UNTS 221. Signed on 4 November 1950; entered into force 3 September 1953. Quoted in Wintemute, *Sexual Orientation*, 261.

45 Ibid., 262.

46 Ibid., 93–5.

47 "The Tide of History and the MoD," *The Times*, 28 September 1999, *Times Law Supplement*, 10–11.

48 Michael Evans, "MoD Sackings Halted After Gays Win Forces Case," *The Times*, 28 September 1999, 8.

49 "The Tide of History and the MoD," *The Times*, 28 September 1999, *Times Law Supplement*, 10; Eric Schmitt, "How Is This Strategy Working? Don't Ask." *The New York Times*, 19 December 1999, IV, 1.

50 European Court of Human Rights ruling quoted in Evans, "European Court," 8.

51 Evans, "European Court," 8.

52 Sarah Lyall, "British, Under European Ruling, End Ban on Openly Gay Soldiers," *The New York Times*, 13 January 2000, A1.

53 "The Tide of History and the MoD," *The Times*, 28 September 1999, *Times Law Supplement*, 10.

54 T. R. Reid, "Britain Ends Its Curbs on Gays in Military," *The Washington Post*, 13 January 2000, A13.
55 Schmitt, "How is this Strategy Working?" 1.
56 Vaid, *Virtual Equality*, 131–2.
57 Ibid., 133.
58 Wintemute, *Sexual Orientation*, 1–2.
59 Ibid., 21.
60 Georgia Code Ann. 16–6–2 (1984) quoted in "The Right to Intimate Sexual Choice," *American Constitutional Interpretation*, eds. Walter F. Murphy, James E. Flemming, and Sotirios A. Barber (Westbury, NY: The Foundation Press, 1995), 1323.
61 Ibid.; Wintemute, *Sexual Orientation*, 31.
62 Ibid.
63 Wintemute suggests that if the Court adhered to the precedents regarding the right of privacy established by *Roe v. Wade, Griswold v. Connecticut,* and *Loving v. Virginia,* it could not have decided *Bowers v. Hardwick* in the manner that it did. In *Griswold,* the Court struck down laws that banned the use of contraceptives by married persons. In *Roe,* the Court struck down laws prohibiting obtaining abortions. In *Loving,* the Court struck down laws banning mixed-race marriage. Wintemute contends that the *Hardwick* decision fails to follow the pattern established by these previous cases: "Although the *Hardwick* majority did not expressly state any general principle defining the right of privacy, their implicit principle might be described as including 'decisions relating to family, opposite-sex marriage or procreation that have traditionally been recognized by the majority as fundamental'. Such a principle cannot rely on any constitutional text supporting the particular categories selected. Nor could the principle explain the decisions in *Roe, Griswold,* and *Loving,* which set aside laws reflecting long-standing tradition condemning abortion, contraception, and mixed-race opposite-sex marriage." Wintemute, *Sexual Orientation*, 43.
64 Ibid., 46–7.
65 "Hawaii Court Lets Gay Marriage Ban Stand," *The New York Times*, 10 December 1999, A28.
66 Carey Goldberg, "Vermont High Court Backs Rights of Same-Sex Couple," *The New York Times*, 21 December 1999, 1, A28; Carey Goldberg, "Vermont's House Backs Wide Rights for Gay Couples," *The New York Times*, 17 March 2000, 1, A16; Mubarak Dahir, "State of the Unions," *The Advocate*, 23 May 2000, 57–60.
67 Some gay and lesbian activists do not seek the right to marry per se, or at least a union referred to as marriage, claiming that the term has been tainted by right-wing conservatism; rather, the goal, according to this opinion should be the legal rights and privileges given by marriage, but referred to as something else, i.e., a civil union.
68 Poll cited in Carey Goldberg, "Forced Into Action on Gay Marriage, Vermont Finds Itself Deeply Split," *The New York Times*, 3 February 2000, A16.
69 Ibid.
70 Weaver and Rockman, "Assessing the Effects of Institutions," 16–19.

71 Baumgartner and Jones, *Agendas*, 233.
72 Rayside, *On the Fringe*, 70–4.
73 Ibid., 70.

5 ASKING THE UNASKED QUESTION: GRAPPLING WITH THE CULTURE
VARIABLE

1 Margaret Carlson, "McCain and his Gaydar," *Time*, 31 January 2000, 43.
2 Verta Taylor and Nancy Whittier, "Analytical Approaches to Social Movement Culture: The Culture of the Women's Movement" in *Social Movements
   and Culture*, eds. Hank Johnston and Bert Klandermans (Minneapolis:
   University of Minnesota Press, 1995), 180.
3 Hank Johnston and Bert Klandermans, "The Cultural Analysis of Social
   Movements" in *Social Movements and Culture*, eds. Hank Johnston and Bert
   Klandermans (Minneapolis: University of Minnesota Press, 1995), 21.
4 Ronald Inglehart, *Culture Shift in Advanced Industrial Society* (Princeton:
   Princeton University Press, 1990) 19.
5 Verta Taylor and Nancy Whittier, "Analytical Approaches," 172.
6 Ken Plummer's notion of a social movement consisting of many overlapping
   social worlds is especially helpful here. The political world is only one part of
   the movement which is also composed of social scenes such as bars, gay and
   lesbian press and mass media, self-help organizations, an academic wing in
   the form of gay and lesbian studies and queer theory, and the growing
   community on the internet. Ken Plummer, "The Lesbian and Gay Movement in Britain: Schisms, Solidarities, and Social Worlds" in *The Global
   Emergence of Gay and Lesbian Politics: National Imprints of a Worldwide Movement*, eds. Barry D. Adam, Jan Willem Duyvendak, and Andre Krouwel
   (Philadelphia: Temple University Press, 1999), 137–41.
7 Taylor and Whittier, "Analytical Approaches," 181.
8 For example, a lesbian or gay man may not be interested in the gays in the
   military agenda, but may want to be able to have a civilly recognized union
   with his or her partner.
9 Ann Swindler, "Cultural Power and Social Movements" in *Social Movements
   and Culture*, eds. Hank Johnston and Bert Klandermans (Minneapolis:
   University of Minnesota Press, 1995), 30.
10 Michel Foucault, *The History of Sexuality: An Introduction: Volume I* (New
    York, Vintage Books, 1990), 43–4.
11 Steven Epstein, "Gay and Lesbian Movements in the United States:
    Dilemmas of Identity, Diversity, and Political Strategy" in *The Global
    Emergence of Gay and Lesbian Politics: National Imprints of a Worldwide
    Movement*, eds. Barry D. Adam, Jan Willem Duyvendak, and Andre
    Krouwel (Philadelphia: Temple University Press, 1999), 61.
12 Taylor and Whittier, "Analytical Approaches," 181.
13 Verta Taylor, "Gender and Social Movements: Gender Processes in Women's
    Self-Help Movements," *Gender and Society* 13:1 (February 1999), 14.
14 Weaver and Rockman, "Assessing the Effects of Institutions," 11.
15 Ann Swindler, "Cultural Power," 39.
16 Hank Johnston and Bert Klandermans, "Cultural Analysis," 5.

17 Taylor and Whittier, "Analytical Approaches," 182.

18 Ken Plummer, "Lesbian and Gay Movement," 137–8.

19 Steven Epstein notes that gay and lesbian rights-based strategies in the United States tend to be quasi-ethnic oriented given the master frames established by the civil rights movement of the 1950s and 1960s. Since the American political structure has historically favored this strategy, gay organizations have often framed the argument that gays and lesbians are born that way, and that homosexuality is not a choice; hence, protection of rights should be accorded to gays as they are any other minority group. This perspective subsumes ethnic, racial, gender, and ideological differences under a unitary gay identity thereby potentially silencing dissenting voices.

20 Johnston and Klandermans, "Cultural Analysis," 18; Swindler, "Cultural Power," 27–31, 38–9; Taylor and Whittier, "Analytical Approaches," 186.

21 The notion of culture as power has been investigated extensively by Michel Foucault, and his insights are discussed in the next section.

22 John B. Dorris, "Antidiscrimination Laws in Local Government: A Public Policy Analysis of Municipal Lesbian and Gay Public Employment Protection" in *Gays and Lesbians in the Democratic Process: Public Policy, Public Opinion, and Political Representation*. eds. Ellen D. B. Riggle and Barry L. Tadlock (New York: Columbia University Press, 1999), 40–6.

23 McAdam, "Culture and Social Movements," 475–7.

24 Ibid., 476.

25 Vaid, *Virtual Equality*, 67 and Shilts, *The Bankd Played On*, 17.

26 McAdam, "Culture and Social Movements," 476–7 and Tarrow, *Power in Movement*, 153–69.

27 Taylor and Whittier, "Analytical Approaches," 168. Ann Swindler posits that frames are not so much the appropriation by some movement organizations of others' techniques, but rather the similar response is structured by the institution itself. In other words, the tactic was formed by the institution. Hence, the non-violence strategy of Martin Luther King Jr., for example, was utilized by American homophiles because these two movements were responding to the same cultural restraints and opportunities as rights-based movements. Swindler, "Cultural Power," 39.

28 Epstein, "Gay and Lesbian Movements," 37.

29 Tarrow, *Power in Movement*, 9–10.

30 Taylor and Whittier, "Analytical Approaches," 168–71.

31 Epstein, "Gay and Lesbian Movements," 40.

32 Ibid., 74.

33 Chandler Burr, "Tony Blair Pushes Gay Rights in Britain," *US News and World Report* (June 15, 1998): 36. A British poll conducted in November 1997 found that 64 percent of Britons support gays in the military, 76 percent are in favor of gay teachers, and 71 percent support equal rights regarding pensions, inheritance, and housing. Yet, 57 percent believe that homosexuality should not be taught as a valid lifestyle comparable to straight relationships. Similarly, a 1996 poll conducted in the United States found that 80 percent of Americans support equal rights for housing and job opportunity while 56 percent contend that homosexuality is always wrong.

34 Barry D. Adam, Jan Willem Duyvendak, and Andre Krouwel, "Gay and

Lesbian Movements beyond Borders?" *The Global Emergence of Gay and Lesbian Politics* (Philadelphia: Temple University Press, 1999), 349.

35 Leon D. Epstein, *Political Parties in Western Democracies* (New Brunswick: Transaction, Inc., 1967), 88.

36 G. William Domhoff, "Who Rules America?" *American Society and Politics*, eds. Theda Skocpol and John L. Campbell (New York: McGraw-Hill, Inc., 1995), 45.

37 Adam, Duyvendak, and Krouwel note that countries with fairly heterogeneous and immigrant-based populations have a historical tendency to tolerate claims made by minority groups (352–3). To exploit this tendency, gays and lesbians must present themselves in a way which recalls characteristics of an immigrant minority, i.e., race and ethnicity as unchangeable traits. Sexual orientation must be viewed in a similar light to achieve any kind of agenda access.

38 Ralph R. Smith and Russell R. Windes, "Identity in Political Context: Lesbian/Gay Representation in the Public Sphere," *Journal of Homosexuality*. 37 (2), 1999, 27–9.

39 David Rayside, *On the Fringe* (Ithaca: Cornell University Press, 1998), 24.

40 Ibid., 50.

41 Ibid., 11.

42 "Equality 2000." A pamphlet produced by Stonewall, 14.

43 David John Frank and Elizabeth H. McEneaney, "The Individualization of Society and the Liberalization of State Policies on Same-Sex Sexual Relations, 1984–1995." *Social Forces*, March 1999, 77 (3), 914.

44 Ibid., 916–17.

45 Ibid., 915–16.

46 Theodore Von Laue, *The World Revolution of Westernization* (New York: Oxford University Press, 1987), 5.

47 William A. Gamson, "Constructing Social Protest," in *Social Movements and Culture*, eds. Hank Johnston and Bert Klandermans (Minneapolis: University of Minnesota Press, 1995), 89–104.

48 McAdam, "Culture and Social Movements," 479.

49 John Knoebel, "Somewhere in the Right Direction: Testimony of My Experience in a Gay Male Living Collective" in *Out of the Closets*, eds. Karla Jay and Allen Young (New York: New York University Press, 1992), 293–300.

50 Taylor and Whittier, "Analytical Approaches," 165.

51 Ibid., 176.

52 Ibid., 177–8.

53 Epstein, "Gay and Lesbian Movements," 63.

54 *The Gay Almanac*, compiled by the National Museum and Archive of Lesbian and Gay History (New York: Berkeley Books, 1996), 81–97.

55 McAdam, "Culture and Social Movments," 480.

56 Kriesi, Koopmans, Duyvendak, and Giugni, *New Social Movements*, 172.

57 McAdam, "Culture and Social Movements," 477.

58 Ibid., 481–3.

59 Ibid., 483.

60　Alexis de Tocqueville, *Democracy in America: Volume I* (New York: Vintage Books, 1990), 32.
61　Edmund S. Morgan, *The Puritan Dilemma* (New York: HarperCollins Publishers, 1958), 93.
62　Ibid., 19.
63　*Constitution*, art. II, sec. 4.
64　De Tocqueville, *Democracy, Volume I*, 53–4.
65　Alexis de Tocqueville, *Democracy in America: Volume II* (New York: Vintage Books, 1990), 107.
66　Morgan, *The Puritan Dilemma*, 46.
67　De Tocqueville, *Democracy, Volume I*, 300–3.
68　De Tocqueville, *Democracy, Volume II*, 6.
69　Inglehart separated the United Kingdom into two entities. Great Britain referred to England, Wales, and Scotland, and Northern Ireland was considered a separate entity since it bore more resemblance to the Republic of Ireland than to any other regions of the United Kingdom.
70　Inglehart, *Culture Shift*, 190.
71　Ibid., 191.
72　Ibid., 190–1.
73　Ibid., 194.
74　This conclusion is further confirmed by studies conducted by Hanspeter Kriesi, Ruud Koopmans, Jan Willem Duyvendak, and Marco G. Giugni in their study, "Gay Subcultures between Movement and Market" in *New Social Movements in Western Europe*.
75　*The Gay Almanac*, 105.
76　Kinsey quoted in D'Emilio, *Sexual Politics*, 7.
77　Epstein, "Gay and Lesbian Movements," 46.
78　*Bowers v. Hardwick*, 478, US 186 (1986), Page [478 US 196].
79　Ibid., Page [478 US 211].
80　Birch, *British System of Government*, 7.
81　Rayside, *On the Fringe*, 35.
82　Lynda Need, "Forms of Deviancy: The Prostitute," *Myths of Sexuality* (New York: Basil Blackwell, 1988), 91–107 and Peter Stallybrass and Allon White, "The City: the Sewer, the Gaze, and the Contaminating Touch" in *The Politics and Poetics of Transgression* (Ithaca: Cornell University Press, 1986), 125–48.
83　Mary Poovey, *Uneven Developments: The Ideological Work of Gender in Mid-Victorian England* (Chicago: University of Chicago Press, 1988), 11.
84　John Ruskin, "Of Queen's Gardens," *Sesame and Lilies* (No publisher information available, 1864), 100–13.
85　Poovey, *Uneven Developments*, 8.
86　Sarah Lewis, *Woman's Mission* (New York: Wiley and Putnam, 1839), 15, 25–7.
87　Poovey, *Uneven Developments*, 8–9.
88　Richard Davenport-Hines, *Sex, Death and Punishment* (London: William Collins Sons and Co., 1990), 124.
89　Jeffery-Poulter, *Peers, Queers*, 43.

90 Lords, *Hansard*, 18 December 1986, 310 quoted in Stychin, *Law's Desire*, 40.
91 Ibid., 329, per Baroness Faithful quoted in Stychin, *Law's Desire*, 41.
92 Ibid., 313 quoted in Stychin, *Law's Desire*, 40.
93 Rayside, *On the Fringe*, 24.
94 Ibid., 24.
95 Davenport-Hines, *Sex, Death and Punishment*, 126.
96 See chapter 3.
97 Jeffery-Poulter, *Peers, Queers*, 43.
98 Davenport-Hines, *Sex, Death and Punishment*, 111–15; Rayside, *On the Fringe*, 26.
99 Jeffrey Weeks, *Sex, Politics, and Society*, chap. 2 and 109, quoted in Rayside, *On the Fringe*, 130.
100 Rayside, "Homophobia," 133.
101 Stuart Weir, *New Statesman*, 8 January 1988, 3; quoted in Rayside, "Homophobia," 125.
102 Rayside, *On the Fringe*, 26–32.
103 Ibid., 43.
104 A 1993 *US News and World Report* poll found that 46 percent of Americans believe that homosexuality is chosen and only 32 percent believe it is innate and fixed. *The Gay Almanac*, 105.

CONCLUSION

1 Lord Arran quoted in Jeffery-Poulter, *Peers, Queers*, 89.
2 Tony Blair, Speech delivered in South Africa in October 1996, quoted in "Gay and Lesbian Rights." Document from the Labour Party Headquarters in London.
3 Stephen A. Tyler, "Post-Modern Ethnography: From Document of the Occult to Occult Document" in *Writing Culture: The Poetics and Politics of Ethnography*, eds. James Clifford and George E. Marcus (Berkeley: University of California Press, 1986), 131.
4 David Smith, "Stonewall Confident of Commons Age of Consent Debate at Eastertime," *Gay Times*, January 1998, 45.
5 Rayside, *On the Fringe*, 313.

APPENDIX: A SURVEY OF SOCIAL MOVEMENT THEORIES

1 Emile Durkheim, *The Division of Labor in Society* (New York: The Free Press, 1984), 70.
2 Robert R. Alford and Roger Friedland, *Powers of Theory* (New York: Cambridge University Press, 1992), 42–4.
3 Doug McAdam, "The Classical Model of Social Movements Examined" in *Social Movements: Perspectives and Issues*, eds. Steven M. Buechler and F. Kurt Cylke, Jr. (Mountain View, California: Mayfield Publishing Company, 1997), 136.
4 Ibid., 41–4.

5 Theda Skocpol and John L. Campbell, "Perspectives on Social Movements and Collective Action" in *American Society and Politics*, eds. Theda Skocpol and John L. Campbell (New York: McGraw Hill, Inc., 1995), 284.

6 McAdam, "The Classical Model of Social Movements Examined," 136.

7 Hannah Arendt, *The Origins of Totalitarianism* (1951) 316–17, quoted in William Kornhouser, "The Politics of Mass Society" in *Social Movements: Perspectives and Issues* (Mountain View, California: Mayfield Publishing Company, 1997), 92.

8 McAdam, "The Classical Model of Social Movements Examined," 137.

9 Samuel P. Huntington, *Political Order in Changing Societies* (New Haven: Yale University Press, 1968), 41.

10 Ibid., 5.

11 McAdam, "The Classical Model of Social Movements Examined," 139.

12 Selznick, 1970, 264 quoted in McAdam, "The Classical Model of Social Movements Examined," 139.

13 Homoeroticism is a consistent though subtle theme in popular war novels including Remarque's *All Quiet on the Western Front* and Heller's *Catch-22*. This point should not be overdrawn; anti-homosexual oppression continued unabated throughout the war. After the war, the domestic anti-communism campaign fostered by Senator Joseph McCarthy, which also contained an anti-homosexual element, exacerbated existing prejudice by positing that homosexuals were an inherent national security risk.

14 Ibid., 49. More discussion on all of these points is contained in chapter 2.

15 More detailed discussion of the Mattachine Society and the Daughters of Bilitis can be found in chapter 2.

16 Ibid., 66.

17 Ibid., 104.

18 Philip Selznick, *The Organizational Weapon*, 1952, 293–4 quoted in Kornhauser, "The Politics of Mass Society," 93.

19 D'Emilio, *Sexual Politics*, 232.

20 McAdam, "The Classical Model of Social Movements Examined," 141.

21 D'Emilio, *Sexual Politics*, 235.

22 Mancur Olson, *The Logic of Collective Action* (Cambridge: Harvard University Press, 1965), 15.

23 Jon Elster, *Nuts and Bolts for the Social Sciences* (New York: Cambridge University Press, 1996), 126–7.

24 The existence and success of large collective action groups, despite their inherent economic irrationality, is, for Olson, primarily attributable to his "by-product" theory. This hypothesis maintains that large organizations become successful economic lobbyists not because this is their primary purpose, but rather as the result of performing some other noncollective function in addition to lobbying. This other function may be the publication of a journal or trade magazine. Since no by-product is foreseeable in our student protest example, the students must be deemed irrational.

25 Dennis Chong, "Collective Action and the Civil Rights Movement" in *American Society and Politics*, eds. Theda Skocpol and John L. Campbell (New York: McGraw-Hill, Inc., 1995), 340.

26 Ibid., 340.

27 Steven M. Buechler, "Beyond Resource Mobilization? Emerging Trends in Social Movement Theory," *The Sociological Quarterly* Volume 34 (2,) 1993, 218.

28 Jenkins, "Resource Mobilization Theory and the Study of Social Movements," 295.

29 Doug McAdam, "The Political Process Model," *Social Movements: Perspectives and Issues*, eds. Stephen M. Buechler and F. Kurt Cylke, Jr. (Mountain View, California: Mayfield Publishing Company, 1997), 173–4.

30 Turner and Killian, 251, quoted in John D. McCarthy and Mayer N. Zald, "Resource Mobilization and Social Movements: A Partial Theory," *American Journal of Sociology* 82 (6) 1977, 1215.

31 McCarthy and Zald "Resource Mobilization," 1236. and Jenkins, "Resource Mobilization and the Study of Social Movements," 291.

32 Buechler, "Beyond Resource Mobilization?" 218.

33 Jenkins, "Resource Mobilization and the Study of Social Movements," 290.

34 Buechler, "Beyond Resource Mobilization?" 218.

35 Theda Skocpol and John L. Campbell, "Perspectives on Social Movements," 285. Also see discussion of issue definition and policy monopolies in chapter 4.

36 Doug McAdam, "Tactical Innovation and the Pace of Black Insurgency between 1955 and 1970," *American Society and Politics*. eds. Theda Skocpol and John L. Campbell (New York: McGraw-Hill, Inc., 1995), 394.

37 Jenkins, "Resource Mobilization and the Study of Social Movements," 291.

38 Aldon Morris, "Black Southern Student Sit-In Movement: An Analysis of Internal Organization," *American Society and Politics*. eds. Theda Skocpol and John L. Campbell (New York: McGraw-Hill, Inc., 1995), 367.

39 Ibid., 370–4.

40 D'Emilio, *Sexual Politics*, 249.

41 John Gallagher and Chris Bull, *Perfect Enemies: The Religious Right, the Gay Movement, and the Politics of the 1990s* (New York: Crown Publishers, 1996), 68–9.

42 This latter question is the focus of both new social movement (NSM) theories and political opportunity structure (POS).

43 Buechler, "Beyond Resource Mobilization?" 222–5, 228.

44 Ibid., 227.

45 Ibid., 230–1. The role of culture is described in greater detail in chapter 5.

46 Alberto Melucci, "The New Social Movements: A Theoretical Approach," *Social Science Information* 19 (2), 1980, 200.

47 Karl Marx, "The German Ideology" in *The Marx–Engels Reader*, ed. Robert C. Tucker (New York: W. W. Norton and Company, 1978), 194–5.

48 Karl Marx and Friedrich Engels, "Manifesto of the Communist Party" in *The Marx-Engels Reader*. ed. Robert C. Tucker (New York: W. W. Norton and Company, 1978), 480–3.

49 Karl Marx, "Marx on the History of his own Ideas" in *The Marx-Engels Reader*. ed. Robert C. Tucker (New York: W. W. Norton and Company, 1978), 4.

50 Melucci, "New Social Movements," 199–200.

51 Hank Johnston, Enrique Larana, and Joseph Gusfield, "Identities, Grie-

vances, and New Social Movements" in *Social Movements: Perspectives and Issues*, eds. Steven M. Buechler and F. Kurt Cylke, Jr. (Mountain View, California: Mayfield Publishing Company, 1997), 280.

52 Ronald Inglehart, *Culture Shift in Advanced Industrial Society* (Princeton: Princeton University Press, 1990), 11.

53 Melucci, "New Social Movements," 218.

54 Steven M. Buechler, "New Social Movement Theories," 308.

55 Buechler, "New Social Movement Theories," 315.

56 Ibid., 302.

57 Ibid., 307.

58 J. Craig Jenkins and Bert Klandermans, 8.

59 See chapter 5 for a further discussion on the connection between subculture and movement maintenance.

60 Herbert P. Kitschelt, "Political Opportunity Structures and Political Protest: Anti-Nuclear Movements in Four Democracies" in *American Society and Politics*, eds. Theda Skocpol and John L. Campbell (New York: McGraw-Hill, Inc., 1995), 321 and Tarrow, *Power in Movement*, 85.

61 Kitschelt, "Political Opportunity," 321.

62 Ibid., 322.

63 Hanspeter Kriesi, Ruud Koopmans, Jan Willem Duyvendak, and Marco G. Giugni, *New Social Movements in Western Europe: A Comparative Analysis* (Minneapolis: University of Minnesota Press, 1995), XV.

64 Ibid.

65 Tarrow, *Power in Movement*, 10.

66 Ibid.

67 Ibid., 16.

68 Ibid., 17.

69 Ibid.

70 While POS and Classical theorists isolate industrialization as a cause of social insurgence, their understanding of this factor is critically different. The latter view alterations in the status quo as direct causes of movements whereas the former see an indirect connection: industrialization restructures the existing political power dynamic thereby enabling a disenfranchised group to have a political voice, but by no means ensuring that it will utilize this voice. See McAdam, "The Political Process Model," 176–7.

71 Tarrow, *Power in Movement*, 86–92.

72 Ibid., 97–9.

73 Patricia Williams, *The Alchemy of Race and Rights*, quoted in Avery Gordon, *Ghostly Matters: Haunting and the Sociological Imagination* (Minneapolis: University of Minnesota Press, 1997), 3.

Bibliography

A Gay Male Group. "Notes on Gay-Male Consciousness-Raising" in *Out of the Closets: Voices of Gay Liberation*, eds. Karla Jay and Allen Young. New York: New York University Press, 1992.

Abelove, Henry, Michele Aina Barale, and David M. Halperin, eds. *The Lesbian and Gay Studies Reader*. New York: Routledge, 1993.

Abramowitz, Alan I. "The United States: Political Culture Under Stress," in *The Civic Culture Revisited*, eds. Gabriel A. Almond and Sidney Verba. London: Sage Publications Inc., 1989.

Adam, Barry. *The Rise of the Gay and Lesbian Movement*. New York: Twayne Publishers, 1995.

Adam, Barry D., Jan Willem Duyvendak, and Andre Krouwel. "Gay and Lesbian Movements beyond Borders? National Imprints of a Worldwide Movement" in *The Global Emergence of Gay and Lesbian Politics: National Imprints of a Worldwide Movement*, eds. Barry D. Adam, Jan Willem Duyvendak, and Andre Krouwel. Philadelphia: Temple University Press, 1999.

Alford, Robert R. and Roger Friedland. *Powers of Theory*. New York: Cambridge University Press, 1985.

American Civil Liberties Union. "Homosexuality and Civil Liberties: A Policy Statement adopted by the Union's Board of Directors" (7 January 1957) in *We are Everywhere*, eds. Mark Blasius and Shane Phelan. New York: Routledge, Inc., 1997.

Anonymous. "Queers Read This: I Hate Straights." (1990) in *We Are Everywhere*, eds. Mark Blasius and Shane Phelan. New York: Routledge, 1997.

Baumgartner, Frank R. and Bryan D. Jones. *Agendas and Instability in American Politics*. Chicago: University of Chicago Press, 1993.

Becker, Elizabeth and Katherine Q. Seelye. "The Military Orders Spot Check of Bases on Gay Harassment." *The New York Times*, 14 December 1999, A1, A25.

Beer, Samuel H. *Britain Against Itself: The Political Contradictions of Collectivism*. New York: W. W. Norton and Company, 1990.

"The Roots of New Labour." *The Economist*, 7–13 February 1998, 23–5.

Bennett, Lisa. *Mixed Blessings: Organized Religion and Gay and Lesbian Americans in 1998*. Washington DC: Human Rights Campaign, 1999.

Bersani, Leo. *Homos*. Cambridge: Harvard University Press, 1995.

Berube, Allan. *Coming Out Under Fire: The History of Gay Men and Women in World War Two*. New York: The Free Press, 1990.

Birch, Anthony H. *The British System of Government*. New York: Routledge, 1967.

Blair, Anthony. Speech delivered in South Africa in October 1996. Received from the Labour Party Headquarters in London.

Blasius, Mark. *Gay and Lesbian Politics: Sexuality and the Emergence of a New Ethic*. Philadelphia: Temple University Press, 1994.

Bowers v. Hardwick, 478, US 186 (1986).

Buechler, Steven M. "Beyond Resource Mobilization? Emerging Trends in Social Movement Theory." *The Sociological Quarterly* 34 (2), 1993, 217–35.

"New Social Movement Theories." in *Social Movements: Perspectives and Issues*, eds. Steven M. Buechler and F. Kurt Cylke, Jr. Mountain View, California: Mayfield Publishing Company, 1997.

Bull, Chris. "A Clean Sweep." *The Advocate*, 22 July 1997, 35–8.

"Firm Partnerships." *The Advocate*, 23 May 2000, 67–71.

Burnham, Walter Dean. "Party Systems and the Political Process" in *American Society and Politics*, Theda Skocpol and John L. Campbell, eds. New York: McGraw-Hill, Inc., 1995.

Burns, Ken. "The Homosexual Faces a Challenge: A Speech to the Third Annual Convention of The Mattachine Society." Published in *Mattachine Review* (1956) in *We are Everywhere*, eds. Mark Blasius and Shane Phelan. New York: Routledge, 1997.

Burr, Chandler. "Tony Blair Pushes Gay Rights in Britain." *US News and World Report*, 15 June 1998, 36.

Button, James W., Barbara A. Rienzo, and Kenneth D. Wald. *Private Lives, Public Conflicts*. Washington, DC: Congressional Quarterly Inc., 1997.

Carlson, Margaret. "McCain and his Gaydar." *Time*. 31 January 2000, 43.

Chong, Dennis. "Collective Action and the Civil Rights Movement" in *American Society and Politics*, eds. Theda Skocpol and John L. Campbell. New York: McGraw-Hill, Inc., 1995.

Clendinen, Dudley and Adam Nagourney. *Out For Good: The Struggle to Build a Gay Rights Movement in America*. New York: Simon and Schuster, 1999.

Comstock, Gary David. *Violence Against Lesbians and Gay Men*. New York: Columbia University Press, 1991.

Cooper, Davina. "An Engaged State: Sexuality, Governance and the Potential for Change" in *Activating Theory: Lesbian, Gay, Bisexual Politics*, eds. Joseph Bristow and Angelia R. Wilson. London: Lawrence and Wishart, 1993.

Cory, Donald Webster [Edward Sagarin]. "The Society We Envisage," *The Homosexual in America: A Subjective Approach* (1951) in *We Are Everywhere*, eds. Mark Blasius and Shane Phelan. New York: Routledge, 1997.

Cruikshank, Margaret. *The Gay and Lesbian Liberation Movement*. New York: Routledge, 1992.

Dahir, Mubarak. "State of the Unions." *The Advocate*, 23 May 2000, 57–60.

Daughters of Bilitis. "Statement of Purpose." (1955) in *We Are Everywhere*, eds. Mark Blasius and Shane Phelan. New York: Routledge, Inc., 1997.

Davenport-Hines, Richard. *Sex, Death and Punishment*. London: William Collins Sons and Co., 1990.

D'Emilio, John. *Sexual Politics, Sexual Communities: The Making of a Homosexual*

Minority in the United States, 1940–1970. Chicago: University of Chicago Press, 1983.

D'Emilio, John and Estelle B. Freedman. *Intimate Matters: A History of Sexuality in America.* New York: Harper and Row Publishers, 1988.

De Tocqueville, Alexis. *Democracy in America: Volume I.* New York: Vintage Books, 1990.

Democracy in America: Volume II. New York: Vintage Books, 1990.

Demhoff, G. William. "Who Rules America?" *American Society and Politics*, eds. Theda Skocpol and John L. Campbell. New York: McGraw-Hill, Inc., 1995.

Dorris, John B. "Antidiscrimination Laws in Local Government: A Public Policy Analysis of Municipal Lesbian and Gay Public Employment Protection" in *Gays and Lesbians in the Democratic Process: Public Policy, Public Opinion, and Political Representation*, eds. Ellen D. B. Riggle and Barry L. Tadlock. New York: Columbia University Press, 1999.

Duberman, Martin. *Stonewall.* New York: Penguin Books USA, Inc., 1993.

Duberman, Martin, Martha Vicinus, and George Chauncy Jr., eds. *Hidden from History: Reclaiming the Gay and Lesbian Past.* New York: Penguin Books USA, Inc., 1989.

Durkheim, Emile. *The Division of Labor in Society.* New York: The Free Press, 1984.

Echols, Alice. *Daring to Be Bad.* Minneapolis: University of Minnesota Press, 1989.

Edge, Simon. "Proudly, Openly, Equally Gay." *New Statesman*, 18 July 1997, 22–3.

Egerton, Brooks. "Gay Politics: A Time to Take Stock." *The Progressive*, May 1985, 25–7.

Elster, Jon. *Nuts and Bolts for the Social Sciences.* New York: Cambridge University Press, 1989.

Epstein, Leon D. *Political Parties in Western Democracies.* New Brunswick, NJ: Transaction, Inc., 1967.

Epstein, Steven. "Gay and Lesbian Movements in the United States: Dilemmas of Identity, Diversity, and Political Strategy" in *The Global Emergence of Gay and Lesbian Politics: National Imprints of a Worldwide Movement*, eds. Barry D. Adam, Jan Willem Duyvendak, and Andre Krouwel. Philadelphia: Temple University Press, 1999.

Evans, Michael. "European Court to Rule Against MoD on Gays." *The Times*, 27 September 1999, 8.

"MoD Sackings Halted After Gays Win Forces Case." *The Times*, 28 September 1999, 8.

Faludi, Susan. *Backlash: the Undeclared War Against American Women.* New York: Doubleday, Inc., 1991.

Ferdinand, Pamela. "Vermonters Rise to Sort Out Law on Marriage." *The Washington Post*, 6 February 2000, A3.

Foucault, Michel. *The History of Sexuality: An Introduction: Volume I.* New York: Vintage Books, Random House, Inc., 1978.

Frank, David John and Elizabeth H. McEneaney. "The Individualization of Society and the Liberalization of State Policies on Same-Sex Sexual Relations, 1984–1995," *Social Forces*, March 1999, 77 (3), 911–44.

Fraser, Michael R. "Identity and Representation as Challenges to Social Movement Theory: A Case Study of Queer Nation" in *Mainstream(s) and Margins: Cultural Politics in the 90s*, eds. Morgan, Michael and Susan Leggett. Westport, CT: Greenwood Press, 1996.

Fussel, Paul. *The Great War and Modern Memory.* New York: Oxford University Press, 1975.

Gallagher, John and Chris Bull. *Perfect Enemies: The Religious Right, the Gay Movement, and the Politics of the 1990s.* New York: Crown Publishers, Inc., 1996.

Gallaway, Bruce, ed. *Prejudice and Pride: Discrimination Against Gay People in Modern Britain.* London: Routledge and Kegan Paul, 1983.

Gamson, William A. "Constructing Social Protest" in *Social Movements and Culture*, eds. Hank Johnston and Bert Klandermans, Minneapolis: University of Minnesota Press, 1995.

"Gay Liberation Supports Law Reform." Essay published by the South London Gay Liberation Front. Archives of Gay Organizations and Activists, London School of Political and Economic Science, London.

Get Real, produced by Stephen Taylor. Directed by Simon Shore. 111 min., Paramount Classics in cooperation with British Screen and the Arts Council of England, 1999. Videocassette.

Goldberg, Carey. "Forced Into Action on Gay Marriage, Vermont Finds Itself Deeply Split." *The New York Times*, 3 February 2000, A16.

"Vermont High Court Backs Rights of Same-Sex Couples." *The New York Times*, 21 December 1999, A1, A28.

"Vermont's House Backs Wide Rights for Gay Couples." *The New York Times*, 17 March 2000, A1, A16.

Gordon, Avery F. *Ghostly Matters: Haunting and the Sociological Imagination.* Minneapolis: University of Minnesota, 1997.

Grey, Antony. *Speaking Out: Writings on Sex, Law, Politics, and Society 1954 – 95.* London: Cassell, 1997.

Guthman, Edward. "The British Are Coming." *The Advocate*, 3 March 1998, 51–3.

Haeberle, Steven H. "Gay and Lesbian Rights: Emerging Trends in Public Opinion and Voting Behavior" in *Gays and Lesbians in the Democratic Process: Public Policy, Public Opinion, and Political Representation*, eds. Ellen D. B. Riggle and Barry L. Tadlock. New York: Columbia University Press, 1999.

Haider-Markel, Donald P. "Creating Change – Holding the Line: Agenda Setting on Lesbian and Gay Issues at the National Level" in *Gays and Lesbians in the Democratic Process: Public Policy, Public Opinion, and Political Representation*, eds. Ellen D. B. Riggle and Barry L. Tadlock. New York: Columbia University Press, 1999.

Hamill, Pete. "Confessions of a Heterosexual." *Esquire*, August 1990, 55–7.

Hamilton, Angus. "New Law, New Rights?" *Gay Times*, January 1998, 32–7.

Harris, Sherry, Todd Haynes, Amber Hollibaugh, John S. James, Simon LeVay, Sarah Schulman, Randy Shilts, and Urvashi Vaid. "We *Can* Get There From Here." *The Nation*, 5 July 1993, 26–31.

Hawes, Dan. *1999 Capital Gains and Losses: A State by State Review of Gay,*

Lesbian, Bisexual, Transgender, and HIV/AIDS-Related Legislation in 1999. Washington, DC: National Gay and Lesbian Task Force, 1999. http://www.ngltf.org/issues/pubs.cfm?issueID=18. 6 May 2000.

Hennessy, Rosemary. *Queer Visibility in Commodity Culture.* Publisher information unavailable.

Herman, Didi. "The Politics of Law Reform: Lesbian and Gay Rights Struggles into the 1990s" in *Activating Theory: Lesbian, Gay, Bisexual Politics,* eds. Joseph Bristow and Angelia R. Wilson. London: Lawrence and Wishart, 1993.

Hoge, Warren. "Britain to Lift Ban on Gays in Military." *The New York Times,* 14 December 1999, A25.

Hoy, David Couzens. *The Critical Circle: Literature, History, and Philosophical Hermeneutics.* Berkeley: University of California Press, 1978.

Hrebenar, Ronald J. *Interest Group Politics in America.* Armonk, NY: M. E. Sharpe, 1997.

Huntington, Samuel P. *American Politics: The Promise of Disharmony.* Cambridge: Harvard University Press, 1981.

Political Order in Changing Societies. New Haven: Yale University Press, 1968.

Huxley, Julian to A. E. Dyson. 17 December 1958. Archives of Gay Organizations and Activists, London School of Political and Economic Science, London.

In and Out, produced by Scott Rudin. Directed by Frank Oz. 92 min., Paramount Pictures, 1997. Videocassette.

Inglehart, Ronald. *Culture Shift in Advanced Industrial Societies.* Princeton, NJ: Princeton University Press, 1990.

Jeffery-Poulter, Stephen. *Peers, Queers, and Commons.* New York: Routledge, 1991.

Jenkins, J. Craig. "Resource Mobilization Theory and the Study of Social Movements" in *American Society and Politics,* eds. Theda Skocpol and John L. Campbell. New York: McGraw-Hill, Inc., 1995.

"Social Movements, Political Representation, and the State: An Agenda and Comparative Framework" in *The Politics of Social Protest: Comparative Perspectives on States and Social Movements,* eds. Jenkins, J. Craig and Bert Klandermans. Minneapolis: University of Minnesota Press, 1995.

Jenkins, J. Craig and Bert Klandermans. "The Politics of Social Protest" in *The Politics of Social Protest: Comparative Perspectives on States and Social Movements,* eds. Jenkins, J. Craig and Bert Klandermans. Minneapolis: University of Minnesota Press, 1995.

Jivani, Alkarim. *It's Not Unusual: A History of Lesbian and Gay Britain in the Twentieth Century.* Bloomington: University of Indiana Press, 1997.

Johnston, Hank and Bert Klandermans. "The Cultural Analysis of Social Movements" in *Social Movements and Culture,* eds. Hank Johnston and Bert Klandermans. Minneapolis: University of Minnesota Press, 1995.

Johnston, Hank, Enrique Larana, and Joseph R. Gusfield. "Identities, Grievances, and New Social Movements" in *Social Movements: Perspectives and Issues,* eds. Steven M. Buechler and F. Kurt Cylke, Jr. Mountain View, California: Mayfield Publishing Company, 1997.

Kameny, Franklin. "Gay is Good" (1969) in *We are Everywhere,* eds. Mark Blasius and Shane Phelan. New York: Routledge, 1997.

Kavanagh, Dennis. "Political Culture in Great Britain: The Decline of Civic Culture" in *The Civic Culture Revisited*, eds. Gabriel A. Almond and Sidney Verba. London: Sage Publications, Inc., 1989.

Kinsey, Alfred C., Wardell B. Pomeroy, and Clyde E. Martin. *Sexual Behavior in the Human Male*. Bloomington: Indiana University Press, 1998 (originally published in 1948 by W. B. Saunders Company).

Kitschelt, Herbert, P. "Political Opportunity Structures and Political Protest: Anti- Nuclear Movements in Four Democracies," in *American Society and Politics*, eds. Theda Skocpol and John L. Campbell. New York: McGraw-Hill, Inc., 1995.

Klawitter, Marieka, and Hammer, Brian. "Spatial and Temperal Diffusion of Local Antidiscrimination Policies for Sexual Orientation" in *Gays and Lesbians in the Democratic Process: Public Policy, Public Opinion, and Political Representation*, eds. Ellen D. B. Riggle and Barry Tadlock. New York: Columbia University Press, 1999), 25–35.

Knoebel, John. "Somewhere in the Right Direction: Testimony of My Experience in a Gay Male Living Collective" in *Out of the Closets: Voices of Gay Liberation*, eds. Karla Jay and Allen Young. New York: New York University Press, 1992.

Kopkind, Andrew. "The Gay Moment." *The Nation*, 3 May 1993, 577, 590–602.

Kornhauser, William. "The Politics of Mass Society" *in Social Movements: Perspectives and Issues*, eds. Steven M. Buechler and F. Kurt Cylke, Jr. Mountain View, California: Mayfield Publishing Company, 1997.

Kriesi, Hanspeter. "The Political Opportunity Structure of New Social Movements: Its Impact on Their Mobilization" in *The Politics of Social Protest: Comparative Perspectives on States and Social Movements* Jenkins, J. Craig and Bert Klandermans, eds. Minneapolis: University of Minnesota Press, 1995.

Kriesi, Hanspeter, Ruud Koopmans, Jan Willem Dyvendak, and Marco G. Giugni. *New Social Movements in Western Europe: A Comparative Analysis*. Minneapolis: University of Minnesota Press, 1995.

Kushner, Tony. "Gay Perestroika." *The Advocate*, 23 December 1997, 78.

"Labour Ditching Gay Rights, Say OutRage!," *Thud*, 5 July 1996.

Lewis, Gregory B. and Marc A. Rogers. "Does the Public Support Equal Employment Rights for Gays and Lesbians?" in *Gays and Lesbians in the Democratic Process: Public Policy, Public Opinion, and Political Representation*, eds. Ellen D. B. Riggle and Barry L. Tadlock. New York: Columbia University Press, 1999.

Lewis, Matthew. *The Monk*. Oxford: Oxford University Press, 1980.

Lewis, Sarah. *Woman's Mission*. New York: Wiley and Putnam, 1839.

Ly, Phuong and David Montgomery. "Stepping Toward Gay Rights." *The Washington Post*, 1 May 2000, A1.

Lyall, Sarah. "British, Under European Ruling, End Ban on Openly Gay Soldiers." *The New York Times*, 13 January 2000, A1, A10.

Marotta, Toby. *The Politics of Homosexuality*. Boston: Houghton Mifflin Inc., 1981.

Marx, Karl. "Marx on the History of his own ideas" in *The Marx–Engels Reader*, ed. Robert C. Tucker. New York: W. W. Norton and Company, 1978.

"The German Ideology" in *The Marx–Engels Reader*, ed. Robert C. Tucker. New York: W. W. Norton and Company, 1978.

Marx, Karl and Friedrich Engels. "Manifesto of the Communist Party" in *The Marx–Engels Reader*, ed. Robert C. Tucker. New York: W. W. Norton and Company, 1978.

Mason, Angela and Mark Watson. "Equality 2000." Produced by the Stonewall Lobby Group, Ltd., June 1997.

McAdam, Doug. "Culture and Social Movements" in *Social Movements: Perspectives and Issues*, eds. Steven M. Buechler and F. Kurt Cylke, Jr. Mountain View, California: Mayfield Publishing Company, 1997.

"Tactical Innovation and the Pace of Black Insurgency between 1955 and 1970" in *American Society and Politics*, eds. Theda Skocpol and John L. Campbell. New York: McGraw-Hill, Inc., 1995.

"The Classical Model of Social Movements Examined" in *Social Movements: Perspectives and Issues*, eds. Steven M. Buechler and F. Kurt Cylke, Jr. Mountain View, California: Mayfield Publishing Company, 1997.

"The Political Process Model" in *Social Movements: Perspectives and Issues*, eds. Steven M. Buechler and F. Kurt Cylke, Jr. Mountain View, California: Mayfield Publishing Company, 1997.

McCarthy, John D., and Mayer N. Zald. "Resource Mobilization and Social Movements: A Partial Theory." *American Journal of Sociology* 82 (6), 1977, 1212–41.

Melucci, Alberto. "The New Social Movements: A Theoretical Approach." *Social Science Information* 19 (2), 1980, 119–226.

"The Process of Collective Identity," in *Social Movements and Culture*, eds. Hank Johnston and Bert Klandermans. Minneapolis: University of Minnesota Press, 1995.

Morgan, Edmund S. *The Puritan Dilemma*. New York: HarperCollins Publishers, 1958.

Morris, Aldon. "Black Southern Student Sit-In Movement: An Analysis of Internal Organization" in *American Society and Politics*, eds. Theda Skocpol and John L. Campbell. New York: McGraw-Hill, Inc., 1995.

Murphy, Walter F., James E. Flemming, and Sotirios A. Barber, eds. "The Right to Intimate Sexual Choice." *American Constitutional Interpretation*. Westbury, NY: The Foundation Press, 1995.

National Museum and Archive of Lesbian and Gay History. A Program of the Lesbian and Gay Community Services Center – New York. *The Gay Almanac*. New York: Berkeley Books, 1996.

Need, Lynda. "Forms of Deviancy: The Prostitute." *Myths of Sexuality*. New York: Basil Blackwell, 1988.

O'Conner, John. "Drawing Rave Reviews after Years Out of Sight." *New York Times*, 21 April 1997, C14.

Olson, Mancur. *The Logic of Collective Action*. Cambridge, Mass.: Harvard University Press, 1965.

Owens, Craig. "Outlaws: Gay Men in Feminism" in *Men in Feminism*, eds. Alice Jardine and Paul Smith, 219–32. New York: Routledge, 1987.

Patton, Cindy. "Tremble, Hetero Swine" in *Fear of a Queer Planet*, ed. Michael Warner, 143–77. Minneapolis: University of Minnesota Press, 1993.

Philadelphia, produced by Edward Saxon and Jonathan Demme. Directed by Jonathan Demme. 125 min., TriStar Pictures, 1993. Videocassette.

Plummer, Ken. "The Lesbian and Gay Movement in Britain: Schisms, Solidarities, and Social Worlds" in *The Global Emergence of Gay and Lesbian Politics: National Imprints of a Worldwide Movement*, eds. Barry D. Adam, Jan Willem Duyvendak, and Andre Krouwel. Philadelphia: Temple University Press, 1999.

Poovey, Mary. *Uneven Developments: The Ideological Work of Gender in Mid-Victorian England*. Chicago: University of Chicago Press, 1988.

Powell, Vicky. "Landmark European Employment Rights Victory for Lesbian Couple." *Gay Times*, November 1997, 41.

"No Promises in Labour's Manifesto." *Gay Times*, August 1996, no page number available. Archives of Gay Organizations and Activists, London School of Political and Economic Science, London.

"Opportunity Knockbacks." *Gay Times*, January 1998, 7–8.

Power, Lisa. *No Bath But Plenty of Bubbles: An Oral History of the Gay Liberation Front*. New York: Cassell, 1995.

"Principles of the Gay Liberation Front." Flyer published by the South London Gay Liberation Front. Archive of Gay Organization and Activists, London School of Political and Economic Science, London.

Radicalesbians. "The Woman-Identified Woman." *Out of the Closets: Voices of Gay Liberation*, eds. Karla Jay and Allen Young. New York: New York University Press, 1992.

Radicalesbians (New York City). "Leaving the Gay Men Behind." *Out of the Closets: Voices of Gay Liberation*, eds. Karla Jay and Allen Young. New York: New York University Press, 1992.

Rayside, David M. "Homophobia, Class and Party in England." *Canadian Journal of Political Science* 25 (March 1992): 121–49.

On the Fringe: Gays and Lesbians in Politics. Ithaca: Cornell University Press, 1998.

Reid, T. R. "Britain Ends Its Curbs on Gays in Military." *The Washington Post*, 13 January 2000, A13.

Richardson, Colin. "Man of the Year, Shame of the Year." *Gay Times*, March 1998, 30.

Riggle, Ellen D. B. and Barry L. Tadlock. "Gays and Lesbians in the Democratic Process: Past, Present, and Future" in *Gays and Lesbians in the Democratic Process: Public Policy, Public Opinion, and Political Representation*, eds. Ellen D. B. Riggle and Barry L. Tadlock. New York: Columbia University Press, 1999.

Riggs, Marlon T. "Ruminations of a Snap! Queen: What Time Is It?!", *Outlook*. Spring 1991.

Ringer, R. Jeffrey. *Queer Words, Queer Images*. New York: New York University Press, 1994.

Rofes, Eric E. "Gay Lib vs. AIDS: Averting Civil War in the 1990s," *Outlook* (1990) in *We Are Everywhere*, eds. Mark Blasius and Shane Phelan. New York: Routledge, 1997.

Rosin, Hanna. "Same-Sex Couples Win Rights in Vermont." *The Washington Post*, 21 December 1999, A1, A14.

Rudnick, Paul. "Out in Hollywood." *The Nation*, 5 July 1993, 36–8.

Ruskin, John. "Of Queen's Gardens," *Sesame and Lilies*. No publisher information available, 1864.

Schmitt, Eric. "How Is This Strategy Working? Don't Ask." *The New York Times*, 19 December 1999, IV, 1.

Schroedel, Jean Reith. "Elite Attitudes Toward Homosexuals" in *Gays and Lesbians in the Democratic Process: Public Policy, Public Opinion, and Political Representation*, eds. Ellen D. B. Riggle and Barry L. Tadlock, New York: Columbia University Press, 1999.

Segura, Gary M. "Institutions Matter: Local Electoral Laws, Gay and Lesbian Representation, and Coalition Building Across Minority Communities" in *Gays and Lesbians in the Democratic Process: Public Policy, Public Opinion, and Political Representation*, eds. Ellen D. B. Riggle and Barry L. Tadlock. New York: Columbia University Press, 1999.

Seidman, Steven. "Identity and Politics in a 'Postmodern' Gay Culture: Some Historical and Conceptual Notes" in *Fear of a Queer Planet*, ed. Michael Warner. Minneapolis: University of Minnesota Press, 1993.

Sewell, William H. "A Theory of Structure: Duality, Agency, and Transformation." *American Journal of Sociology* 98 (July 1992): 1–29.

Shea, Lois R. "Analysts Cautious on Gay-Rights Loss." *The Boston Globe*, 12 February 1998, B1, B17.

Shefter, Martin. "Party, Bureaucracy, and Political Change in the United States" in *American Society and Politics*, eds. Theda Skocpol and John L. Campbell. New York: McGraw-Hill, Inc., 1995.

Shepherd, Simon and Mike Wallis, eds. *Coming On Strong: Gay Politics and Culture*. London: Unwin Hyman, Ltd., 1989.

Sherrill, Kennith. "The Youth of the Movement: Gay Activists in 1972–1973" in *Gays and Lesbians in the Democratic Process: Public Policy, Public Opinion, and Political Representation*, eds. Ellen D. B. Riggle and Barry L. Tadlock. New York: Columbia University Press, 1999.

Shilts, Randy. *And the Band Played On: Politics, People, and the AIDS Epidemic*. New York: Penguin Books USA, 1988.

Sinfield, Alan. *Gay and After*. London: Serpent's Tail, 1998.

Skocpol, Theda and John L. Campbell. "Perspectives on Social Movements and Collective Action" in *American Society and Politics*, eds. Theda Skocpol and John L. Campbell. New York: McGraw-Hill, Inc., 1995.

Smith, Barbara. "Across the Kitchen Table: A Sister-to-Sister Dialogue" in *This Bridge Called My Back*, eds. Cherrie Moraga and Gloria Anzaldua. New York: Kitchen Table: Women of Color Press, 1981.

"Where's the Revolution?" *The Nation*, 5 July 1993, 12–16.

Smith, David. "The Age of Consent is My Life." *Gay Times*, September 1997, 32–6.

"Government Promises Equal Age of Consent within Two Years." *Gay Times*, November 1997, 39.

"Stonewall Confident of Commons Age of Consent Debate at Eastertime." *Gay Times*, January 1998, 45.

Smith, Ralph R. and Russel R. Windes. "Identity in Political Context: Lesbian/Gay Representation in the Public Sphere." *Journal of Homosexuality* 37 (2), 1999, 25–39.

Spencer, Colin. *Homosexuality in History*. New York: Harcourt Brace and Company, 1995.

Stallybrass, Peter and Allon White, "The City: the Sewer, the Gaze, and the Contaminating Touch" in *The Politics and Poetics of Transgression*. Ithaca: Cornell University Press, 1986.

"Statement of Purpose of the Mattachine Society" (1951) in *We Are Everywhere*. eds. Mark Blasius and Shane Phelan. New York: Routledge, 1997.

Stockwell, Ann. "Yep, She Rules." *Advocate*. 20 January 1998.

Stychin, Carl F. *Law's Desire: Sexuality and the Limits of Justice*. London and New York: Routledge, 1995.

Swindler, Ann. "Cultural Power and Social Movements." in *Social Movements and Culture*, eds. Hank Johnston and Bert Klandermans. Minneapolis: University of Minnesota Press, 1995.

Tarrow, Sidney. *Power in Movement*. New York: Cambridge University Press, 1994.

Tatchell, Peter. "Labour Landslide Against Section 28." *Capital Gay*, 14 October 1988. Page number unknown. Archives of Gay Organizations and Activists, London School of Political and Economic Science, London.

"New Labour, New Hype." *Gay Times*, January 1998, 19–20.

"Soliciting for Change." *Gay Times*, October 1997, 37–40.

Taylor, Verta. "Gender and Social Movements: Gender Processes in Women's Self-Help Movements," *Gender and Society* 13:1 (February 1999), 14.

Taylor, Verta and Nancy Whittier. "Analytical Approaches to Social Movement Culture: The Culture of the Women's Movement" in *Social Movements and Culture*, eds. Hanks Johnston and Bert Klandermans. Minneapolis: University of Minnesota Press, 1995.

"Collective Identity in Social Movement Communities: Lesbian Feminist Mobilization" in *American Society and Politics*, eds. Theda Skocpol and John L. Campbell. New York: McGraw- Hill, Inc., 1995.

Thomson, Rachel. "Unholy Alliances: The Recent Politics of Sex Education" in *Activating Theory: Lesbian, Gay, Bisexual Politics*, eds. Joseph Bristow and Angelia R. Wilson. London: Lawrence and Wishart, 1993.

"Tide of History and the MoD." *The Times Legal Supplement*. 28 September 1999, 10–11.

Tom Robinson Band. "Glad to be Gay." *Power in the Darkness*. LP. Chris Thomas, producer. Capitol Records, 1978.

Toner, Robin. "A Gay Rights Rally Over Gains and Goals." *The New York Times*, 1 May 2000, A14.

Tourraine, Alain. "An Introduction to the Study of Social Movements." *Social Research* 52, 1985, 749–87.

Tyler, Stephen A. "Post-Modern Ethnography: From Document of the Occult to Occult Document" in *Writing Culture: The Poetics and Politics of Ethnography*, eds. James Clifford and George E. Marcus. Berkeley: University of California Press, 1986.

United Kingdom. *Report of the Committee on Homosexual Offenses and Prostitution (The Wolfenden Report)* John Wolfenden, Chairman. New York: Stein and Fay, 1963.

United States Constitution of 1787.

United States Senate Investigations Subcommittee of the Committee on Expenditures in the Executive Department. "Employment of Homosexuals and Other Sex Perverts in the U.S. Government" (1951) in *We are Everywhere*, eds. Mark Blasius and Shane Phelan. New York: Routledge, Inc., 1997.

Vaid, Urvashi. *Virtual Equality: The Mainstreaming of Gay and Lesbian Liberation.* New York: Anchor Books, Doubleday, 1995.

Vogel, David. "Representing Diffuse Interests in Environmental Policymaking" in *Do Institutions Matter?* eds. R. Kent Weaver and Bert A. Rockman. Washington, DC: The Brookings Institution, 1993.

Von Laue, Theodore. *The World Revolution of Westernization.* New York: Oxford University Press, 1987.

Weaver, R. Kent and Bert A. Rockman. "Assessing the Effects of Institutions" in *Do Institutions Matter?* eds. R. Kent Weaver and Bert A. Rockman. Washington, DC: The Brookings Institution, 1993.

  "When and How Do Institutions Matter?" in *Do Institutions Matter?* eds. R. Kent Weaver and Bert A. Rockman. Washington, DC: The Brookings Institution, 1993.

Weber, Max. "Politics as a Vocation" in *From Max Weber: Essays in Sociology*, eds. H. H. Gerth and C. Wright Mills. New York: Oxford University Press, 1958.

  The Protestant Ethic and the Spirit of Capitalism. New York: Charles Scribner's Sons, 1958.

Weeks, Jeffrey. *Against Nature: Essays on History, Sexuality, and Identity.* London: Rivers Oram Press, 1991.

  Coming Out: Homosexual Politics in Britain, from the Nineteenth Century to the Present. London: Quartet Books, 1979.

  Sexuality and Its Discontents. London: Routledge and Kegan Paul, 1985.

Willer, Shirley. "What Concrete Steps Can be Taken to Further the Homophile Movement?" *The Ladder II* (1966) in *We are Everywhere*, eds. Mark Blasius and Shane Phelan. New York: Routledge, 1997.

Wilson, Angelia. "Which Equality? Toleration, Difference or Respect" in *Activating Theory: Lesbian, Gay, Bisexual Politics*, eds. Joseph Bristow and Angelia R. Wilson. London: Lawrence and Wishart, 1993.

Wintemute, Robert. *Sexual Orientation and Human Rights: The United States Constitution, the European Convention, and The Canadian Charter.* Oxford and New York: Clarendon Press, 1995.

Wolfenden, Sir John. *Report of the Committee on Homosexual Offenses and Prostitution (The Wolfenden Report).* New York: Stein and Day, 1963.

Yang, Alan. *From Wrongs to Rights: Public Opinion on Gay and Lesbian Americans Moves Towards Equality, 1973–1999.* Washington, DC: National Gay and Lesbian Task Force, 1999.
  http://www.ngltf.org/issues/pubs.cfm?issueID=18. 6 May 2000.

INTERNET SITES

Sylla, Mary. "Baehr v. Lewin: Will Equal Protection Lead to the End of Prohibitions on Same-Sex Marriages?" *National Journal of Sexual Orientation Law.* Volume 1, Issue 1.

<http://www.cs.cmu.edu/afs/cs.cmu.e . . . garians/njsol/baehr_equal_prot.txt>
(14 September 1997)

"Equal Rights." *The Labour Party-Policy Guide.*
<http://www.labour.org.uk/views/policy/society/rights.html> (16 September 1997)

"Lesbian and Gay liberation over the years: 1970."
<http://www.pride.org.uk/1970.html> (16 September 1997)

"Lesbian and Gay liberation over the years: 1971."
<http://www.pride.org.uk/1971.html> (16 September 1997)

"Lesbian and Gay liberation over the years: 1972."
<http://www.pride.org.uk/1972.html> (16 September 1997)

"Lesbian and Gay liberation over the years: 1976."
<http://www.pride.org.uk/1976.html> (16 September 1997)

"Lesbian and Gay liberation over the years: 1980."
<http://www.pride.org.uk/1980.html> (16 September 1997)

"Lesbian and Gay liberation over the years: 1982."
<http://www.pride.org.uk/1982.html> (16 September 1997)

"Lesbian and Gay liberation over the years: 1988."
<http://www.pride.org.uk/1988.html> (16 September 1997)

"National Gay and Lesbian Legislative Update – 30 June 1997." *National Gay and Lesbian Task Force On-Line.*
<http://www.ngltf.org/press.leg975.html> (10 October 1997)

Adams, Jr., William E. "Can We Relax Now? An Essay about Ballot Measures and Lesbian, Gay, and Bisexual Rights after Romer v. Evans" *National Journal of Sexual Orientation Law.* Volume 2, Issue 2.
<http://sunsute.unc.edu/gaylaw/issue4/adams2.html> (29 October 1997)

Cox, Barbara J. "Are Same-Sex Marriage Statutes the New Anti-Gay Initiatives?" *National Journal of Sexual Orientation Law.* Volume 2, Issue 2.
<http://sunsute.unc.edu/gaylaw/issue4/cox3.html> (29 October 1997)

Fajer, Marc A. "Bowers v. Hardwick, Romer v. Evans, and the Meaning of Anti-Discrimination Legislation." *National Journal of Sexual Orientation Law.* Volume 2, Issue 2.
<http://sunsute.unc.edu/gaylaw/issue4/fajer.html> (29 October 1997)

Supreme Court of the United States. "Romer, Governor of Colorado, et al. v. Evans et al. certiorari to the supreme court of Colorado No. 94–1039. Argued October 10, 1995–Decided May 20, 1996." *National Journal of Sexual Orientation Law.* Volume 2, Issue 2.
<http://sunsute.unc.edu/gaylaw/issue4/romer.html> (29 October 1997).

"Gay and Lesbian Milestones on TV."
<http://www.religioustolerance.org/hom_0042.htm> (29 October 1997)

Cook, Blanche Wiesen, Ken Sherrill, and Alisa Solomon. "Bibliography: Lesbian and Gay History, Politics and Culture."
<http://maxweber.hunter.cuny.edu/polsc/ksherrill/biblio.html> (30 October 1997)

"1997 Capital Gains and Losses: Introduction." *National Gay and Lesbian Task Force On-Line.*
<http://www.ngltf.org/97cal/intro.html> (5 January 1998).
<http://www.hrc.org> (13 August 1999)

Index